921 BRA

D1084751

Then I heard the voice of the Lord saying, "Whom shall I send? And who will go for us?"

And I said,

HERE AM I, SEND ME! HERE AM I, SEND ME!

HERE
AM
I

HERE AM I, SEND ME! HERE AM I, SEND ME!

Dr. Willys K. Braun

An Autobiography

OTHER BOOKS BY THE AUTHOR

Advance of the Church in Africa
Evaluating and Escalating Church Growth
in the Third World
Pastoral Evangelism in Africa
Roots and Possible Fruits of AD2000
Evangelism Resources

Library of Congress Control Number: 2006922839
ISBN: 1-933858-03-6

For more information, contact
Evangelism Resources
425 Epworth Avenue
Wilmore, Kentucky 40390
Phone: (859) 858-0777
Fax: (859) 858-2907
Email: eroffice@qx.net
Web: erinfo.org

DEDICATION

This wee trip down memory lane is dedicated to my incredible wife who – to date – has for 60 happy years walked very close to God and sensed His will for us. She loved me as I was and quietly exposed me to missions at Wheaton College until one day I discovered for us both that the Lord was calling us to missions. She has recognized when God was leading me into new enterprises for Him, but not without questioning me carefully on occasions. I have observed God's special love for her through the years and I understand it. She has read His Book through over and over, has lived its precepts and proclaimed them for 70 years in American, African and Indian churches, in conferences, schools and books. She has been faithfully His as she has been faithfully mine. I am what I am, largely because of her.

FOREWORD

Periodically in human history there are men and women in various sectors of society who rise above their fellow human beings. They stand out as leaders. Some of these bless the world; others curse it. Their influence for good or for evil affects untold people.

There is no question but that God wills those who are gifted with ability and with power to influence the masses to use these gifts and abilities for good.

The tragedy is, though, that some do not. Others led by His Spirit and controlled by His love do. Some of them stand across the horizon of time as lofty peaks of servitude and holy influence. In their field of service they contribute far beyond their own powers or abilities, however stellar these may be. They are empowered of God to do so.

In the field of modern missionary history, one of these towering peaks of personality and service is Willys Braun.

To the everlasting benefit and blessing of multitudes, the young lad Willys came to an altar of surrender to Christ, of death to self and of obedience to his personal heavenly vision. He answered God's divine call to become a missionary and to dedicate his all to what many Christians consider God's highest, noblest calling.

While the Lord was dealing with Willys, He was also speaking to a young woman. He and Thelma found each other, as God had planned. They have spent sixty-two years living out what has to be one of the most beautiful of all love stories, sharing together the romance of a life in extraordinary missionary service.

One does not think of Willys only, but always of Willys and Thelma. It has been said countless times that behind every great man there is a great woman. There she stands, Thelma, sharing in a beautiful partnership with Willys the joys, the dreams, the victories, the sorrows and the defeats of God's calling and appointments.

After their marriage they went out under The Christian and Missionary Alliance for thirty years of service in the Congo. One July evening in 1976 the ultimate of their missionary visions came to fulfillment and Evangelism Resources was born. The will of God has been their consuming passion.

The greatest treasure for any in heaven will be the redeemed who are there because someone brought the Good News of the Gospel to them.

Great will be the company of those in Glory who made it home safely because of the lives of Willys and Thelma Braun.

So in grateful anticipation of the Father's welcome one day, I want to say the best thing and pay the highest tribute to my beloved friends and colleagues, Willys and Thelma,

Well done, good and faithful servants . . .

BUT, the end is not yet and there is much for them yet to do.

Dr. Harold Spann
September 10, 2003

TABLE OF CONTENTS

INTRODUCTION

God created. Man recorded. A few blocks from where I write there are two libraries built by Asbury Theological Seminary and Asbury College for their students. They have a combined collection of 300,000 books – so far. The construction cost of those buildings was about $15,000,000. A quarter century later these buildings will be deemed to be too small and much larger ones will have to be built.

Man has recorded his own thoughts, words and actions and those of others from the dawn of time. He records infinite details about animals, birds, reptiles and insects that live in his world now or that ever lived here. They vary in size from dinosaurs and whales to microscopic forms. They live hundreds of years or a few hours. Plant life, atoms, molecules, chemicals, rocks, volcanoes and hurricanes, nothing escapes the curiosity of humankind. And all observations and learning are recorded endlessly by men who give all their years to their particular universe of study, even if it is so small that a thousand of them together would not be large enough for an invisible chigger to stand on. God created. Man recorded.

In view of this flood of information and opinions which fills not only huge libraries but enormous dumps outside of every city in the world, it does not seem immodest for me to add my bit of recorded history to the clutter. God regarded me as worthy of life for nearly 85 years as of now. I realize that a sea turtle lives even longer, so I do not regard length of years as the only or the best criterion of worth, but it is perhaps one. At least it adds to the pages to follow.

Many humans in childhood adopt a very low opinion of life's significance or of their own in the world. They find their place by looking into the mirror of their parents', teachers' and friends' attitudes toward them. If there is no admiration, no applause, no sparkle in the eyes of their society's glance at them they accept the verdict that they are common dust and build a common lifestyle out of that dust. India has built a caste system based on this self-evaluation of hundreds of millions of people who see no beauty, no hope, no value in themselves because their society is their only mirror in which they see themselves.

God provided mankind His own mirror for His own people to gaze into – it is the face of Jesus Christ. Not a painting or a sculpture – but the unseen yet well-known face of God in human form who valued man so infinitely much that He left heaven, left eternal glory, eternal justice, eternal goodness and eternal life to enter our warped and flawed humanity to teach us, to exhibit holiness, compassion, divine power and love. Then He took on Himself what He hated most about us – our damning sin – and paid the price of our evil in dying for us.

What is my real value? What I see in my peers who walk past me unseeing? Or who burst into talk in the middle of my sentence? Or who no longer invite me to their fun times? Or who belittle me when and where it hurts most? If so, I should have followed my grandfather's counsel and lived my life repairing cars until I could no longer hold a wrench.

By the grace, the limitless unmerited favor of God, I saw another reflection of myself in the face of Him who so loved me. Repairing vehicles, manufacturing shoes, running my own business, serving society as a sociologist – all were passing responses to society's mirror. In God's mirror I discovered a world of men, women, boys and girls for whom Jesus provided salvation, and I read His call in the New Testament to go and announce His good news far and wide.

A fellow fresh out of college needs help to cross an ocean, set up a home, feed a family and preach the Word. It would require three more years to take the steps outlined by the Alliance, but they were good years and they had only 365 days each. Like other years, they passed. Then the great adventure began and continues until now, 56 years later.

It has taken me to over sixty nations on five continents, not as a tourist, but as a very purposeful ambassador of God. In Africa my writings ministered to over 500 bishops and other heads of denominations and soon may reach 1000 more over ten years in English, French and Portuguese. Students came to our International School of Evangelism from 26 nations. Whole African nations launched countrywide movements of evangelism. One of them maintained its movement for over 25 years.

In Asia Portable Bible Schools were held all over India and Bangladesh and, now, Myanmar and Nepal, adding over 11,000 men trained to the 30,000 in Africa. Currently there are 25 schools of evangelism in Asia, and ER-sponsored literature goes to about 800 heads of denominations in four Asian nations.

The funding basis of these ministries is Evangelism Resources, which was begun in 1976. Currently income is about $750,000 a year. ER is a mid-sized mission amid the over 700 American missions measured by income. Its home staff is tiny. Its overseas missionaries are few. Our money goes to Africans and Asians who are doing what we could never do and what no other missions are doing. It would require $3,000,000 a year to staff our overseas schools with American missionaries, the way missions normally do. Said differently, we could train only 100 students a year instead of 700 with our income.

Our God is amazing. He began with me where I was: small, no star in anything, timid, a very poor student, no speaking ability, no singer, no musician, no Bible student, broke, with no trade to support a family. My personal report card affirmed what I saw in my society's mirror. Future prospects: grease monkey.

Enter – salvation, the indwelling Holy Spirit, Thelma with her vision for missions. Wheaton. Nyack. Language study. The face of Christ with its love and assurance that "I can do all things through Christ who strengtheneth me" was not just for Paul. All He needed was an empty vessel longing to be filled.

Fifty-six years of His filling are what the bulk of the pages that follow is all about. They are about Christ in a poor candidate for service. If in some pages my flesh hides Him, I will have failed to rightly depict the reality. But if here and there you see His empowerment and guidance, this recital will be accurate and worthy of publishing.

There will be some repetition, some mediocre writing. With a full-time job at the ER office these chapters were rapidly sketched in evening hours. My intent is not to produce a best seller – or even a worst seller – but to get on paper some incidents of my life. If I have not adequately covered yours, get out your pen and start writing your

3

story. This is mine, my walk with God and the amazing woman He gave me to make up for my many shortcomings.

SECTION ONE

FAMILY

1

EUROPEAN ROOTS

Sweden was the homeland of my mother's ancestors. Swedes were a warlike people. In the 700s Vikings terrorized the seacoasts of many nations, plundering villages and cities at will. For nine centuries Sweden's navy and armies conquered large territories and by the mid-1600s it was one of the greatest powers in Europe until Russia overwhelmed its navy in 1708. The nation sent out explorers on history-making voyages to North America and until today Swedes are found in the forefront of missions in Asia, Africa and Latin America. They are an international people.

My great-great-grandfather, Olaf Bjorn, born in 1782, was a valiant soldier called "The Bear" by Sweden's king. My Aunt Amelia recounted this to me when I was a boy. Dorothy, my sister, visited relatives in Sweden and found official records of Olaf. There was a note saying he was physically handicapped. Perhaps he was seriously wounded in war. He was also a farmer and fisherman.

There have been no bulky, bear-like offspring of Olaf in our family, to my knowledge. Great-great-great-great-grandson, Josh Braun, is the closest thing to a bear in height, but he does not yet have the girth to be bear-like. Sorry to let you down, Olaf.

Andreas Olsson Bjorn
Born in Sweden 1824
Father of Matilda Ross;
Grandfather of Lillian Ross
Braun; Great-grandfather of
Dorothy and Willys Braun

Olaf Bjorn's son, Andreas Olsson Bjorn (1820-1906), my great-grandfather, was said to be a

7

physician and farmer. He lived to be 86 in a time when 60 was considered to be very old. There has been unusual longevity in later generations of the family. Life expectancy in 1940 was 65 years of age. My mother excelled that by 18 years, her daughter by 23 years. And I am already twenty years beyond that.

Andreas Olsson Bjorn had a daughter, Matilda, who married Joel Brynteson in 1872 and they had three daughters, Amelia, Alma and Selma. Times were then very hard in Sweden. Joel, my grandfather, was a farmer but also a man of action. He took his family to Norway hoping for a better life. He did not find it. Many Swedes were going to America in those years. In 1878 he went alone to America. Two years later he sent money for Matilda and the three girls to sail to New York and travel to St. Louis and to a farm 50 miles south of St. Louis near what is still a small village, Bonne Terre. These French words mean fertile soil.

In America his very fertile wife bore Anne, Oscar and Frank. In American schools Betsy Ross, designer of the American flag, was a much-admired heroine and it is no surprise that when the cry to abandon the difficult Swedish name, Brynteson, grew to a crescendo, the name Ross supplanted it. As part of the Americanization of the family, the Swedish language was dropped and English was used 100% of the time. I never heard Swedish spoken, even by Amelia who lived seven years in Sweden and clearly remembered much of its culture.

At some point the Bonne Terre farmer bought good bottomland on the banks of the Mississippi. Crops were excellent. But the river did not flow straight in a secure bed. A glance at the map reveals an outlandish series of endless bends from St. Louis to the Gulf of Mexico. To go 570 miles south it travels 1300 circuitous miles, cutting a swath ten miles wide through Missouri, Illinois, Kentucky, Tennessee, Arkansas, Mississippi and Louisiana. The Ross farm was there one day and gone the next as floods covered its acres and sliced out a new river bed on them.

It is interesting to reflect on Joel Ross, the man. He had taken his family from Sweden to Norway, had crossed the Atlantic to America and moved inland to St. Louis, the starting place for points west. He settled down in Bonne Terre, bought high-priced bottomland on the river, had six children and then got caught up in talk about a coming event called the Oklahoma Land Rush. In 1889 he sold his farm, bought up a stock of trading goods, loaded it and his family into a prairie schooner and traveled southwest by west toward Oklahoma.

A bit of history may clarify what the Ross family would find in Oklahoma. Between 1830 and 1842 the U.S. Army forced 15,000 Cherokee Indians out of eastern states to trek 1000 miles to Oklahoma. These were not wild, warring enemies. They were part of what were called the Five Civilized Tribes. They had lived with settlers over a hundred years and were socially advanced. Thousands died on the trip westward through Tennessee, a corner of southeast Kentucky, Missouri, the northwest corner of Arkansas and into eastern Oklahoma. Indians call that awful experience the Trail of Tears.

They crossed the Mississippi just south of Cairo, Illinois, where the Ohio adds its waters to the great river. Incidentally Cairo, 100 years later, is where my own canoe trip from St. Louis to New Orleans ended. Four days of campfire cooking ruined my digestive system. I rested up a day in Cairo and hired a truck to take the canoe and me back home.

Fifty years after the Indians trailed westward from the river to Oklahoma, Joel Ross' wagon and family reached the Trail of Tears and followed it to the Oklahoma border to wait for the opening signal. A pistol shot rang out at noon, April 22, 1889 and the Oklahoma Land Rush began. Joel's wagon lurched forward with another 50,000 new settlers who became Oklahomans that day. They obtained land near what is now Eddy, according to Cousin Esther. No Eddy is listed on current road atlases. It may not have survived. The larger territory was called the Cherokee Nation.

Esther tells of an incident in which Joel's eldest daughter Amelia, then in her early twenties, overheard some white settlers planning to give free liquor to the Indians on the day they were to receive government payment for their lands. Their goal was to get the Indians drunk and steal large sums of money from them. Amelia told the local Cherokee chief what she had heard and he warned his people not to drink any liquor. The tribe was so appreciative of Amelia's tip that they held a feast in her honor, at which she was queen.

Thirty years later Aunt Amelia told me that a Cherokee brave brought horses to her father as a dowry for her hand in marriage. Joel refused, but the idea was not far-fetched. Cherokees were affluent and had schools, churches, a government, laws and courts. As poverty struck the new settlers, marrying daughters to prosperous Indians became quite common. Ten years ago a Tulsa pastor told me, "There's a lot of Indian blood in Oklahomans today."

Grandfather's trade goods were eventually sold and he left Oklahoma and returned to St. Louis where he turned to drink and died at 54. America had not been kind to him. His adventures were courageous but, as a man of the soil, he probably would have fared better staying on his Bonne Terre farm.

His wife Matilda gave him a seventh child after their return to St. Louis, a girl whose name was Lillian. She was to become the mother of Dorothy and me. If Grandpa had prospered and stayed in Oklahoma, this last child might have married an Indian and Dorothy and I could have been what whites called mixed-breeds. What might have been is always interesting to contemplate.

For followers after the Lord Jesus Christ, we see His divine hand on a mother of seven, a widow, and on the generations which would follow her.

2

MATILDA

I never saw my Ross grandparents. Both died before I was born. But after Joel's death his widow, my grandmother Matilda, was to become God's role model for her children, her grandchildren, her great-grandchildren and her great-great-grandchildren – so far. Matilda walked with her Lord and 82 offspring have followed her.

She outlived her husband only seven years but in that time she came into contact with the Plymouth Brethren Assemblies at a time when revival was stirring among them. They were Baptistic in doctrine, after the teachings of an English Bible scholar named Darby. He taught that the Scriptures call for assemblies of laymen who study the Bible daily and come together around the Lord's table every Sunday in meditation. Any brother could call for a hymn to be sung a cappella, or could read a portion of God's Holy Book and bare his heart regarding his understanding of the Lord's intent in those verses.

I grew up in the Assemblies and can testify to the profound worship and sense of awe in those Sunday services. There was no pastor. Laymen, businessmen, some very prosperous, some laborers, were the evangelists on Sunday nights, the prayer leaders on Wednesday nights and the Bible teachers on Friday nights.

My mother took Dorothy and me to church three times on Sunday and on Wednesday and Friday. Women were Sunday school teachers and active in visitation to homes. They also had cottage prayer meetings for women neighbors. When phones became available my mother had a long list of families she called regularly. A typical conversation lasted as long as the person on the other phone wished to share her problems, and toward the end of the conversation Mother would comfort and encourage her friend. Her words had meaning, for everyone knew she was a widow, working hard to keep her house and her two children during a depression unlike anything America has experienced since. Powerful, wealthy men all over the nation lost everything in a stock market that plunged and broke banks from coast to coast. There were many suicides.

Aunt Amelia (Ross) Bossert,
Uncle John, and John, Jr.

It was Matilda's faith and courage that shaped her five daughters and two sons. And that faith was passed on to their children and their children's children for five generations. Of those children, my own life was greatly influenced by my pious mother and her sisters, Amelia and Selma, her brother Oscar and her brother-in-law, John Bossert. He filled in, off and on, as a father figure in our home during years when he had to leave his wife Amelia and two children on his farm and return to work as a die maker in a St. Louis company.

He was a greatly beloved uncle. When he came from work we had fun together through the meal and doing dishes. Then fun stopped as Uncle John brought his Greek Bible and resource materials to the cleared kitchen table and earnestly studied verse after verse in the original. Why did he do this so steadily? Like all the Brethren laymen, he was set to learn God's Word thoroughly.

Matilda Ross had no child named for her. Matriarch of generations who would live devout, separated, worship-filled lives, she was not honored or even remembered by the dozens of offspring whose lives she so profoundly shaped. Matilda is not a Bible name; it is not a modern name, so it is unlikely that there will be a baby Matilda in the future. But let it be said and remembered that God gave through her to her children's children for generations an enduring faith that has reached out to many nations of the world and, at home, has blessed the lives of her seed in a national culture that is rapidly degenerating.

Bless the name of this woman in our past who saved us from so much grief and pioneered for us the Trail of Heavenly Blessings.

3

MOTHER

I do not have the skill of a novelist to weave a spellbinding tale about my mother, but the content for one was there. Born in a Swedish immigrant family which had suffered bankruptcy in the Oklahoma land rush, tiny Lily was to see her parents die, then grow up as the ward of her single sister Amelia.

Mother's culture was mid-western Bible-belt. She did well in school but I am unsure of how much schooling she had. Surely she finished grammar school and probably high school. In later life her circle of friends included many college professors who were at home with this warm, loving lady. But marriage came early in life, and children too, so there was no time for college. Nor had any of her immediate family gone to college, nor her husband-to-be.

Her teen years were filled with school and church and family. By now Amelia, a cook in a hotel, was married to a widower of French origins, John Bossert. Mother related to him as a stepdaughter living in his St. Louis home until she married a young artist, William Braun, of German parentage.

I recall Aunt Amelia's story of how Lillian met William. He was a fervent witness for Christ in a Brethren Assembly and spoke at a street meeting which Mother and Amelia attended. "I'm going to get him to walk me home," Lillian whispered to her big sister. She did.

Courtship letters in the collection Mother and my sister kept and which I now have were not about his love for "Dearest Lillian," but about his adoration of God. His prose sounded like that of a medieval monk rather than that of a college-age boy wooing a fair maiden. What a vocabulary of praise, what a passionate paean of total dedication, not to a woman, but to God! This was a rare suitor of any age, and they were married soon after.

Among those letters was one from a missionary in Spain. He was replying to the young artist in St. Louis who apparently had written to him offering to join him in mission work. The tone of the reply has an arrogance about it not atypical of Brethren elders in their relationship with younger men. In a few words he crushed the dreams of the young applicant for overseas service. Were there other aspirations of this man and his wife to be about God's business full-time? Both are gone now and I never thought to ask when they lived. Somewhere, somehow a turning away from the elders of the Assemblies grew in the heart of the young man and he wanted nothing so much as to "go out the door," leaving St. Louis and its Assemblies and elders forever.

Lillian (Ross) Braun
Mother of Dorothy and Willys

Chicago was the second-largest city in America and only 300 miles from St. Louis. The time came when he had established a paying business and he was eager for his family to move to Chicago. Importunate letters spelled it out over months but Mother could not, would not go to Chicago. Was it her strong attachment to her family, her church, her friends? Christian women were familiar with the lovely words, "Whither thou goest, I will go," and the wedding vows of "forsaking all others" were well known. But Mother did not join her husband there.

My guess is that she was already aware that he was no longer the humble servant of the Lord whom she had loved and married, so she made a decision which would make her a lifelong widow.

William wanted a divorce. His old employee Alice, a gifted artist, was now with him in Chicago. Mother refused a divorce. Her

14

husband planned a way to make her seek a divorce. He secretly visited his parents in St. Louis and demanded that they invite my big sister, six-year-old Dorothy, to visit them. Dorothy did so and was quickly carried away by her father to Chicago and placed in a Catholic boarding school. Alice was around to "mother" her on weekends.

A year of that and Mother gave up hope of rebuilding her family. She went through with the divorce, reclaimed Dorothy and moved from South St. Louis, where her in-laws lived, to North St. Louis, where her relatives lived. I recall the Lee Avenue four-family house with its outside toilet and its round clothes-washing tub put in the kitchen for baths.

Several years later Mother put a down payment on a small cottage with four rooms and a basement and yard. By then, Dottie and I were both in school. Mother did beautiful smocking on little girls' dresses and women's blouses. She also made slips and other dainty bits of clothing. Obviously she also received alimony.

We lived carefully but comfortably. My allowance was five cents a week and I could earn extra pennies by keeping my shirts clean enough to wear two days. We never had enough money to pay off the house mortgage or to buy a car. But we ate well, were happy and never felt poor. Never! A coal furnace in the basement heated the house. It was my job to shovel coal, shake down ashes, remove them from the furnace, spread them around the water drain in the concrete floor and sprinkle them thoroughly. Why? There were two reasons. One was to save little unburned coals to throw in the furnace. The other was to reduce the ashes as much as possible because it cost money to have ashes hauled away. In the Great Depression one needed to be careful to save every possible penny.

An interesting thing about Mother was that she had great compassion for the poor. Frequently hoboes came to our door and explained that they were starving. I never saw one turned away. A dish was set on a tray with utensils and Mother would divide the food she had made for our next meal, put a large serving on our guest's plate and serve him out on the front porch. With no man in the house she never permitted strangers to come in, but so many came that we decided the hobo-grapevine passed the word around freely that a good meal could be had anytime at 1907 Agnes Street.

When summer vacation arrived I went gladly to Uncle John's farm. I imagine these summers on the farm began when I was about eight. They ended when I went to college. Mother had fewer worries when I was on the farm. She and Dorothy had the house and the months to themselves. They must have enjoyed that. It never occurred to me until now that my time on the farm sweetened for a decade the dear old summertime for 1907 Agnes. I suspect the ladies were just as unready for vacation to end as I was. But when the opening of school was only days away I was welcomed home like a little hero. That status lasted several hours.

Mother was a good cook. She had for Sunday noon meals a single woman, elegant and interesting, who came a long way each Sunday to our Assembly. Beef, mashed potatoes, gravy, string beans, a half-pear in a square of lime Jell-O salad and tapioca for dessert was standard fare then. I discovered very early that when we had women guests, I could be a star entertainer – for about four and a half minutes, with hilarity galore. But as if an alarm clock silently went off in each female head, eyes turned glassy and I just felt a very strong urge to change careers and locations. I never could understand how popularity could blossom – and fade - without explanation or discussion.

But women were not Mother's only guests. She made sure that every visiting missionary and evangelist, musician and Bible teacher came for a Sunday meal. There were dozens of homes represented in that Assembly, but it seemed to be understood that

16

Lillian Braun's Sunday noon table was the place at which every passing preacher would eat. Apparently it wasn't only the hoboes who knew about 1907 Agnes Street. There was Mr. Gilbert, a handsome man who looked a lot like the TV detective Perry Mason. Mr. Arthur Rodgers was another. I rode with him across Missouri and part of Kansas to an Assembly conference. We became close friends. After the services I slept in a friend's home and hitchhiked home about three hundred and fifty miles. I was in high school then.

Mother had remarkable faith in God. She did not oppose my owning a shotgun as a youngster and going on long hunting trips. She accepted my making a rowboat and buying a canoe and let me start a 1300-mile canoe trip on the Mississippi River. She must have known I would never make it to New Orleans, but she let me find out for myself. I hitchhiked all over New York, Pennsylvania and Ohio, crossed the continent from Seattle, Washington to St. Louis, thumbing with a homemade sleeping bag for nights. She never hassled me. She just made the bag to my dimensions and kissed me "Goodbye" and "Welcome" again when I returned. I was her only son. I did ridiculous things. I risked my life over and over, not out of bravery or to save the world, but out of inexperience and stupidity. Mother showed a courage I cannot explain.

Through our growing years, Mother did fear sickness. She could see no way her children would be cared for if she were incapacitated. It scared her. I remember her fasting for weeks for health reasons. I do not recall her being sick but I knew she was frequently afraid she had a dangerous illness. On one occasion she was right. Her appendix was inflamed. In those days a ruptured appendix ended in death. And in those days the operation was considered a major and dangerous one. A five-inch opening was standard and it took a week to heal enough to get out of bed. I know. I had one. But Mother's was at least six years earlier. She gathered Dorothy and me for prayer before leaving for the hospital. She let us know that she might never see us on earth again. And she gave us a verse from the Bible to hold on to. "Underneath are the everlasting arms," she breathed. Everything went well and after a week, a pale and enfeebled Mother returned to her children and life started up again.

The depression was hard on farmers. Crop prices were down and Uncle John's farm had no bottomland. His fields were on rocky hills and harvests were poor. He built a large poultry unit in an effort to make money, but his gleaming white leghorn hens and crates of white eggs brought small income. A milk-fed calf might bring $17 and a big aluminum cream can a few bucks, but after a few years of struggle, Uncle John would have to return to Schleters factory in St. Louis as a die maker. Where did he live? With us. Remember? Aunt Amelia and Uncle John raised Mother. It was logical that he find a home away from home with his "step-daughter." And it gave our family a man to balance the ratio.

Uncle John's presence in the house changed things a bit. We had only one bedroom which Mother and Dorothy used. I slept on a folding cot in the dining room. It had a slipcover during the daytime. When Uncle John was with us we opened a hideaway davenport at night, which we shared. He was a happy addition to our lives and, in a way, evened up the score of my months on the farm each year.

Back to Mother - she was attractive and, I am confident, could have remarried. But she believed the Bible forbade that and lived as a widow 59 years after the divorce. She loved the Lord, had devotions with us, dragged us to church – a long walk – at least five times a week, prayed for us, loved us, worked hard for us, taught a Sunday school class for decades. With what result?

Both of her children lived as she lived – trusting, serving and loving the Lord Jesus Christ. Both were graduated from Wheaton College. Dorothy went on to earn a doctorate in Christian Education and to serve her entire professional life teaching it to hundreds of young people. I, by the grace of God, had four years in college studies, two years of French study and was awarded a Doctor of Divinity degree by Asbury College, based on mission service in Africa.

If Mother had joined her husband in Chicago, Dorothy and I would probably have shaped our lives quite differently. From eternity's viewpoint, from any viewpoint, she made the right choice. I salute her memory. She chose a narrow, rocky road but it led to heaven for her, for us and for the many who met Jesus on our global journeys which her life, along with Thelma's, made possible.

4

DOROTHY

My sister was born a year after our parents married. Mother was eighteen, her husband twenty. The home Mother grew up in was one of love and piety. Her new home also was until I was born four years after Dorothy. I do not think I caused the sea change that occurred in this idyllic family, but the year after my birth our father left St. Louis with a strong aversion for it which never died. When Dorothy was seven she was taken secretly to Chicago until Mother agreed to a divorce.

Dorothy was returned home after the divorce and our family moved to North St. Louis near Mother's relatives. Dorothy's time in the Catholic boarding school during her stay in Chicago apparently contributed to her schoolwork, for she finished high school with high grades a year ahead of most.

After graduation she studied secretarial courses and obtained excellent employment in a prominent securities firm. Her daily contact with the socially elite Rexford family proved to be an excellent finishing school for her in her twenties. In that period Dorothy gave me a $10 birthday present – ten days at a boys' camp at Cedar Lake, Indiana – for three years in a row. I was 15, 16 and 17 then. In the last camp I took Christ into my life as Savior. For that I am eternally grateful.

After I graduated from high school and added a year at Missouri University I worked for three years. Mother stopped working. Dorothy's salary and mine enabled us to live comfortably and new furniture replaced the old. In 1938 I left St. Louis for Wheaton and a year later Dorothy left for Moody Bible Institute. Mother found employment once more and sold the house on Agnes Street.

At Moody Dorothy became the secretary of a noted author-preacher, Dr. Harry Ironside, pastor of the large Moody Memorial

Church. Dorothy's role was to take down his sermons in shorthand and type them up for collection in book form. His appreciation for my sister is evident in many letters written to her over seven years after she left Chicago. And many helpful checks were sent to her as she studied at Wheaton College in Illinois, served as a missionary with Mother in Pikeville, Kentucky and did post-graduate work in Biblical Seminary in New York City and at New York University. Dr. Ironside was Plymouth Brethren and a national figure in his time.

Dorothy appears even in her early years as a devoted servant of the Lord Jesus. In St. Louis a typical Sunday saw her attend three services, play the piano for them, teach a Sunday school class and give out tracts to the sick in a hospital. In her college days she was still giving out tracts in hospitals. In post-graduate study periods she taught Sunday school in large Presbyterian churches – definitely non-Brethren.

In 1948, Thelma and I were in our third year in Belgian Congo and Dorothy began her teaching career at King's College. For fifteen years she built up the department of Christian Education, at first at its Wilmington, Delaware campus and later at the Ossining campus in New York. We visited Mother and Dorothy often there during three furloughs, each furlough with a new baby boy.

Dorothy and Mother lived life to the full in the King's College period. Dorothy went to London in summer with a publisher of Sunday school materials. She and Mother visited us in Switzerland and traveled with us around Europe in 1962 on a family tour. She came to see us at Lukula in Congo in 1965. Her diaries recorded a woman full of energy, on the run in scholastic circles. Mother was very much at home with professors, evangelists, college presidents and visiting celebrities of the Christian world. It was a far cry from the Assembly where we grew up.

And it was to get better. Biola College in La Mirada, California invited Dr. Dorothy Braun to teach in its much larger Department of Christian Education. She and Mother moved into a fine house worth twenty of the houses we grew up in, in a beautiful neighborhood adjoining the college. It was ideal. An olive tree in front and an avocado and a fig tree in the backyard reveal the climate. Roses bloomed until Christmas time. What a paradise!

For twenty years Dorothy taught her classes in Biola and some in Talbot Seminary as well. She wrote Sunday school lessons and songs for Christmas and Easter. She bought a business and hired others to run it. For a brief time she was engaged to marry a fine college staff member, but then decided to remain single. She chaired the CE department – the second largest in the school. Life was full to bursting.

In 1970 my family had a furlough in La Mirada. We lived two blocks from Dorothy and Mother. Chris was a college senior that year and Paul and Phil fitted happily into the C&MA church and their respective schools. It was a splendid year with many family events and ended when we were assigned to New York to head the Alliance Key '73 program.

In 1977, Mother was dying of cancer and I flew out to be with her and Dorothy. A doctor was able to remove the kidney blockage and Mother survived to live another year. Three years later Dorothy retired from Biola. In 1982 and 1983 she made a leisurely trip through Europe and Asia visiting many of her graduates on mission fields. On her return she was engaged by Asbury College in 1984 to teach Christian Education. The following year she taught in Asbury Theological Seminary. She went back to her home in California in 1986 and stayed there for five years, then moved back to Wilmore, Kentucky to be near Paul and Nancy and Thelma and me.

For seven years Dorothy had a nice apartment near downtown Wilmore. As the years passed, she needed more and more help in the laundry, cooking and other daily needs. Finally, on the advice of her physician, she was moved into a beautiful retirement home in nearby Lexington, then to one here in Wilmore when it was available. There she enjoyed family visits and Sunday excursions to church for a couple of years, with good health and peaceful spirit as those quiet days went by.

In November 2001, while I was in India, Dorothy fell and her right hip was shattered. She was taken from lovely Wesley Village to a Lexington hospital where doctors operated on the bone. She was temporarily moved to a Lexington facility to recuperate, but severe pain took away her will to live. Day after day she drifted further away and was moved to a hospice unit where in peace and dignity she slept away early Sunday morning, two days before Christmas. Nancy was the only one of us with her as she took leave of her exhausted body to be ever with the Lord.

Many caring friends came to the funeral home on Friday afternoon and the memorial service on Saturday of the same week. Thirty guests came to our house and Thelma was helped by close family friends in supplying a memorial meal.

· · · · · · · · · · · · ·

Dorothy Braun

Dorothy was the first to earn a Ph.D. in our family. She distinguished herself in her profession. She was steady as a rock spiritually. She was a generous member of the Evangelism Resources Board for many years and was very helpful to her missionary nephews, whom she loved dearly. She had literally hundreds of correspondents and dozens of close friends, most of whom have preceded her to glory.

I suppose if I had been asked to design an ideal sister I could not have imagined one equal to Dorothy. By caring for Mother lifelong, she gave up marriage and kept us free to do God's work in Africa and Asia. God has not missed all the above, nor have we.

Dorothy's farewell ended the matriarchal triumvirate of Matilda, her daughter Lillian and Lillian's daughter. The transformation of Matilda at the time of her salvation led a small army to faith in Christ. My mother maintained total dedication to her Lord, and Dorothy, who had no daughter to whom to pass on the torch, taught about 3000 college students who now serve her Lord all over the world.

5

THE BRAUN PARENTAGE

The family migrated from Germany under contract to work for an American who lived near New Orleans. He paid their ocean passage. At that time the German family's name was Koehler. I do not know how long they worked for their sponsor, but the way I heard it they met a steamboat captain whose name was Braun. He plied the Mississippi River and arranged with them to board his craft at midnight and leave New Orleans for St. Louis.

Mrs. Koehler, my great-grandmother, left her husband and married Captain Braun who then adopted the children and gave them his name. There is a bit of a parallel here in that my Swedish grandfather decided his Swedish name was too difficult for Americans to pronounce and had the family name changed.

In my own childhood there was a Koehler family in the Brethren Assembly we attended. Mr. Koehler was a handsome man and he had a pretty, shy daughter named Virginia who was somewhat younger than I. Decades later I would learn that she had married my old friend Charles Todd, owner of a national chain of over 30 cleaning franchises and an important manufacturer of industrial uniforms. He joined our Evangelism Resources Board and he and Virginia attended annual Board meetings until her illness made that impossible. We visited the Todds many times and they entertained our St. Louis friends in a memorable gathering at their spiritual retreat center in western Illinois. Virginia passed away in 2000.

The Braun family tree in Germany is not known to me. Fern, my cousin, made notes and told us of her research but what I know from personal experience was that my grandmother and grandfather had a prosperous life, lived in a very nice house in South St. Louis and always welcomed Dorothy and me on our seasonal visits. They maintained the German language and used it extensively. "Come back soon, ain't it?" was a favorite farewell. Grandma served a rarity for us, a luscious, soft rye bread with thick butter. Wonderful! Perhaps that is as good an example that I can give of the economic difference between those Brauns and my widowed mother who struggled to keep a ten-cent loaf of white bread on the table.

Here is how the Braun family tree looks:

1. Great-Grandpa Koehler (replaced by Great-Grandpa Braun and Great-Grandma Koehler, changed to Braun).
2. Their only child known to me was my grandfather William Braun, whose wife was Minnie.
3. Their children were William H., Minnie, Corinne and Charlotte.

Jacob Wiebert,
Grandmother Minnie's father

Grandmother Minnie's father was Jacob Wiebert, 1837-1896, who was born in Germany and emigrated to Illinois. He fought for the north in the Civil War. Aunt Minnie married Joseph. Both were devout Catholics and understood and respected my call to missions. They had a prosperous home with expensive paintings and chinaware, lived a happy life and died rather early with no children.

Aunt Corinne married a Mr. Koch whom I don't remember. She had a daughter Fern, who is my age and is a longtime friend. Aunt Corinne had a popular downtown restaurant. When I visited St. Louis I'd stop by to visit her. She served scrumptious fudge sundaes and was a very sweet lady.

I recall that she gave me chickens when I graduated from grade school. This may seem to be an unusual gift but at that age I was sold on chicken farming – copying my Uncle John's poultry farm. I built a solid little chicken house in the backyard and kept chicken feed and fresh straw in it. They gave lots of eggs, which my mother bought from me, helping cover my costs for chicken feed purchased from a large store a mile away. All of that in a city neighborhood is unimaginable today, but most city people had been farmers and the transition to today's urban regulations was still decades away. Outdoor toilets were still widely used then.

Aunt Corinne listened to TV evangelists and found saving faith in Jesus.

Aunt Charlotte, bless her heart, had remained at home, caring for her father, mother and her mother's brother, her Uncle Will Seibert. She saw all three through their final illnesses and buried them, then married an older man whom she cherished until he died. A second marriage to another elderly gentleman followed. It ended with his death. Then Aunt Corinne sickened and Aunt Charlotte kept close contact with her until her death.

Not many people's lives in our society are encumbered by six illnesses and burials and losses, as was Aunt Charlotte's life. Yet she was ever a cheerful, thoughtful person and a talented artist who designed cloth prints for Ely Walker, a large St. Louis dress manufacturer. I was keen on art in high school and Aunt Char invited me to try my hand at designing cloth patterns at her home. My teenage

Beloved Aunt Char,
artist and loving caregiver

hand did not have the professional perfection required. One trial was enough to prove that. Her patterns were truly exquisite.

Aunt Charlotte became a follower of the Lord. In later years she lived in retirement with her aging boxer dog. She loved to give Thelma pieces of her jewelry bought by her two prosperous husbands. We stayed at her home often when in St. Louis and had good times together. On each visit she gathered the family together for a dinner at the Bevo Mill, famous for its Olde Germany ambiance and food. She is with Jesus now.

Fern, my cousin, married a Mr. Maushund and had a daughter Loyce, who as a very pretty collegian married a winsome scientist who maintained his ties with relatives in Turkey and visited them often. He was 100% American in culture and was always warmly friendly to Thelma and me. He and Loyce had two children, both well educated.

That exhausts the family except for my half-brother, born to my father and his new wife Alice. His name is William, or Bill, and he is ten years my junior. He is well educated, brilliant, charming, single and has filled the house with his beautiful oil paintings to the point where it resembles a very crowded museum. A wooden bust of his father sculpted by him joins other art experiments around the piano, which he plays skillfully. He never married.

A wooden bust of William H. Braun, carved by his son, William

"Comparisons are odious," it is said. But in my years of sociology study there were many instructive case studies of families, and I see some value in making a few observations about these two American families. They were both European immigrants, both Lutheran, both what we call nominal Christians. Grandpa Ross died a poor farmer and a drunkard. Grandpa Braun died a prosperous city man. So far, there was a rather uneven playing field, with no place for God on either side.

It was Grandma Matilda Ross's discovery of the transforming power of Jesus Christ as Lord and Savior that changed the future for generations of her offspring.

The Braun side of the family was prosperous, gifted, law-abiding, urban, close-knit and loving. I am describing ideal American citizens, am I not? But the Bible was not their book and Jesus Christ was not embraced as their personal Savior except in the later years of several individuals. So what? In our society, so nothing. They were, are, very good people.

And what about Matilda's offspring? Remember, they were a farming family. After the death of Grandpa Ross, his widow and children moved to St. Louis. Farmers new to a city have few skills to offer employers. Not one of Matilda's children owned a house, except my mother. A surprising number died young. All were poor. But all were devout, incredibly happy in their love for Bible truths and for the God who wrote them. Church was their society, their culture and their life. They were rich in faith and holiness, and these were what Matilda's grandchildren inherited from her and her children. Empty talk? Not at all. Matilda's offspring now number 83, of which 14 were Brauns. They include musicians, artists, builders, college and seminary professors, businessmen, pastors, missionaries, authors of books and editors of magazines. They have ministered powerfully in Africa and Asia. Overall, they are as prosperous as the Braun families, often highly educated and, in a word, blessed of God. They too are good citizens, loyal Americans, and followers of the God Matilda discovered and taught them to love and obey.

This I see as a case study our American society could see replicated by the millions, all across these fertile plains, if it would only look. Its message is simple; "It pays to serve Jesus. It pays every day. It pays every step of the way." Sons and daughters of Matilda, faithfully follow the Lord God and He will faithfully bless your life and those who are your heirs.

6

FATHER

In this chapter I want to note the similarities of my father's life and my own. Both of us seem to have repented and come to the Savior at or about age 17 through the ministry of the Plymouth Brethren. He was preaching on the street at age 18. I was teaching a Bible study for young men at that age. He wrote to a missionary in Spain offering to be a missionary there. He was advised by the man in Spain to ask the local elders to send him. Another letter to a missionary in the Philippines indicated a

William H. Braun

continuing concern for missions. He never got to the fields. I did, not with the Brethren, but with the strong mission program of the C&MA – for a lifetime.

Like my father, I enjoyed art. He made it his profession for about seven years, then moved into sales of cosmetics and eventually opened his own company, Imperial Brands. Throughout my decades I engaged in drawing, sculpture, painting, carpentry, carving, architecture, illustrations for publications, slide shows and collections of dozens of paintings. My father's house in North Hollywood, California has dozens of fine oil paintings which his wife and son painted and there were more dozens, unframed, rolled up in a closet. In our love for art we were similar.

In his late teens he was a man on the move. He married at 20, had partnerships with two very successful St. Louis artists in whose large homes I spent many happy hours. They were fine Christian men, both very active lifelong in their Assemblies. A written contract with one gave my father thirty dollars a week and the other man only five. A letterhead in the collection was handsomely designed for the company of Braun and Walters. My father's name was first, indicating that he was the senior partner – at 18, 19, 20 or 21.

In his family life he was articulately loving. A large number of letters written from other cities always began and ended with loving titles and phrases and he wrote often of his love for his "babies."

There is no clear indication when his whole life changed nor why. The saintly, loving, preaching Christian artist turned away from St. Louis and the warm testimony of a believer.

When I was 32 and the family was back in the US on furlough, he called and asked me if I would be willing to run his business in Chicago. I thanked him but told him my years were given to the Lord and I could not accept his offer. It had no attraction whatever for me. I had tasted and seen that the Lord is good. I was the happy man who trusted in Him. As I reflect on the fact that William, his son by his second marriage, was then 23 years old, out of college two years and a brilliant student, I suspect that son did not want to be tied to the family business. Probably his parents wanted him to go with them to California as well. He did, and he cared for them until they died.

My relationship with my father was always that of dissidence. We wrote from time to time but my goal could only and always be to bring him back to Christ. His goal was to be admired and loved as he was. I wanted my earthly father to be in heaven with me for endless fellowship. He wanted only a surface, felicitous posturing as if everything was jolly fine. I never wanted to anger him or hurt him. I only wanted to restore him to saving faith. He would have none of it.

A verse my father loved to quote to me was "Honor thy father and thy mother." My mother I honored always. I honor my father as well as the fervent street preacher and passionate extoller of the Lamb of God in his courtship days. I honor him as a Christian businessman and as the applicant for missions in Spain. I honor him for his loving letters to the wife he left behind with two tots.

But there is a dateline beyond which the honorable father was in no sense a spiritual or moral role model. I do not write this in anger, but in wistful sadness. I only indicate that in obedience to God, I honor my father for years in which I did not know him. Beyond those years I could only pray for his salvation and speak or write of my Father who is in heaven.

7

ST. LOUIS

The pony was safer than the tricycle!

Few memories attach themselves to the flat in which my earliest years were spent on Lee Street in North Saint Louis in the 1920s. I recall a tricycle and a high-speed chase after a rooster which ended in a crash and a bump that pushed up beyond belief on my head. I remember an outdoor toilet in the back yard and being bathed in a round, galvanized tub. I remember long rides in streetcars to attend missionary services in a suburb called Maplewood, which ended

Willys with
grade school diploma

in my total collapse in slumber and being carried home by my Uncle John. I remember a tree with branches similar to those of ash trees - but they broke easily. I learned that to my hurt.

Mother moved us to a new house near Hyde Park when I was about seven. It had a nice bathroom and a full basement where I played and developed skills in carpentry and, later, built a ping-pong table. This was a home full of love for fifteen years, long enough for me to graduate from grade school and high school, to attend freshman year at a branch of Missouri University and to work for a few years, then to study at Wheaton College.

Hyde Park had a large pond which was home to schools of sunfish. An average hour of fishing yielded four or five little fellows - just enough to make our kitchen smell of fried fish - a nauseating odor to my sister Dorothy. I'll never understand fish. One day they were ravenously hungry and I pulled in over seventy. I recall reclaiming

32

a one-half inch segment of worm from seven fish before it disappeared. One day I got a bite and pulled up a large snapping turtle which was so heavy the little hook straightened out and the turtle swam away.

Hyde Park pond froze over in winter and I would sled down the surrounding hill onto its busy surface. There I learned to ice skate, only to find my ankles preferred to bend out at a most unproductive angle. Roller skating was more fun. I could speed around the smooth asphalt roads for hours. But ice skating, as an art form, eluded me forever. I remember my buddy, Harold Wright, saying one day, "Catch me, Bill." He was about three feet away. I lurched eagerly forward but he was on the other side of the pond. Clearly I was not meant to be a part of the Ice Follies, though the idea of folly does seem applicable to my efforts on the ice.

I did better wrestling, playing football and baseball. But there was this thing with my fingers. I seemed always to have a bluish black fingernail. As a catcher, sizzling balls tipped slightly by a batter arrived, but not in my catcher's mitt. Carpentry contributed its share of black nails, as did car doors, moving rocks or lumber, or carrying a canoe. The world was full of black nails for me. None of them deterred me from adding another. It was just part of being a kid, an adventurous kid.

Knights played a major role in my grade school days. Mother dressed me in short pants with knee-length golf stockings. An admired older fellow shouted at me one day, "Knight so bold, and he wears half socks." I saw nothing unsuitable about half socks. Knighthood was in the spirit of a man, not in his socks. Horse and rider contests were all the thing in those days and pulling other riders down was the greatest of sports.

The Carnegie Library across from our Clay School had books on chivalry with magnificent engraving block illustrations. The stories made an avid reader of me. But best of all they were as thick as a Manhattan telephone book, with heavy hard covers. A book like that slammed down on another knight's head produced a rewarding thump and brought him down - but not out. My own head has a slight hollow between the front and the back. You may remember Perry Winkle. Whether our bent for literature helped form my skull I do not know. But knighthood truly flowered on the way home from the library.

The Mississippi River was only five blocks from my home. To reduce erosion of the west bank, the city fathers had trucked in rough granite blocks of about a cubic yard in size. These were bumped up against each other into a very irregular surface with ups and downs and wide cracks between stones. A favored sport was to run a block on those stones, feet flying in long jumps, short hops up or down faster, faster, faster. Oh, for a bit of that pep and agility today!

The river was a fascinating magnet to me and to my friend, Johnny Thiesse. I had a single-shot 22 rifle and we would take a box of shells down to the river and shoot at safety matches. In those years guns were common and hunting was what men did. I bought my first shotgun when it and I were about the same height. Squirrels, rabbits and doves were valued for food, and a boy who brought meat to the table was a hero. I often took my shotgun on the streetcar to hunt in fields on the edge of the city and no one thought anything of it.

Johnny was a businessman at age 14. He convinced me that there was money to be made repairing bicycles, so we rented a nearby garage and set up shop. He said we needed to buy broken bikes and repair and sell them. We bought bikes. We bought parts, re-spoked wheels and painted the vehicles. I don't recall selling any. Certainly the world didn't beat a path to our atelier.

Then Johnny had another idea for the garage - boat building. So we went to a lumberyard, bought lumber and built a rowboat with oarlocks and oars. The craft was heavy as lead. I imagine we hired a truck to take it to the river. We put it in the water and watched it fill up and settle on the bottom. Chatting with river people who had boats tipped us off to what we had to do. It was called caulking. We bought the cotton threads we needed and pressed them into all the cracks and daubed it all with tar. That made our boat watertight and fun to row around the huge river. But it cost money. We parked the boat with a houseboat man for a princely sum each month. Winter came and each month we paid for an unused boat. By spring we wearied of this heavy tax and sold the boat - for just about what the lumber cost. Our boat-building days ended at that point. A much-used canoe was purchased for $14 and that, added to a $12 racer bike, increased mobility considerably.

Our family never had a car except for a month when I risked my savings for college to take a carload of St. Louis boys to Dallas, Texas for a boys' camp. When we returned, I sold the car and lost very little in the deal. But the racer bike is what opened up the city of St. Louis to me. I recall one Saturday singing in time with the pedals, "There was a tailor had a mouse, Hi diddle um cum fiddle. They lived together in a house. Hi diddle um cum fiddle." There were more verses and I would go into high gear when "terrin tandem" came up. That song was good for miles of exploring the gateway to the west in all of its neighborhoods.

A favorite area was Lindell Boulevard where stately mansions looked out over the city's famous Forest Park, site of a world's fair before my time. It was a day when the park was safe for all night and day. There was the great zoo with animals from around the world. Africa's huge pythons and India's cobras were there with the anacondas of South America. One day keepers were feeding a twenty-foot python which was too lethargic to eat. I was asked to hold a yard of him straight. A keeper came with a five-inch fire hose full of ground beef and a long shover. The snake's mouth was opened and the hose shoved a foot into its throat. With a rush forward the man with the shover swooshed the ground meat into the snake's stomach and the job was done. We carried the lazy fellow back into his cage. I fell in love with God's creatures and until today find the TV programs about animals to be fascinating.

Forest Park has a splendid art museum, a classic setting for young people who crave beauty. The hours I spent in its marble halls were thrilling. There were gorgeous paintings by American and European masters. I still remember a landscape of an evening in which the sun streamed through breaks in the clouds in dazzling shafts as real as life. I recall ivory carvings from the orient, a statue of Abraham Lincoln with every detail of this earthy president marvelously replicated. There was a marble girl inspecting a frog and there were, yes, real knights in armor. I saw no half socks, but they could have been hidden under the plates and chain mail. Probably were. But I could sense that those warriors had the same noble urge to battle as I had.

The bird house, the elephants, lions, gorillas, apes and open pits of bears were endless attention-getters. I drew buffaloes close up. One old bull charged the fence where I was sketching and I almost went to heaven right there. I must have really made his rheumy-eyed day.

Willys, a student
at Missouri University

Once a year the South Side Assembly had a Sunday school picnic and our family was always invited. Why? Well, the leading elder of the Assembly was a commercial artist and had once been a partner with my artist father. Mother and Mrs. Hendricks remained close friends. The Hendricks had two sons about my age and that strengthened the bond.

I recall a summer when I was old enough to hit home runs in the picnic softball game and old enough too to appreciate an especially winsome young lady who attended that Assembly. A large lagoon had been created in the park and canoes could be rented. I secured Gladys' agreement to go for a canoe ride after the supper was over. I had been canoeing for years and had a most enjoyable hour paddling the quiet waters with this lovely friend. Little did I realize that she would be engaged and married to Richard Schramm before the next picnic. We were older than I knew.

Across from the park, in a well-lighted room behind one of the stone mansions, a group of university students met for a fencing exercise. They wore the standard reinforced white garb and wire masks. They had foils with buttons on the ends and they attacked and retreated with the slender foils seeking to strike through to register a touch in a vital area. There were also matches with epees and they were much noisier and far more dangerous. It was a magic setting and I recall a

36

handsome fencer seated at a table with his chin gracefully supported by the interlaced fingers of his upraised arms. It was a perfect pose for a striking photograph and I have found myself trying to imitate it on occasion, but with no impressive results. However, I did buy old foils and masks and fenced on occasion. The fencing equipment even went to Congo with us in 1945 - a perfect waste of space, but too cherished a memory to leave behind. Youth . . .

After high school I attended a depression-inspired branch of Missouri University in the downtown YMCA in St. Louis. It was not until Christ came into my heart that my mind turned to serious study. Both occurred when I was seventeen, far too late to benefit my high school records. But going to college opened doors in my mind, some to bless me, some to curse. I came to the conclusion one day that I was unable to write one sentence in correct English. The college offered an hour of remedial English an hour before regular classes began. I walked the two miles to the school an hour early all winter. A Jewish professor patiently rid me of childish usages common to my crowd and helped me understand the underlying structure of our language. A set of books added greatly to my vocabulary and I gained confidence that I could indeed write and speak correctly. It was probably the best thing that happened to me in that university.

The worst thing that happened was the overpowering conviction that all I had believed about God and Scripture was false. Professors gave powerful "proofs" of evolution for which I was totally unprepared. Young people see nobility in standing for truth. Suddenly "truth" was the enemy of all I had believed to be true. I was devastated. I continued to go to church with my mother and sister. My real friends were Christians. But they had not faced these professors and their unanswerable alternative to faith.

For two years I wallowed in unbelief. I found a few non-Christian friends who lived comfortably with disbelief. But I found no comfort in them. I tried to start a small business of my own but that hope was dashed. I attempted to court a Christian girl and that ended in a deep feeling of rejection. I was outside, looking into the society of which I had been a happy part.

Perhaps it was these combined tensions which made my nose bleed and bleed one night. I could not stop it and I felt I was weakening.

Lying on my cot it seemed to me the Lord of heaven said, "You have a choice to make me your Master or...." I don't recall the alternative but whatever it was, I didn't want it. I wanted a divine Master. And that is what He became that forlorn night - for the next 61 years, so far.

Evolution? It is no problem. "In the beginning my Master created the heavens and the earth." I have never doubted it since my nose stopped bleeding. I have never questioned the love and wisdom of my Master, nor the integrity of His Book. I have served Him over six decades and He has lavished His love on me and mine. The cold, hopeless, godless efforts of man to explain his world apart from the Creator-Savior God can only lead to emptiness of soul. God has a far nobler life than that for those He made in His own likeness.

One part of Brethren teaching was shed slowly over a long period – the notion that other denominations were not biblical. One Sunday I left Wheaton for a mass rally of Christians and saw tens of thousands of people singing my Brethren songs! It was most confusing. There may have been other Brethren there, but not everyone was Brethren - yet they were all singing "our songs" printed in a tiny black book without music. Wheaton itself was an eye-opener with exuberant Christians from denominations I KNEW were liberal!

How God ever brought this exclusionist preacher to travel the world and find great Christians in every denomination as preparation for leadership in launching nationwide movements of evangelism that won many, many liberal pastors to saving faith and a saving message on two continents I'll never know. But He did.

I have found amazing Brethren churchmen around the world heading exceptionally large ministries. They have impacted India by sheer spiritual power. Many churchmen there have Brethren roots but now lead independent agencies of great vigor. I do not count my years in the North Side Assembly as a misfortune, but as God's choice – thanks again to Matilda and Mother's piety and obedience.

8

THE FARM

John Bossert married Anna, one of Matilda's daughters. Anna died young and, after a period of grieving, John sought to marry her sister Amelia, Matilda's oldest daughter. She felt called to the mission field and resisted the importunity of her brother-in-law. But while the Brethren do support many, many missionaries around the world, St. Louis Assemblies had not sent any of their own. Amelia was not sent out and she finally agreed to marry. She had kept my mother after Matilda's death and now Lillian was ready to marry. Amelia, oldest of the children, finally was free to marry John Bossert.

John and Amelia decided to buy a pioneer's log cabin and farm in Franklin County, 60 miles west of St. Louis and only 50 miles from Bonne Terre, where she had lived as a young girl. She must have welcomed the idea. Farm life could be a very happy way to live.

The family traveled by train to Leslie, a dying town with a closed bank, a closed mill and a closed post office. One business that was still open was the saloon, notable for its collection of red fox pelts, added to each winter. Furs were very popular those days, so popular that hunters could no longer find raccoons, mink or muskrat. Only possums and skunks were left, and the former would bring a day's wages and the latter two and a half days. It was great fun to follow the dogs at night in hopes of treeing a possum or holing up a skunk. And a winter's catch worth $60 was not a small matter.

There was also a general store in Leslie operated by Messrs. Strehlman and Gerkin, two hard-working retailers with almost anything a farm family needed, from dress materials, to farm machinery, to seed and chicken feed. To me, its sights and smells, the round wood stove heating it and most of all, the dignified, daring, all-knowing farmers who drifted in from unknown areas, with their horse-drawn buggies, surpassed anything I experienced in St. Louis. Here was drama, down-to-earth wisdom and the amazing reality of families who lived from the soil in log cabins they had built with their own hands.

It was this segment of America's society that the St. Louis Bossert family entered at the town of Leslie. They probably found a farmer who would load up their belongings in his wagon and haul them to their farm three miles away. They would have bought flour, salt, sugar and other needs at the store in Leslie to begin life on their land.

From the age of six to seventeen I spent an average of four months a year on that farm. In the early years I was picked up at the train station by my cousin Johnny, ten years my senior, in an old, cracked leather buggy housed in a log shelter when not in use. It was pulled by a dappled gray named Mark and a brown horse named Pete. My cousin Amelia, three years my senior and named for her mother, who then became known as Meelie to distinguish her from her daughter, would take bridles to these horses when they were free in the pasture, bridle them, lead them into a deep ditch so we could jump on their backs, and then we would roam the pasture part of the sixty-acre farm.

They were work horses used to pull wagons loaded with hay or winter fodder or the buggy to town, as needed. They were not riding horses and no saddles were available. But they were friendly, serviceable members of farm life and were well treated.

One ride fresh in memory seventy-five years later began as a familiar jog through young oaks in the pasture at late dusk. Suddenly a nearby piercing, human-like scream panicked the two horses and no less their child riders. The animals bolted back toward the barn at a frenzied gallop and pulled up in a jolting stop at the barbed wire gate. I leaped off Pete and, in the dark, ran to open the gate. Fumbling in the dark for the pole, I felt a barb go deep into the corner of my eye, just missing the eyeball. I ignored the pain, found the gate's pole, unlooped the wire over the pole and the horses rushed in to what to them was safety. We put them in their stables and rushed to the cabin to tell our experience to Aunt Meelie and John. They listened and decided it was a lynx or cougar warning us away.

My Uncle John and Aunt Meelie were the closest thing I had to maternal grandparents. They had served as parents to my mother until she married. In my youth Uncle John was often away in St. Louis earning money to keep the farm going. Little John, as he was often called, was the farmer and man of the house. In hunting season he would take me to farms abandoned by their pioneer families. Each had its own graveyard. All were in the process of decay, some more advanced than others. A generation had farmed the poor soil. Their sons and daughters had abandoned the land and left their homes to fall.

Aunt Meelie,
queen bee of the
congregation

A state road from Leslie passed about a third of a mile from the farm, and the mailbox was on that road. It was my chore to go for the mail each day and the trip took me over rail fences onto the land of what we called "the Old House." Like my uncle's, it had a little two-story log cabin. Its wood-shingled roof had rotted through and upstairs rain was soaking old clothes and letters left behind. Usually I paid no attention to the cabin, but on occasion when rain caught me near it I would find shelter in it. One day I was reading letters written by German farmers. English and German were interspersed, but the messages were clear. They told of sickness and of crops and neighbors. And they told of the arrival of the railroad track to and through Leslie.

While reading I became aware of big bumblebees buzzing around and discovered they had made a nest in the damp, rotting clothes. Having been badly stung by bumblebees on various occasions, I regarded them as enemies to humankind. The walls downstairs had been plastered over rough, four-foot plaster laths. These were open to view and I took one, returned upstairs and began to swat the enemy as they rose heavily from their nest. One came in from the outside and looked me over before attacking, giving me time to swat it. This was a very small nest and soon its few workers were hors du combat. The rain ended and I left a bit of history behind to get the mail.

The Old House had a small pond and I circled it often to seek frogs for food. One day I saw an enormous snapping turtle lying just below the surface. It, too, was an enemy of man, fish and animals. I looked for the biggest rock I could lift and dropped it on him. It was of no significance to this mammoth reptile. He simply paddled slowly into deeper water.

Good fishing at the farm

One day I had my gun up at that pond and saw a seven-foot snake lying on the bank. Very, very unwisely I tried to kill it by banging the wood stock on it. The stock broke off and I learned the intricacies of making a replacement. Very, very unwisely I used the same gun in the same way to kill a winded antelope twenty years later in Belgian Congo with the same shameful result. Some things we never learn well.

God met my heart by that pond one day and I did learn His lesson for life. Cousin Amelia knew there were crawfish in the murky waters of the pond. She shaped a circle of a strong piece of wire and sewed a piece of mosquito net on the circle, shaped as a shallow net. To this net she attached four cords with which to put it in the water and pull it out. She packed some chicken gizzards, string, a pan, salt and matches and we two walked to the pond to catch crawdads.

This was accomplished by placing the net out in the pond where we could see it and throwing a piece of gizzard tied to a line out in the deeper water. When the line registered active tugs, Amelia slowly pulled it in over the net where we could see and catch the rascals. It worked so well that in a short time we had a pot full. The next step was to boil them. It had rained recently and the wood and grass were not yet dry. As head of operations, Amelia put some sticks and grass together and struck matches one after the other. None started a fire. With the last match in her fingers she stopped, thought for a minute, and said, "Will, let's pray." So we bowed our heads and she asked Jesus to light the fire. We raised our heads and she struck the last match. It began a blaze which boiled the water and cooked the crawdads for two kids on their knees before Him. It began a blaze in my heart as well, one that is still burning bright after many years.

I was the only male in our home in St. Louis, so was outnumbered by my mother and sister. On the farm, Johnny was often farming and my companions were Aunt Meelie and young Amelia. Added to that on occasions was my cousin Esther, who was my age. It was a feminine world much of the time and I think this prepared me for a long and happy marriage. All of those females taught me how to live comfortably with them and to walk humbly with my God.

My Aunt Meelie kept her two children, plus Esther and me when we were there, fed and on schedule through lonely years when her husband was earning money during long depression years. Little John built a 100-foot-long chicken house, an incubator cellar and a brooder house in a courageous effort to make the farm pay. He plowed, planted and harvested wheat, oats and corn to feed the cows, horses, chickens and pigs. He hunted and fished for meat and fur.

Aunt Meelie planted a large garden each spring and canned or stored its produce for food through the winter. She was an excellent cook and city friends loved to sit at her table and eat squirrel, rabbit, possum, chicken or pork - with all the trimmin's. When Uncle John visited the farm on occasional weekends he would take his wife on walks on a road through the woods and share his dreams with her of financial success raising chickens and of a big farm house and a car. I ran up the road ahead of them looking for lizards to throw rocks at. They liked my antics. They laughed at my efforts, which encouraged me to show off more and more.

There were tender evenings on the porch where little John played his Sears-and-Roebuck guitar and we sang and chatted until bedtime in the sweet summer evenings. Uncle John was not a popular preacher in the Assembly in St. Louis. Too much Greek, I suspect. But on the farm he managed to bring from forty to sixty farmers together each Sunday morning at the house of the Hellings, a prosperous farm family with ten children, including some full-grown, strong sons who worked hard and made the farm pay. Uncle John preached the Word with zeal several years and there was talk of building a church.

Those were happy years. Aunt Meelie was the queen bee of the congregation and she took her position seriously. She was a bright and shining matron at the Sunday meetings. A marriageable son and daughter added keenness to her social demeanor. There was lots of laughter and good will and not a small amount of courting and marriage - wonderful times for all.

And then money ran out and Uncle John left for St. Louis where his job was always awaiting him. Church services ended. The depression lowered egg and chicken prices. Life on the farm became more lonely, more difficult.

I recall one summer day when little John and I returned from town, having sold large cages of white leghorns to Strehlman and Gerkin and bought chicken feed and a sack of flour. When Johnny stopped the team in front of the cabin to take the sack of flour into the house, Aunt Meelie came out and saw that a nail in the wagon had opened a hole in the sack, letting a tablespoon full of flour to leak out. To her this was a devastating crisis. She cried like a baby. There was no end to the battle of life for her.

But one Sunday afternoon a nearby gunshot opened new vistas of anguish for this lady. Hunting on Sunday was taboo with Uncle John. But Uncle John was in St. Louis. His son, an adult now, felt that hunting was a quiet, restful way to spend a Sunday afternoon. He had hunted that day and came home by the barn where he fed some hay to the horses and returned to the house. His sister later went out to the animals to do her daily chores, saw her brother's gun leaning against the barn and picked it up to carry to the cabin.

She was an able gun handler, a good hunter. Did her dog frisk around playfully and jump up, pulling the trigger? We do not know, but the back of Amelia's skull was blasted off. Her mother and brother found her and did what farmers had done for thousands of years. They prepared her for burial and placed her on her bed. The neighbors came from far and wide. Uncle John and I rushed out to the farm and saw the lovely girl asleep on her bed. I also saw fragments of her brain high on the side of the barn. We buried Amelia under a great oak in the cemetery in Leslie, not on the farm plot. Already, I suspect, the thought was in the minds of her parents that one day they would leave the farm.

Uncle John and I, shocked and grieving, went home to St. Louis, but not long afterward Uncle John moved to the farm to be with his wife. The church services were begun again and Johnny sought the Lord as Savior and was baptized. This comforted his parents. A bit later Marie, one of the Helling girls, caught Johnny's eye and they were married and fixed up the brooder house nicely for a home. A baby girl was born and life seemed promising once more. But money ran out and back went Uncle John to his work in St. Louis, Aunt Meelie with him. They established themselves in an apartment where peace and comfort reigned.

By that time I had graduated and was employed in the headquarters offices of the International Shoe Company. Our family saw the elder Bosserts regularly at church. But Uncle John missed the preaching he loved so much on the farm. One fall evening he asked me to go with him to a warehouse where homeless men could get a bowl of soup and a cot to sleep on free. He was scheduled to speak to the men about his Lord.

Uncle John was well qualified to speak to such men, for in his youth he had been a man of the road who drank, smoked and brawled from city to city between jobs. He knew the life and the vocabulary and deep needs of these men. And he could tell them that the day he turned to the Savior he was transformed, never to drink, smoke or brawl again. The crisp fall air and the joy of sharing Jesus with those men combined to restore vitality to my old uncle's stride.

He was young in spirit as we walked block after block toward home, enjoying each other. But when we reached Delmar, a very busy street, I looked to my left to see what cars were coming down toward us and missed seeing that my uncle, on my right, had dashed out to the center line, while I waited on the curb. Suddenly brakes shrieked and my beloved Uncle John's body flew through the air to drop unconscious on the boulevard. A young driver had crossed the line at the intersection, not seeing the man standing there.

An ambulance took us to a hospital where a doctor told me Uncle John needed blood for a transfusion. I did not hesitate to give it but as soon as he had the blood, he told me my uncle was dead. I realize now that there was no blood typing. Had the doctor simply lied to get free blood? If so, so be it.

The driver had clearly broken the law several ways but my aunt told policemen, "God's will was done. Suing this young man will not bring my husband back to me. I forgive him in Jesus' name." She returned to her apartment, lonely once again.

Without Uncle John's financial help, there was no hope for the young Bosserts of living on the farm. They auctioned off the animals and furniture, went to St. Louis and moved in once more with Aunt Meelie, who loved the baby and company. Johnny found employment in a factory, stamping out metal parts in a giant press. He hated it. Marie hated it. He went to work. She went to bars. Before long Marie left her husband and daughter, divorced and re-married.

Johnny, baby Florence and Aunt Meelie lived together. Florence became an attractive, warm Christian young lady and married a young man. Aunt Meelie, the Swedish immigrant, went to be with her Lord. Johnny sold the farm lands and built a very nice house for his daughter, her husband and himself and lived out his remaining years with them, a quiet but respected Christian.

At that time, Thelma and I were missionaries with three boys, none of whom knew anything about the Bosserts and their long, important role in my life. During my years visiting the farm I wanted nothing more in life than to be a Missouri farmer. God had something else in mind for me, but those rural years made life on a jungled mountaintop easy, comfortable and happy. There wasn't much difference except the people were black and spoke a language we quickly learned.

9

THE BRETHREN

As a child and youth I accepted what I regarded as the theology of the Plymouth Brethren among whom I lived. Salvation proceeding from personal repentance and faith in Christ's sacrifice for sin and His resurrection was the constant preoccupation. Every Sunday evening was a gospel service. Sunday morning was for the breaking of bread, a people's forum where any man could preach, pray or begin a hymn - always a cappella.

These communion services were often emotional as the sufferings of the sacrifice were described in crushing detail. Tears flowed easily in the presence of the bread (a loaf) and the cup - one love cup. And "When I Survey the Wondrous Cross" was sung passionately like a glorious paean of victory in Christ. There was worship, real, palpable worship in those services. And only the saints gathered in those non-public meetings were permitted to give tithes to the support of the Assembly. After all, there were no pastors or staff to pay. Utilities and perhaps building payments or repairs composed the very low budget.

Sunday school, Wednesday night prayer meeting and Friday night Bible studies completed the five-service weekly schedule, except when there were special weeks of evangelism or Bible teaching by one of the rather numerous traveling preachers. They were a colorful lot. Mother always invited them to a splendid Sunday noon feast so I got to know some of them. Arthur Smith had held the first chair in the Toronto Symphony Orchestra, as I remember. His violin, after dinner, sobbed and pealed, double-stringed and plucked so movingly I bought a fiddle from a second-hand store and began imitating the maestro. Mother paid for lessons all winter and I reached a nearly recognizable "America the Beautiful" before the weather warmed up

47

enough for baseball, when I obeyed Stephen Foster's advice, "Hang up the fiddle and the bow...."

To fill out the picture of the Brethren a bit more, I must mention Maplewood Assembly. A remarkable number of prosperous professional and businessmen led that group, taking part in preaching and teaching, praying and calling on the sick. It was, I think, the ideal Assembly. It was not immune from the near-fatal virus of the St. Louis Assemblies which drove away so many children of Brethren families. A smooth transition of young men into a welcome sharing of the ministries seemed impossible. The age gap deepened as godly men grew older and their sons, at 21, still seemed to them to be immature children. They lost so many to churches which welcomed them - or to the world where they disappeared.

But missionaries liked to preach at Maplewood. As a missionary, I understand why. There was good attendance and unusual wealth, both very attractive to overseas lay preachers wanting to build a church or school or medical dispensary. Mother took us to some of these missionary meetings. I don't remember the messages now, but one man from Africa had spread out a huge lion skin on the platform and, after the service, I joined other little boys sitting on this very flat king of the beasts. Somehow I found myself by a paw, armed with terrible claws. My fingers examined these and, oops, one slipped off the bone core. I was horrified. I was frightened. I was thrilled. The claw was quietly deposited in a pocket and became an item in my tin box of treasures which on occasion I buried in the garden, as all pirates do. To this day I feel the Lord hooked me for Africa with that claw.

Harold Harper, an unknown pair of Welshmen with fine voices, an Englishman with the look of a prophet and others preached in our city. As an adolescent I begged the prophet to let me be his Elisha and go with him. I wanted to be exactly like him. He kindly required that I finish high school. I never saw him again. Arthur Rogers was a warm-hearted evangelist whom I greatly liked. When he drove from St. Louis to meetings in Kansas I went with him. I recall sharing with him a sense of loneliness. It was true, the gang I grew up with included no known Christians. They became fine athletes and won the city baseball championship in Sportsman's Park, but they grew into activities in which I could not join. I felt abandoned. Christian youth my age were in other Assemblies, but the old men had driven all young men away from mine.

Mr. Rogers' only advice was to be faithful to God and to show myself friendly to others. We reached his Kansas Assembly and after a service and meal there, with some black families included, I hitch-hiked 400 miles across Kansas and Missouri to my home. And, believe it or not, I can't recall one person who drove me that distance. (Hitchhiking was honorable in those depression days. Not many people had cars and those who did were generally affable people's people, extroverts who welcomed a neat young fellow to brag to. Perhaps they were bored being alone too. Certainly they weren't worried about giving a boy a ride.)

One more incident in the Brethren Assemblies returns to mind. At one evening service we had an exciting visitor, a turbaned Indian Christian. He was invited to speak, this big, exotic visitor, and he told a heart-breaking story of persecution of his large family because they were Christian. Yet there was a note of faith and determination to serve God, no matter the cost. The elders were deeply moved. They rallied around this poor brother and many dollars passed unseen from elder to Indian in heartfelt handshakes - Brethren style. The Scripture for this method of giving is to let not your left hand know what your right hand is doing and, if you give your gifts before men you already have your reward.

Well, the newspaper, not long after that, ran an article about a certain Gunaseka Rama Hathamya, a big St. Louis African-American whose real name may have been closer to Andrew Jones, who wore a towel around his head and was shaking down the churches for money to rescue a mythical wife and many children in India. He had collected large sums of money to the delight of his real St. Louis family.

Gunaseka Rama Hathamya - name to charm with. Depression-bound St. Louis lacked little in creative scams. People were out of work and found many new ways to survive. Gunaseka had only to cross the river to thrill the churches of Illinois.

I owe the Brethren a deep experience of conversion and surrender to Jesus my Lord. This has been foundational and upon it the Master has built whatever followed. I have maintained a robust expectation that God can use laymen in powerful ways and was unordained during perhaps half of my missionary years with the Alliance. In fact, I spent ten years teaching about 200 pastors from whom many would be ordained – before the leadership learned I had not been ordained in the rush to get us to Africa.

My days in St. Louis were drawing to a close, unknown to me. I rejoined the young men of the Assemblies. I had seen dozens of them leave the fellowship and never return. With an older friend, Joe Boge, I called the remaining young men to a meeting to study the Bible and to open a discussion on how to save the future of the Brethren gatherings. Already the once-large North St. Louis Assembly had fallen apart because of bullish old cranks who destroyed each other and drove out the younger men.

Young men's Bible class
Willys at left end of top row

The Young Men's Bible Study met each month and was the healing, uniting force that staunched the flow of men out of the congregations. It went on for many years until the young men were strongly entrenched leaders in their various Assemblies.

At the same time I created a voice of youth to youth in a monthly paper called *Today and Tomorrow*. It was welcomed throughout the Brethren of St. Louis and it too was continued long after the Lord opened the door for me to go to Wheaton College.

My returns to St. Louis were few and short after that. Through the decades my friends have gone to glory. I have no family there on my mother's side and only a cousin and her family on my father's.

Life moves along and proves over and over that you can't go home again.

10

SHOES

After the year in Missouri University, I got a job with the International Shoe Company, headquartered on Washington Boulevard in downtown St. Louis. Its ten-story office building filled the block, and a ten-story warehouse filled an adjoining block. It had 15 name brands, such as Mother Goose and Star Brand, and one of every seven pairs of shoes sold in America was made by this company. Some 60 shoe factories, a canvas plant and a rubber plant dotted the mid-western states - a very impressive empire.

My role was an humble one. I liked art and have an eye for it. The art department of this huge company had a brace of designers who earned five times my salary. They drew some beautiful and some ugly fashions on paper. A pattern department made metal-edged hardboard cutting patterns to cut leather for a model of each design. A sewing room with ten ladies sewed the model together and gave it to me. My job was to get a basswood form like a foot of the right model and tack the leather upper on the last so the men who made up orders for the factories could decide whether to have the model manufactured and, if so, how many of each size.

It was a pleasant job and I roamed every nook and corner of those twenty floors learning how business was done. After a year I was made a receptionist in the purchasing department. Charm was not expected. A steady stream of salesmen of sharkskin, lizard, snake, sheep, goat, cow and horse hides came to see one or more of the buyers. Buttons, buckles, shoe laces, shoeboxes, cotton, rubber, counters, metal toecaps and taps were in demand. When there were no salesmen, piles of orders were awaiting separation, filing or mailing. It was another learning experience. I liked business and had friends in various businesses. The Junior Chamber of Commerce was attended as well as business machine fairs. Suddenly the world was opening up very wide.

The third year I was assigned to the sales area of one of the 15 brands. The section I worked in had two functions, the first of which was to design shoes for misshapen feet. There was the two-foot-long shoe of the Allton, Illinois giant, Robert Wadlow. Grotesquely twisted feet were copied in plaster and shoes cut to fit them. Here was a little window into a segment of life's abnormalities entirely new to me.

The second function of the department was to sell off stocks of shoes which were not selling. Accurate lists of styles and sizes available, with prices slashed, were sent out to shoe-store owners and they would order as they wished. My job was to take their orders to about ten different desks where each was processed and recorded by hand. A computer would have handled the whole thing with one operator, but the word computer at that time could only describe someone who worked with figures.

Some of the workers were angry men who hated their endless recording and made life unpleasant for me. Others were friendly and a delight to deal with. Ten flights of stairs were my orbit day after day. I took them on the run whether up or down. Walking to work in the early morning and home in the evening added to the muscle-building my legs experienced daily. The only break in the eight-hour day was a half hour to eat the two sandwiches, a cookie and apple which Mother packed for me.

A month's salary was $60. Mother used $55 to cover the house payments, food, clothes, fuel, etc. My $5 I banked for the future. Mother bought all my clothes. I worked Saturdays as a shoe salesman at Famous-Barr Department Store, giving me $20 extra per month for the bank. I didn't realize that selling in the department store was preparing me for a year or two later when I would sell my cork belts in most of the great department stores east of the Mississippi.

I had no hesitancy in saving rather than spending. The depression made even children profoundly aware of the worth of a nickel. All society focused on economic survival. The hundreds of dollars saved, when the time came, would give me courage to leave St. Louis for college.

But there was one major event to occur in these work years. The company arranged for about 40 young workers to study a course on shoemaking overseen by a Christian staff member. Her face is clear in my mind but her name is not. Miss Viola Schesky seems about right. I was one of her students and she urged me to excel in that school. My high school grades were abominable. My university year was very good. But the subject matter of this course was something that fascinated me. I came out number one in the end.

When I applied to Wheaton, Miss Viola was one of my references. I think her recommendation overcame the normal reaction to my high school records. I was accepted into the school and began with a 19-hour schedule my freshman year.

There is an explanation to the dramatic change in my grades. I had come to terms with my God and grasped His promise, "If any man lack wisdom, let him ask of me, who giveth liberally and upbraideth not." No day passed without my holding up this promise to my Lord. Bless His Name! He gave what I lacked liberally. And He never upbraided me for asking. What a God we serve!

The shoe company experience made a man out of a boy. I left it and St. Louis for Wheaton College in September 1938, eager most of all to get to know my Lord better.

SECTION TWO

SEVEN MORE YEARS
OF STUDY

"The Tower" Blanchard Hall

11

WHEATON COLLEGE

Ruth Todd was back in St. Louis from Wheaton College for the Christmas holidays. Ruth was the daughter of a Christian millionaire – the only one I knew. She breezed into a group of Assemblies young people, every eye on her, and told us of her marvelous school and her exciting experiences there. I was a working man, settled for life, I thought, in the St. Louis business world.

Ruth planted a seed that grew from that December day to an August day, when like my father before me, I left St. Louis for Chicago, then for Wheaton, 25 miles west of the second largest city in America.

What were my goals in going to Wheaton? The major one was to have time to learn more about my God. Wheaton required many hours of Bible study in classes under gifted teachers. Wheaton placed me among 1300 students, mostly Christians, learning for a life of piety and service. Wheaton had compulsory daily chapel services where great churchmen of the nation spoke to our hearts. Wheaton professors were God-inspired men and women, role models, living out their own testimonies as they taught. Four years of such a heaven-oriented society would give me ample time for God to shape this vessel. My "clay" was both pliable and eager.

Heroes of the American Church of the '30s and '40s came to Wheaton College and spoke in daily chapel services. Dr. Harry Rimmer wrote books against evolution which greatly reinforced my faith. He spoke in chapel one day and I went backstage afterwards to express my appreciation.

Another speaker was R. G. LeTourneau, the manufacturer who invented powerful road-building machinery with tires as high as a man. He told us God gave him many great new ideas in bed for his machines and he wrote a fascinating book, *God Runs My Business*. I slept in his home in Texas during a week of missions in his church.

He showed me six-inch steel plates being cut by a torch, to be made into precise cogwheels. In a storage lot was the steel-walled mold for the walls of a whole house. He could pour the walls in one day, cutting the cost of a home greatly. The building unions wouldn't let him make houses that way so the huge mold rusted away. Mr. LeTourneau was a genius and a powerful speaker.

In four years, one heard about 700 evangelical leaders from all over the world.

Of all the speakers that spoke in chapel, none was so popular or so loved as the president of Wheaton, V. Raymond Edman – an ex-C&MA missionary to Ecuador. His wife's serious illness kept them from continuing their ministry overseas but Dr. Edman's passion for unreached peoples was contagious for Wheaton's brave sons and daughters true.

Raw teenage "kids" that came to that school in that period would change their world. Evangelists (Billy Graham), theologians (Carl F. H. Henry), mission founders (Bob Evans), Bible translators (Clarence Nida), global radio broadcasters (Paul Freed), Senate chaplain (Richard Halverson), national movement mobilizer (Kenneth Strachan), global boys' clubs (Joseph Coughlin), trainer of Russian pastors (Peter Deyneka), and seminary professor in Japan (Phil Foxwell) are but a few who come to mind. There were many more who were giants in their area of service to the Lord whom they learned to love and obey at Wheaton.

My second goal at Wheaton was, quite frankly, to learn whom God had chosen to be my wife and partner. Among the 600 young ladies in the school I had not the slightest doubt that there was that one whom He had selected to share with me all of the unknown years ahead, a faithful, strong, God-filled partner in every phase of life.

I dated a few classmates, attractive, lively girls, but – just girls. One semester passed with no word from the Lord. Then there she was in the dining hall, the only girl at a long table of men, keeping them all excitedly entertained. That was 63 years ago – entertaining, exciting, happy, fruitful years.

But a special chapter is devoted to that story. It is titled "Thelma." What else?

The third goal was to gain an education that would equip me to be God's eager servant for life. Much time was spent earning money and much more courting Thelma. I was keenly aware that it would take a daily miracle from God if I were to pass my courses. So I daily prayed for God's wisdom as His Word urges those who lack wisdom to do. To my amazement, I was number six in a class of 325 freshmen. That is equivalent to two out of a hundred, as compared with my high school rating of about 60 in a hundred. God heard my prayer. I was an honor student and a member of Phi Gamma Mu, the national social science honor society, excelling all my dreams.

There was also a profound longing to learn more about this world. My 21 years had been divided between St. Louis and the Leslie farm in depression years, two pinpoints on a globe 24,000 miles around its waist. I had taken out library books on psychology, philosophy, chemistry and history, but learned only enough to discover the vastness of what I did not know. Wheaton would open my mind in my chosen field of sociology and anthropology. Sociology was to equip me to be useful in American society which had so many desperate, poverty-stricken families, and anthropology was, well, it was to enlarge my knowledge of the peoples of the world.

Memorizing page after page of college textbooks was not the only way to get good grades. One frosty morning on my way to school I found a fat red squirrel who must have bounced off a speeding car. I had shot many squirrels to eat on the farm, so I felt very comfortable picking him up for an examination. He was in perfect shape and an idea began to form. If I boxed him, cleaned the meat off his skeleton and set the bones in a shallow frame of hot paraffin – with an acorn in his paws –, would the zoology prof increase my grade? It worked out that he would, and the skeleton was put in a display case for specimens where it may remain to this day.

One vacation took me to Arkansas to explore some caves that Indians had used over hundreds of years. I made no great finds but collected pottery shards and bone tools that, along with Indian curios bought in northwest Canada, so pleased the librarian that I was permitted to display these items in a natural setting in several cases in the library. Anthropology, my minor, was an excitingly real science to me.

Still on the subject of displays, in my junior year I asked permission to use one of the display cases in a busy hallway where everyone passed every day. It was still depression time and my major in sociology, along with success making and selling cork belts, seemed to convince the administration that I qualified for a case. Every week a new display was put up and each had a positive message for fellow students. A classmate named Joe Bayly also had a showcase and we carried on a friendly competition. Joe became a big name in InterVarsity and wrote two very unusual books on soul-winning and on coming dangers of government euthanasia.

One day I visited the office of college President Oliver Buswell and described a project I had in mind. It was to erect a 4- x 8-foot plywood "slate" like those used in grandfather's school. Each day I would write an inspiring Scripture verse on its black surface. It would face the Stupe where all students went once a day. He gave his approval. A half-hour later I passed him on a sidewalk and he looked at me as if he had never seen me before. He was a brilliant Greek scholar but I suspect the mass of verbs and nouns of that language had used up all of his memory usually reserved for people. The giant slate, after some months, was blown over in a storm and I didn't replace it.

My fourth goal was to pay my bills so I could stay in school. In depression America it was not easy to do that. No help came from church or family. I was alone – with God.

I arrived in Wheaton with savings of $300 from three years of work. It paid the first semester's fifteen hours of college and four hours of make-up high school geometry. Every free hour was spent in the library studying or working to earn next semester's tuition. I was on my own. Mother and Sister could not help me. My relatives, who could, did not. The Assemblies' young men forgot the role I had played among them. The wealthy elders, too, had no interest in my need or my future. God would be my only help and I would graduate debt-free with a debt-free wife and a car as proof of His faithfulness.

Earning money for the next semester was essential. Wheaton College had an employment office which townspeople called to request student workers to cut grass, scrub floors, rake leaves, paint walls, clean out gutters or do whatever they themselves did not want to do. The pay was 35 cents an hour, not counting the time it took to get there. In those days students did not have cars, but bikes were useful. I had my racer bike, and it cut the time it took to go to a job in Wheaton, Glen Ellen or Lombard.

By Christmas I had earned about $60 and, unwisely, I took it to St. Louis when I hitchhiked home. Someone told me of an agency in the city where people planning to drive to a distant city could register their time of departure. Individuals wanting a ride could sign up, for a minimal price, for a place in such cars. It sounded good to me but I worried about possible theft of my $60 - the fruit of 171 hours of work and 40 hours of bike riding to and from work places. One learns by doing. I mailed my money to Wheaton and never saw it again.

I felt this was discipline from my Lord. My father, who had little sympathy for my faith and commitment to Christ, had sent a one-time gift of $100 to me. I felt I should not use it. My needs were to be met by work and by God's enabling, not by those outside the household of faith. This was a Brethren principle which I believed. In cashing my father's check, I felt I had forsaken my own standards. The loss of my hard-earned $60 was accepted as a mild reminder that obedience is better than sacrifice.

For three years I was employed by the Stupe – the student supply store, as janitor. It was a steady source of income and, being on campus, it eliminated long bike rides. I also worked for Phil Foxwell, a professional magician who was won to Jesus and was now a fellow student. Phil was a genius. His father acted as his agent and contracted magic shows in high schools, men's trade unions and even at Wheaton College. Phil loaded his car with props and we drove to his shows. Of his courses, Greek was his greatest challenge. At every stop-light Phil went over his recent Greek studies. The sun visor was covered with little cards showing conjugations.

In view of his fabulous memory I wondered why he bothered. One very popular part of his shows was the distribution of pages of a half-dozen current magazines, all mixed up, throughout the audience. He then invited anyone to call out the name of the magazine and the page that he or she held. With no hesitation and no written notes, Phil called out the content of that page – for a full ten minutes.

I was the stooge. It was my job to prepare the guillotine that would slice wickedly through a cabbage before his assistant, a beauty queen from Michigan, rose out of an empty little house and then put her neck into the guillotine trough to be cut off with, of course, a hysterical scream.

Phil married the queenly daughter of Dr. Buswell, Wheaton's president. They served a lifetime as missionaries in Japan as professors in a Presbyterian seminary. Wonderful people.

Willys in Alaska with Ernest Young, soon afterward a Professor of Anthropology

Earning money was a powerful learning experience. On my first summer vacation I went to Alaska. In these days of plane travel, that sounds simple enough. But in 1939 it included a drive to the west coast with a wreck halfway there, hitchhiking to Vancouver, British Columbia, riding railroad cars inside and outside in the rain and on the locomotive's cowcatcher, a trip on a steamer to Ketchican and hitchhiking down the western coast and eastward to St. Louis – all without benefit of a hotel or restaurant over 5000 miles.

In Prince Rupert on the Pacific I made a felicitous discovery. At low tide the shore was covered with starfish. Wheaton used starfish in its zoology laboratory. I found some five-gallon tins, bought formaldehyde and packed starfish in each tin. Tops were soldered on and the tins were shipped to Wheaton to be purchased by the lab.

The boys' camp in Texas, where I had been a leader the past two years, invited me to come down. I did. I recall going out in the pasture to bridle a large saddle horse. As I approached he reared up on his hind legs, offering to kick my head off. A horse looks mighty big that way. When he came down I got the bridle on him, mounted and rode to the camp mailbox. There was a letter from Thelma that I read at a joyous full gallop back to camp. Wow! That's livin'!

On my return to St. Louis I was faced with the reality that "livin'" would not get me back in Wheaton. I focused and came up with some items to sell. There were two pictures painted on redwood with background areas etched with sand blasting. A photo album was added and four cork belts with pictures on small cork plaques laced on rawhide thongs. There were four styles: school, sports, Mexican and Chinese. I designed these and hand-painted sample belts. With these and order blanks with the company name of College Boy Co-op I hitchhiked to various college bookstores and showed my wares. Vassar gave me my first order. With it in hand I went to New York and showed my belts to the buyer at Macy's. She looked at the Vassar order and made out a larger order. I went from store to store in New York and Philadelphia, down the east coast and back to St. Louis, hitchhiking and staying in YMCAs all the way.

Where did I get the idea for the belts? Thelma told me about some belts she had seen made at a girls' camp. I took her idea and lo, the belts were the only things that sold of my entire kit. Love that girl.

I had an impossible task ahead of me. It was one thing to paint a sample belt. It would be something very different to paint hundreds of them. The Lord opened a way. It was my custom to speak of Wheaton and of my faith in Christ with each driver who picked me up. One driver showed an interest in what I was doing. I described my belts and the job awaiting me. "Have you ever heard of silk screening?" he asked. I had not. He told me the basic principles and when I reached St. Louis I went to the library and found a book that filled in the details. Silk and the plastic-like sheets to cover and adhere to the silk on wood frames and paint were purchased. I cut out each color of each belt's plaques. There were five plaques on each of four belts and five colors were cut for each belt, a total of twenty screens.

Cork sheets had to be purchased and a table set up on which the sheets could be painted by scraping paint across the screen. The paint went through the holes cut in the plastic – squish! One color done for a belt. Squish, squish for hours and the ordered belts were painted. Then came the punching of four holes in each plaque – for hours –, the threading of plaques on rawhide with a cork sombrero added as the buckle, and the belts were ready to be boxed and mailed out. Tuition money would come from prestigious department stores in the east for my second, third and fourth years at Wheaton.

Pearl Harbor blasted our nation in 1941. Vacation time came and again the need to earn money became a priority. An idea came to me that since much of the war was fought with ships, a collapsible boat, which took little space, might be useful to the war effort and later to fishermen and duck hunters. Paul Freed was a good friend who had a $900 debt and needed to earn money. Together we obtained government purchase orders in Chicago to buy the materials we needed to make a boat. I recall living on an occasional sandwich for weeks.

Finally our boat was finished. It had airtight galvanized prow and stern held in place by iron bars. The passenger part of the boat was of canvas with a plywood bottom. It looked great. We took it to a pond, where I later proposed to Thelma, and put our creation on the water. Fine! Until I stepped into it. At that point it earned its name, "collapsible boat". It folded and went to the bottom. Next day we evaluated our situation and concluded that this boat had no future. Our partnership ended.

The summer was passing and I had no money for the next semester. There was only one option open to me, a sales trip to the department stores of the east. I left my partner and headed out, thumbing my way from city to city. Wheaton had a well-known slogan, "Wherever you go, you represent Wheaton." I had my own slogan. I represented my Lord. So after small talk with drivers good enough to help me reach my destination I'd mention Wheaton College and my call to missions overseas. This opened the door to sharing my love for the Savior which sometimes met with agreement, sometimes with silence.

Once an older woman stopped for my raised arm and I hopped in. After awhile I spoke of my calling and it opened a floodgate of the weirdest stories I could imagine. She spoke of well-known evangelicals with whom she had been associated, I believe as a musician. One was an honored college president who was a popular speaker. Another was a famous Christian industrialist. The gist of her story was that these icons of evangelicals harvested bags of money in services, then went to expensive hotels to celebrate together. Her implications were that this was all crass commercialism. I knew Christian colleges were very lean in those depression years and had to do all they could to raise money for buildings. And I knew the industrialist was a multi-millionaire with a fascinating story of God's guidance in his life. Christians would love to hear both speakers. And I know how pleasant it is, after a great but demanding service, to relax with friends over a chocolate fudge sundae. But this woman saw these men in a shocking light and I wondered at her reaction against them. Maybe they found a musician with a better voice and a better spirit.

Hitchhiking in those depression days was common and acceptable, but not by all drivers. On one occasion I found myself still far from a city in open farmland at night. Cars were few and people were in a hurry to get home. Hours passed and I was weary. I sat on my suitcase waiting for headlamps to appear and turned to prayer. I should have done so earlier. I asked the Lord to stop the next car and as I opened my eyes a car swooshed by. So much for prayer. But brake lights went on way down the road and the car backed up, back, back, back to me and my suitcase. To my amazement a young fellow and girl, obviously courting, welcomed me into the back seat and took me to my distant destination. My presence didn't advance their romance, I'm sure, and I suspect both wondered why in the world they ever picked up a stranger on an evening of fun. I knew.

I loved to travel in my teens and covered the nation, north, east, south and west, meeting hundreds of drivers of cars of every vintage. Some drunk high-schoolers from a back-hills town picked me up, crowded me in and flew crazily down the road mile after tense mile. I was so glad to escape that tin-lizzy and am sure my prayers alone preserved their lives and mine for one more day.

On my return, Paul asked me if I would make my belt-making equipment available to him and approve his selling west of Wheaton. He went west, sold a pile of belts, paid off his $900 debt and began designing new kinds of women's belts, which he sold to J. C. Penney and Woolworth's 5 and 10. Paul would be my best man when Thelma and I married. We would work for him making his belts at Nyack College and he would go on to begin Trans-World Radio, a global Christian broadcasting mission.

. . . .

Department stores bought my belts as never before and after a really big order from a famous New York store I telegraphed Thelma a terse message, "The Lord says, 'Go ahead'." To us both that translated as, "Let's get married before school opens." I returned to Wheaton, made up all the belts I needed and shipped them to the stores. I was free to be married. Checks had started coming from the sale of belts so I had money to go to Mansfield on a bus. My friend Paul Freed was to be my best man. He joined us at the Mansfield Alliance Church and, in the black suit which had been bought for my high school graduation years earlier, I stood with Paul waiting for the lovely lady of my life.

Having to earn money leads to a multitude of unexpected situations, acquaintances and learning experiences! Mrs. Eleanor Roosevelt was a busy member of government in depression years. One of her interests was college students struggling to pay tuition. Dean Wallace Emerson, later to become president of Westmont College in California, was one of my sociology professors and the overseer of some government funding. He offered me a job. Indeed, he created a job for me. It was to interview all freshman students and to counsel them regarding their majors and their goals. An office was provided for this and I took very seriously this well-paid assignment.

When Thelma and I married, she was a graduate and I a senior. We now were renting an apartment, buying our food, paying for a car and all of my school expenses. She taught school full-time but her income alone was not enough. So I applied for a job on campus teaching grade-school students crafts in the school shop. I also obtained a coaching job in another town's primary school. With the counseling, together we had four jobs and with all of them, a month could end with eating a can of beans for supper.

We were not in poverty but we knew the value of a nickel – even a penny - in that year. Yet when the year ended we were debt-free and had a car, free to move on to Nyack Missionary Training Institute for the two years of C&MA training required for missionary candidates.

Wheaton had been a liberating, mind-expanding, wife-finding, God-calling, maturing and empowering experience that would influence and encourage us lifelong.

Oh Wheaton, dear old Wheaton, live forever,
Brave sons and daughters true
We will e'er uphold thy colors
The orange and the blue.

Sixty years ago it sang its way into my heart. I arrived at the town's train station on the Chicago-Aurora-Elgin commuter train in late August. A tall student with a college station wagon invited students into the car and delivered them to the school. I later learned his name was Billy Graham and he was often seen with a classmate of classic beauty, Ruth Bell.

Except for a few men who inhabited the fourth floor of Blanchard Hall, male students lived in rooms of private homes. The depression left many families unemployed and in need of income. The Ice family with an unemployed father, a very busily employed mother, two teen-age daughters and a fat, bouncy terrier, opened their home to three men.

One was Phil Worth, who ultimately became pastor of Collingswood United Methodist Church for 26 years. The church was large, prosperous and strongly evangelical. Dr. Frank Stanger had pastored it before Phil and left it to become president of Asbury Theological Seminary. Phil was a lot of fun as a housemate. We spent hours together and I learned that he had played his trombone with Percy Crawford, founder of King's College. Phil served as a board member of King's for a long time and later was a board member of Evangelism Resources.

Phil courted a girl of our Old Stone Church, Dorothy Cramer, and married her - another tie with this college friend. Dottie developed a Bible-teaching ministry which was absolutely superb. Hundreds of women left their busy lives behind to hear from God

Dr. Harold Spann and Phil Worth

Phil and Dottie Worth

through Dottie's lips. I know because I sat in on some of her services and was deeply moved by them. She spoke at dozens of centers and conferences and had a radio program called *Women Alive* which was widely broadcast.

All through our mission years, when the Brauns returned to America for furlough, an invitation would come from the Worths to preach in their church. We shared the pulpit with Dr. Ford Philpot, Sam Kamalesan, Oswald Hoffman, Stephen Alford and numerous other noted preachers on those occasions.

About the trombone - in the Ice house days, one night Phil serenaded a passing fancy living in Williston Hall. I wish you could picture the event. Williston, the multi-storied women's dorm, along with Blanchard, the Student Union and Pierce Chapel form a large, park-like square. Our tall, stripling hero stands in the moonlight below the large porch, blasting the night with his skillfully played romantic tune, a bright moment in time in Wheaton's long role as maker of marriages. But happily, this one fizzled out. Dottie is a gem!

Another housemate was Phil Saint, a professional artist, son of a famous stained-glass window producer. His windows grace some of the most prestigious buildings in the east. Phil was an eager, committed, mature Christian artist. He was a popular chalk-talk artist and, of all things, color blind. He had a girl friend who helped him by arranging his chalks in precise order. She was slender and lovely and Phil loved her dearly. I recall the morning we were both shaving in the Ice house bathroom, using the same mirror. The air was charged that morning with a special electricity. My neighbor was ecstatic. When he finished shaving he pulled a diamond ring out of his pocket and said, "Look at this. Kay and I are to be engaged today!!"

They were, but it didn't last long. Kay returned the ring and accepted a bigger one from a heavy, older student named Al Smith, the Al Smith whose chorus books would dominate church music for two decades. Phil rebounded almost as quickly as Kay in the broken relationship and married a sweet classmate who went with him to South America where they served long and effectively as missionaries. Phil's brother Nate was one of the martyrs of the Auca Indians and his sister Rachel, also a missionary in Auca country, stayed on in that country ministering to the murderers of her brother and his friends until nearly the end of her life.

These and others who shared the Ice house were dear friends. They occupied an attractive bedroom with central heat. My room was an unheated, tiny, ex-food storage room behind the kitchen with just enough room for a cot and clothes hangers. Three of its four walls were open to the icy blasts of Illinois winters. Only by leaving the door open a bit was a modicum of warmth brought into my quarters. Needless to say, my evenings were spent in the warm library of the college and I used my room for only eight hours of every twenty-four.

Every Sunday, for three years, I attended the Brethren Assembly in Lombard in the mornings and Wheaton Tabernacle Sunday evenings. Seven services a week plus Bible classes in college kept my spiritual tank topped-off in those four years. The bus trips to Lombard brought Brethren students together and they were an interesting group, There were Armerdings – one of whom became president of the college later. Tom Parks of Vancouver, British Columbia became president of our sophomore class and founder of the Spokesmen's Club, which dominated all class officer elections until we all graduated. Don Monroe was the son of a wealthy Canadian doctor. Don had a photographic memory. He made top grades by lazily flipping through the pages of his textbooks. One girl was the daughter of a nationally known Christian publisher. The Brethren were well represented. And the Lombard Assembly had some remarkable Bible teachers equal to any of Wheaton's profs.

The Great Depression was a time of humility and compassion. Survival was the focus of millions of unemployed families. There were some students from wealthy backgrounds, but I heard no arrogance or class distinction rhetoric. It was understood that the nation was in trouble. Yet Wheaton had its standards for dress, and they showed up best in pop-concert evenings when men wore tuxes and women long, formal dresses.

Tom, my chem lab friend, was class president, an eloquent, handsome man. But he had no tux and a lovely daughter of the Grace Line (ocean liners) asked him to be her date at an open house. I had an extra suit and gladly made it available to Tom. I was with Thelma in the women's dorm when news came that after dinner, in the girl's apartment, Tom had bent over to retrieve a fallen paper and the back seam of his pants exploded. In utter shock he backed into her bathroom and surveyed the damage.

There was a dignified old grandma in the dorm who did sewing for the girls who lived there. Tom's pants were rushed to her for repairs, while, pants-less, Tom waited out the endless evening in the bathroom. At last the awaited knock on the door came, the pants were delivered and Tom dressed, bid his date goodnight and fled. The romance had ended and I don't think Tom ever thanked me for the tux.

Looking back, I realize all too well that God alone made Wheaton possible to me. My high school grades were pathetic. I had no financial support. No one in our church or society, to my knowledge, had gone to college. My earning power, working six days a week, was $960 a year – all work and no play. And there was no light at the end of my tunnel in pre-Wheaton days in St. Louis. It was treadmill all the way.

The search to know God better is what motivated the sudden decision to go to Wheaton. It was a case of seeking first the kingdom of God. "All these things" that were to so enrich the decades to follow were hidden behind the curtain of time to me, but known by the King. I shudder at the thought that it could all have been lost if the Spirit of God had not opened the door to me of one of the world's most admired Christian colleges, Wheaton, dear, old Wheaton.

12

THELMA

Mansfield, Ohio, was where she was born. Her mother told the doctor her name was Thelma Mae. It must have been a stressful day for the doctor for he wrote Elba May on her birth certificate and that is what appears on her passport decade in and decade out. Airport security guards frequently point out the discrepancy between her plane ticket and passport and give us a long, searching look. So far, they have accepted our explanation about the forgetful doctor.

Four brothers were growing up in the house where she was born. The youngest of them, Elwood, was already ten. Clyde, the oldest, was sixteen. To the whole family she was "Princess." That was the first of a long string of pet names. In my time on the bridge she has been Peaches, Pumpkins, Lum, Honey, Babes, Sugar and, most often, Gracie. She has responded to all with equal aplomb.

State champion flautist

At three, her little fingers began stretching across the ivory keys of a piano and in not many years she became a splendid conference and church pianist. I have watched her play a medley of hymns without a note in front of her, with such feeling and depth that whole audiences have

Drum major of high school band

been mesmerized. And her skill remained through her fifties, sixties, seventies and eighties.

Was it her mastery of the piano which contributed to her confidence as a young teen so that she excelled in everything she attempted? She won the state championship as a flautist. It seems strange to me that I have never heard her play the flute. It was a passing fancy. Her grades were the best in high school. She was major domo of her school's marching band and editor of her high school paper. I visited her high school decades later and saw her name engraved on a marble plaque, as "Most Outstanding Student" of the 1937 class of 350.

But that was a small part of Thelma's activities. She was the pastor of a thriving Baptist church and the annual records of the district superintendent give her congregation excellent marks for the years she filled the pulpit. When her mother died, a notebook of newspaper clippings came into our possession - dozens of articles about the girl evangelist who had held a crusade of services in cities of Ohio and Pennsylvania. No side show, these crusades. I've read through some of her sermons of that period and they were spiritual meat.

Those were the teen years in which most young people are driving their parents crazy, demanding adult "rights" and acting like spoiled infants at the same time. I have never been able to visualize the Thelma of those years to my own satisfaction for I had never met a girl like her. When we met at Wheaton she was 18 and a sophomore. High school, pastoring, crusades, et al were in the past. She was working her way through college, making top grades and facing the future like all the rest of us.

I have often wished I knew her in earlier years and often stare searchingly at pictures of her of high school days. How could she have lived so adult and so full a life in her teens? I had no answer except the very special intervention of God.

Thelma went to Wheaton in 1937. I arrived a year later. The year of college and years of work before Wheaton made me several years older than my classmates. They were maturing years in which one after another of my friends paired off and married. I had grown up with my mother and sister, a female household. And in my mind, it was time to seriously seek a wife.

Yet here was an area of concern which gripped my heart. I was completely unnerved at the prospect of choosing a girl to marry. In this I collapsed in the arms of my Lord. There were splendid young women at Wheaton College, daughters of famous Christians, some rich, some stunningly beautiful. And I was intensely lonely for the lady God wanted me to meet and to marry. I had a few dates and in classes friendships were formed. One was with a girl who would become a medical doctor, a missionary to Nigeria and die in the frightening lhasa epidemic around 1969.

Wheaton had two dining halls attached to Williston Hall: Upper, for students with more money, and Lower, for those with less. The depression again. I was, of course, a diner in Lower. Long tables for ten or twelve students had bowls and platters of food and students came in by ones or twos and sat at the table being filled at the moment.

One evening I was the last at a table. I bowed my head, gave thanks for the food, asked God for wisdom and served myself from the bowls of food. Only then did I become aware of the composition of the group at the table. All but one were men and the single girl was clearly undaunted by this fact. Later I learned that she grew up with four brothers and had early learned to cope in their world. At this table on this evening she was having a superb time keeping the others happily engaged in interchanges. Having come in late, I felt out of it and was trying to eat fast and catch up with the group when the girl's voice turned my way with a question about my sweater-knit shirt. I did my own laundry to save money and knit shirts required no ironing so I wore several styles of them. This one had a regular collar but it also had a sweater-like neckline, seeming to be a sweater over a shirt.

I explained the shirt's unusual feature to her and went back to my food. I marveled at the lady's ability to hostess the entire table but was a bit miffed at my own role during the meal.

A week or two later there was to be a pop concert to which students would go with dates. I had no one in mind until I found myself at a table with the vivacious entertainer who asked about my shirt. I was near her this time and she was fun. Time and place were right. I asked if she would attend the pop concert with me. She would.

I dressed in my tux in the tiny room I called home and called for Miss Thelma Still early that evening at the receptionist's desk at Williston Hall. Her room was called and I was announced. In a few minutes, dressed in a flowing, formal gown and silver-strap slippers, the lady of my life floated down the wide steps to our first date.

She fascinated me from the beginning. No giddy, unsure high schooler, this one. She walked and talked with confidence and warmth. I don't recall the music of the United States Marine Band but our walk downtown for a malted milk, on fresh snow, the chat over the malt, the sense of wanting to know this enchanting person better remain bright, clear memories. And she wouldn't soon forget the evening because walking a late winter, snow-covered street in open slippers landed her in the dispensary for a day or two.

Soon after came spring break and I asked Thelma if I might carry her suitcase to the train station when she started home to her family in Ohio. She liked that and I waved her off, feeling a special loneliness. I wrote a long letter to her at her home and received a shocking reply. Her father, so eager to see her, had died of a heart attack while she was traveling homeward. Instead of the exciting vacation she expected, she arrived in a home suddenly bereft of father and husband and filled with mourning and bewilderment. Visions of her sorrow and shock filled my thoughts and I set myself to receive her back at school with daily attentions which would relieve her sadness as much as was possible.

She stepped off the train into a new relationship. We ate together every possible meal. After classes and work we explored the town of Wheaton on every side. I came to love her deeply and became very worried about this. Why? I did not trust my own judgment. So after a Sunday dinner I went to my bare, cold room to meet my God.

For hours I prayed and read His Word. In my vigil, seeking God's guidance I read Psalm 16, "The lines have fallen unto me in pleasant places - fullness of joy."

To me, my Lord was saying, "I have chosen her to be your wife." I was deliriously happy. I was early that evening, eagerly looking for her at the dining hall. I couldn't wait to tell her of my love, my deep concern that God reveal His will for us and the joyful assurance I had that He had confirmed my desire as His own. She received this report by her smitten friend with sweet pleasure. But I recognized that while she was happy for my certainty she had no comparable conviction of her own. I had a dear friend focused on me. I would have to win her lasting love by more than talk.

So I set to work. Wheaton assigned a post box to each student. I obtained the numbers that opened Thelma's combination lock and every day made sure to deposit in it a flower, or a poem, or a drawing, or a piece of fruit or candy, or a suggested date. There was never a day for two and a half years when she did not receive a symbol or declaration of my love. I had no trombone to blow like my friend Phil Worth, but my serenade flowed out of a mailbox as unfailingly as the sunrise.

As we bonded in daily meals, study time in the library and walks home, I learned more of the incredible girl the Lord was giving to me. Early I heard her play the piano - exquisitely. And she sang in a husky, low voice songs and poems I had never heard before. I learned little-by-little of her astounding familiarity with God's Word.

One of the Brethren's basic tenets is expressed in the verse which instructs women to be silent in the church, counseling them that if they had a question, they should ask their husbands at home. How was I to deal with this? Thelma had answers, not questions. But she was invited widely to be anything but silent! And she probably had seen more people find salvation than I would all my life. That was the deciding point for me. Jesus had promised that "your sons and your daughters will prophesy." My love was Mrs. Still's daughter and God had called her to prophesy powerfully to tens of thousands of lost men, women and children. I could only marvel at the grace of God in her life and praise Him.

On a Thanksgiving afternoon in my junior year and Thelma's senior year, we were playing ping pong and suddenly I realized that God was calling us to be missionaries. I had been a very serious sociology major and had plans for a master's degree and a Ph.D. The chairman of the division of social studies, Dr. S. Richey Kamm, counted me as one of the few students who would make a life in that field. By God's enabling, I was an honor student and a member of Pi Gamma Mu, the honorary society for the social sciences. He was a missions-minded Christian and congratulated us for our calling, but there was evident disappointment at losing from his field a student in which he had hoped.

While the ping-pong game was the moment of decision, it was not the whole story. Thelma arranged dates for her Plymouth Brethren friend to attend numerous missionary conferences of her denomination, the Christian and Missionary Alliance. She had a great love for missions and she wanted me to share her passion for a lost world. I never felt she was pressuring me to do more than listen. Every Sunday morning I went to the Brethren Chapel in Lombard and, since there was no C&MA church in or near Wheaton, she attended the church of her choice. On Sunday evenings we attended the Tab, where Dr. V. Raymond Edman, professor of political science and an ex-missionary of the C&MA in Ecuador, held students spellbound. When Dr. Edman became president of Wheaton College, a student was chosen to replace him, a handsome young man named Billy Graham. We learned later that he had once asked to be a C&MA pastor but was judged to be too young . . .

Dr. Edman was in charge of the college week of missions and he built each year's program around spectacular C&MA missionaries. We never missed, thanks to Thelma. We even went in to Chicago to a church pastored by a man named A. W. Tozer. He was good. I didn't realize how good. He and his many books are known around the world.

These are the influences which preceded my discovery that God was calling us overseas. She would never say it this way, at least not out loud, but I suspect she received my great statement with the thought, "Dummy, I knew it all the time."

Before she graduated I proposed - something I had been doing every day through my gifts of love. I faced her departure as I would

Wedding bells were ringing

cancer. It was unthinkable to spend a year with her mailbox 300 miles away. But we did what we could. I bought a diamond, the chapel bells rang out the announcement and she returned to Mansfield.

She had many friends and our wedding was a happy occasion. My mother and sister were there and Thelma's mother. Both mothers were widows and I can imagine their thoughts as the only son of one and the only daughter of the other wed and went their blissful way, out of their lives and toward an as-yet-unidentified mission field. Pride, joy, loneliness and loss must have battled each other in those hours.

After the wedding a loving church family, the Carl Oswalts, had a reception for the guests, and pictures were taken by friends who had cameras. Compared with weddings of today, it was utter simplicity. In its entirety, it possibly cost less than one layer of a modern wedding cake. But it was beautiful and spiritual and the knot we tied has endured for 57 years so far.

Thelma had made a down payment on a used Plymouth car and we left our dear friends for a honeymoon trip to the Blue Ridge Mountains of Virginia. Actually it went on through Georgia and reached Florida before we turned back. To save money - a very scarce commodity for the new couple - we set up cots in forests along side roads some nights. I recall the pleasant voices of a mountain family one night. They seemed no more than a hundred feet away. Their dogs didn't sense our presence and we were gone by dawn.

It was not our first trip together. After a month-long trip through British Columbia and Alaska in my first vacation, I went to Arkansas to collect Indian artifacts from caves and then served as a counselor at Camp Tejas in Texas. Back in St. Louis I prepared my belt kit, went selling in the east, made and shipped belts and had time to take a bus to Mansfield to visit Thelma's home. I arrived in the afternoon and was amazed to learn that we were to leave in two hours for Wheaton in Thelma's old car with the prophetic name of Jezebel. In my old-fashioned heart I would never permit my daughter to drive off into the night with a boy for a college 300 miles away. But the Lord never gave me a daughter to protect. And I suppose Thelma knew her young man.

Whatever moral dangers the situation might have had were dismissed by Jezebel. I spent most of the night jacking up the car, taking off lug nuts, removing tires, patching tubes and reversing the operation for a series of at least four flats. We pressed on wearily through the night and reached Wheaton in early dawn, dirty, disheveled and totally bushed. That was our only trip together until we were married.

The trip through the Smokies was a revelation of facets of my new wife which I had not discovered earlier. For example, we happened on a huge black bear on the road and I stopped and opened the window to take a picture. Thelma felt this was inadequate behavior. "Better get out of the car," she suggested, "and get a good picture." A young swain wants above all else to please his bride. I got out and the bear ambled past me five feet away. I got an excellent close-up. We continued up the mountain road. Around the first curve were large signs, "Danger, bears. Don't get out of the car or open windows." Ho hum . . . Almost a widow after three days of marital bliss.

Another memento of that trip was a wild drive at night in mountain country through some of the tightest curves I've ever experienced in the blackest of nights. Thelma was driving when a delivery truck passed us and she determined to keep it in sight. My nerves were gone. My hope was gone. My faith was gone as we plunged into the black hole of the night, twisting and bouncing. In those days people didn't use drugs but I'm certain Thelma was on some kind of high. She drove with gleeful abandon mile after mile until we reached a town with a motel where I was able to get her foot off the accelerator.

Thelma, I learned later, was a roller coaster fan. Why was I not surprised? She took Disney Land on the west coast and Disney World on the east coast in stride and any others in between. Bears, snakes, buffalo and revolutions I can face, but rides on cars on man-made rails in the sky are not for me. Bravery, and perhaps lunacy, come in many shapes and forms.

Our gas ration stamps and money were fast running out as we drove back toward Mansfield. We coasted downhill on many a mountain and arrived at Thelma's home broke and out of gas stamps. Friends enabled us to drive back to Wheaton where belt checks were accumulating.

My best man, Paul Freed, deep in personal debt had a request. "Will you let me sell your belts west of the Mississippi and use your silk screens to make the belts?" Of course I agreed. He was a charming salesman, tall, handsome, a dashing figure, and he sold belts everywhere he went. Soon he was out of debt and had capital to create new styles of wood-bead belts on bright silk cords. He sold masses of these to J. C. Penney for years afterward.

An incident in our young married life during the year occurred when the Russian Cossack Chorus came to the college for a pop concert. The school sponsored a poster contest with a prize of two free tickets. Sounded good to me and I submitted a poster which won the two tickets. After supper on the evening of the concert we had a free hour before dressing. Tired out from a long day we thought a rest would be good. We stretched out for a few minutes and woke up when the concert was over.

That was not the end of the story. I was called into the office of Dr. Peter Stamm, brother of the martyr, John Stamm of China. He eyed me solemnly and said, "Willys, about your poster. Wheaton takes a dim view of it." I had no idea what he was talking about and indicated as much. He said, "You printed on it, 'As Russian as vodka.' Really, for Wheaton . . ?" I had the impression that vodka was like Sanka, a kind of coffee. He disabused me of this lack of worldliness and let me go. So much for posters.

As vacation approached, I proposed to Thelma that we make up a big batch of cork belts to help pay our way through two years at Nyack Missionary Training Institute in New York. This was a requirement for would-be missionaries of the C&MA. It was a reversal of the past when I sold belts before making them.

We bought materials and made a mass of belts. Paul Freed gave us samples of his belts to sell as well and we drove off to make a killing in the belt business. But we couldn't sell either our belts or Paul's. And life was much more costly driving a car and living in motels. We exhausted our money and had to wire Paul for a loan.

This was a crisis. God had sold my belts for three prosperous summers. Paul's belts were in hundreds of Woolworth and J. C. Penney stores. Now He did not prosper us. We went to prayer. I said, "Lord, if you want us to stop trying to sell belts, show us by enabling us to sell well tomorrow." The next day was brilliant, like the best of the past years.

Duplicity is not an admirable trait in a servant of God. But after such a great day, I wanted to go on selling. But the hand of the Lord was not on us. We bowed to His will and returned to Wheaton to pack up our belongings and go to Nyack Missionary Training Institute for the two years required for future C&MA missionaries.

The Bible was Thelma's book. She read it systematically, she read it from cover to cover, over and over. She reveled in Bible commentaries, broadening and deepening her understanding of the text. She was a Bible student lifelong and the best of Bible teachers. For our ten years training future pastors of the C&MA in Congo, she gave her best to hundreds of eager men and the few women who studied in the Kinkonzi Bible Institute.

It is hard to identify the most important service of a lifetime given to God, but I suspect that these years teaching young preachers in Congo-Zaire were the most productive for Thelma over the long term. Time given to shaping the faith and message and character of many hundreds of God's messengers multiplies the coverage of the gospel magnificently and, in the case of the International School of Evangelism, actually multiplied the school itself thirty-one times so far, making it a global ministry.

Over 35 years Thelma has been writing her *Jottings* articles in *Congo Mission News*, Dr. Ford Philpot's *Story Teller* and in Evangelism Resources *NEWS*. They mix humor with good story telling and spiritual insights. Over nearly a quarter century, *ER NEWS* readers have volunteered from every part of the country, "We read *Jottings* first." Sheer stubbornness on our part has denied her page one for *Jottings*, the place it deserves. But obviously we have fooled nobody by keeping it on the last page. *NEWS* may be the only mission news which is uniformly read backwards.

There are books in Kikongo translated by Thelma in the 1950s. One is Philip Newell's popular *Revelation*. I carved four linoleum blocks for a four-color rendition of the four horsemen on the cover. It was a handsome addition to a dozen other titles used in training future pastors. In those pre-Independence years, a new book about God's Book could sell 3000 copies in a few months. Congolese laymen were eager followers of the Lord.

It amazed us to see how the masses turned their back on God in favor of a return to pre-Christian violence as Independence drew near. Over 200 foreign missionaries were slaughtered by gangs of vandals and civil war has gone on ever since.

One booklet Thelma wrote in Kikongo has been printed in numerous languages. It is titled *He Married a Princess* and its message to women is that "the King's daughter is all glorious within." It calls women to see themselves as God's glorious, beloved and honored daughters and to live on that exalted plain in their daily lives. Clearly I married a princess. I always knew it.

The book Thelma wrote as a text for 200 class hours of portable Bible schools has been printed in dozens of languages and has taught about 40,000 men so far. Her teaching skills shine throughout the 40 hours of Old and New Testament survey, 40 hours of doctrine, 40 hours of homiletics, 40 hours of village pastoral duties, 20 hours of personal holiness and 20 hours of denominational information. The text is titled *Called to Shepherd God's People*. Ten thousand copies were published in Russia and many thousands in English, French, Spanish, Creole, African and Asian languages. India alone has some thirteen translations.

Thelma had three sons. There were many fine missionaries in the C&MA field and they had attractive sons and daughters, but almost none returned as missionaries. The three Braun boys returned as missionaries, two to Zaire, one to Ivory Coast. I have often wondered why so few returned and why all three of ours did. When we get to heaven perhaps God will explain this to us. If so, their mother will get most of the credit, I am sure.

Thelma has lots of friends. One in particular brightens her life. June Eisemann, our next-door neighbor, has the ability to say "hello" on the phone and evaporate 60 years from my wife. Excited chatter punctuated with frequent peals of laughter fill five minutes or so with sheer delight. I wish I could do that for her. Since I can't, I'm very thankful that June can. Every wife needs someone like June to roll away the years and flood in sunshine. June's husband, Wes, is a great neighbor and ER's assistant treasurer. We talk shop or gardens or rabbits or drought or whatever is current. Over nine years we've enjoyed each other enormously. But it's our ladies who light up like flashlights on the phone day after day. It's lovely to hear those two. Decades haven't changed anything for them. Praise God.

I painted a portrait of Thelma when she was 21. It was my first serious oil painting and it wasn't bad. We took it to Belgian

The Eisemanns, Wes and June,
partners, neighbors, dearest friends

Congo and I hung it over the fireplace. Our table was in the living room and I sat looking at Thelma, every meal, and past her at the portrait. One day I decided I could perfect the painting and I got out my paints and began. Unfortunately, I could never get the palette tones the same as the painting and what I did was no improvement. Discouraged, I threw out the painting.

Years later in Kinshasa I befriended a young African student in the Academy of Fine Arts. He did beautiful pencil portraits of three evangelists for me. A year later he was doing colored pastels and I gave him a small photo of Thelma which he copied, life sized, in pastels. It hangs over our piano, beautifully framed.

Those who read *ER NEWS* know that every *Jottings* is accompanied by a fresh picture of Thelma. I've always thought of this as putting our best foot forward. Somehow, everything seems better with a recent snapshot of her with the word, *Jottings.*

Thelma's role in the nearly quarter century of Evangelism Resources has been that of teacher and perfecter of the broad, deep flow of Christian literature we have produced. So many titles, so many languages went through her computer, her fingers, her brain. If we have communicated well the vision and passion and goals and achievements of these global ministries, much of the credit is hers. Again, her hundreds of friendly notes to partners of ER, sent along with gift receipts all year, every year, have kept the allegiance keen on the part of many good friends.

Overseas she has traveled thousands of miles by train, taxi or plane, often in very uncomfortable circumstances. She has slept on hard beds, in suffocating heat, with mosquitoes and other critters sharing the space, and kept her cool. Whatever travel includes, even overnights spent in chilly airports to save the cost of hotels, Thelma has accepted with good grace.

When the International School of Evangelism was opened in Kinshasa, Thelma taught hundreds of students from dozens of nations of Africa. Her godly piety not only taught men a positive attitude toward God and His Word. They were also shown that God was pleased to have His Word taught by a woman to ordained, experienced, degreed and honored men of God. They called her Mama Braun and saw God at work in her. Letters received from these graduates never, never fail to greet Mama Braun.

When Latin American Mission requested the C&MA to second us to the Office of Worldwide Evangelism-in-Depth for all Africa, my assignment took me on long trips all over Africa. For months at a time I was away from home and Thelma filled the role of both parents for her children. Happily we were housed on a school compound with other families with children as close friends.

This whole book could be filled with Thelma alone. She may write her own sometime. But as I close this chapter I want to add an unshakable conclusion I have drawn about my wife. God loves her in a very special way. So often confirmations have occurred. Her Lord treats her like a princess, too.

13

NYACK

We shipped great cartons of unsold belts to Nyack and drove there for year one, arriving penniless. We were housed in Wilson Hall with other families. There were two rooms. One had a little sink and a two-burner gas plate, a table and two chairs. We assumed it to be the kitchen. The second had a bed and dresser. The floors were of ancient, splintered soft wood, uncovered. The overall decor would best be described as "bare depression style." A bathroom at the end of the central hall served four families.

But the college was helpful. It paid fifty cents an hour to students who made improvements. I built cupboards along the kitchen wall where the gas plate and sink were and a long desk for study. On a city street I found a large roll of discarded linoleum awaiting the garbage man. It was worn bare of any original color but it covered the splintery floor well. We bought blue enamel and painted a first coat, then using a sponge we added a pattern of lacy white. It looked clean and bright, as did the other additions to those drab rooms.

We needed an income. Thelma was hired to teach freshman English in the school. I got a job at Gairs, a carton manufacturer. It printed boxes for major brands. My assignment was to toss heavy-gauge cardboard head-high into a giant press. I worked opposite a taciturn, big Swede who weighed twice as much as I. He was bored with his job but found it amusing to grab 150 pounds of cardboard on his side, requiring me to grip the other side, and together we heaved it high in the air. Fun, fun, fun. A few tons later, my hours ended, I punched the time clock and went home - exhausted.

After a time they needed help in the folding area. After sheets of cardboard were printed and die-cut to shape, they were fed through machines that folded and glued them at a dizzying pace. These ever-hungry monsters demanded 100% concentration and all the unbroken coordination a person could muster. It gobbled up vast stores of boxes, permitting relief only if a box jammed in the works, shutting off the machine.

But it was the unearthly din of countless boxes clacking against guides and machinery, row after row, roaring at top speed that was carried home when work was done and replayed itself in the mind until sleep came.

One moonlit fall night I returned from the factory with the noise still loud in my ears and proposed a climb up the mountain. The weather was crisp and both men's and women's dorms were dark. The hillside was covered by dry fallen leaves and they made a bit of noise as we climbed. Our backs were to the dorms and we didn't notice when a few lights went on. But we did hear excited men's voices muffled by distance. Looking back we could make out a small army of students streaming up the mountain with flashlights. It was spooky. I pulled Thelma behind a large rock and waited. Soon a flashlight shone at our feet and then our faces. "Hi, what's all the excitement?" I asked.

The Old Stone Church

"Oh, we heard leaves crackling and thought soldiers from the camp were peeping Toms by the girl's dorm," he answered. The men returned to bed and so did we. In chapel the president made a mild remark about couples taking moonlight walks on the mountain. Seems it was frowned upon, but kindly.

One day news came that the Old Stone Church was seeking a pastor. One candidate, brother of a famed Christian leader, had already had a Sunday. Thelma - the experienced pastor - and I, a Sunday school teacher at best,

86

visited the elders and a Sunday was chosen for us to candidate. "Us" is the right word. Thelma played the piano and wowed them all. A young organist was ecstatic to have such a partner. Thelma sang, her haunting voice swelling earnestly through the wee auditorium. And Thelma suggested my two sermons of the day. In my old black suit I preached my first and second pastoral sermons, gesturing where Thelma had suggested.

Painted glass window

The elders called us, Thelma and me, and I left Gairs. Our income from two years of offerings averaged $13 a week. It required a day for sermon preparation, a day for Sunday services, half a day for Wednesday prayer meetings, time for visiting, two weeks for a boys' camp and the purchase of a car for pastoral duties. We had sold the Plymouth to pay tuition at Nyack. In return we preached 300 sermons, trained a choir, built the Sunday school up to 60 students, had evangelists in for weeks of meetings, sponsored a missionary conference which raised thousands of dollars, held a boys' camp, gave married students ministry opportunities and painted a six-foot-high Salsman's head of Christ on glass for the window over the entry.

Those were two happy years. Paul Freed came and we made belts for him to pad out our income. In the second semester of our second year Paul said, "Why don't you show J. C. Penney your belts?" I took some of them into their imposing New York offices and gave the purchasing agent the old spiel about Vassar, Macys, Sacs, and company. He agreed to try them out and gave me an order for belts for a half dozen stores. As a result, the whole stock was sold. We paid all our school bills and had some money left over.

God had reached into my life at age seventeen. My sister had arranged for me to attend a Brethren boys' camp for three years. In this my third year, the camp evangelist was Alf Gibbs of Pretoria, South Africa. He was middle-aged, paunchy, impressive, friendly. He was especially good at tennis and could chop a lob over the net which actually bounced back over the net on his side - a neat trick. He had large old-fashioned glass slides of *Pilgrim's Progress*, and he was terrific. I had heard dozens, hundreds of preachers as a boy and slept through most of them. This man gripped my heart and that of many of the boys.

One night there was a roaring bonfire and marshmallows to roast for the kids. I had my full share. Then Mr. Gibbs called us to circle around for a testimony meeting. I had no testimony. I was a quiet rebel in my heart. One by one some of the best athletes of the camp got up and declared their faith in Jesus Christ as Savior and Lord. I had shut out sermons by adults successfully but I couldn't ignore these fellows. They had something real, something I needed. That night I felt as if I were a frog kicking to get out of the grip of God. Finally I stopped kicking and accepted His offer of salvation and life.

At Nyack, remembering how God had entered my life at that camp, I felt a great debt to other boys and organized a boys' camp in an abandoned army camp base. We got ration stamps from the boys' parents and went into New York City to buy needed food stocks.

Tents, all ready for the boys

These we took to the camp and the boys came. Camp started and was a lot of fun and a lot of work. Parents helped prepare food and kept stomachs happy. I believe we exhausted our food a day early but nobody cared. Camp had been great and almost every boy left with a testimony of faith in Christ.

Back to the extra money we had. I persuaded Thelma to let me buy some used army tents, cots, utensils and sports equipment and pulled together a team of mature students to take this portable unit to towns where there were strong C&MA churches. They were to hold boys' camps in rural settings outside of those towns. To make it all acceptable, I inveigled the annual council, held in Nyack that year, to let me describe the camps and get a vote of approval. In the huge, highly structured annual councils of today, it would be unthinkable for an unknown student to pop up and be included on the august program of famous men. But in 1942 things were humbler and we had strong friendships with several members of the national board of directors. Believe it or not, my presentation drew enthusiastic applause.

The camp leaders held a few camps, but the wife of one had a baby and the proud young father dropped out - and so did the others. Not all ideas are great ones. Years later we shipped the tents to Congo where they housed students at the Kinkonzi Bible Institute.

Dr. A. B. Simpson, founder of the Christian and Missionary Alliance, had had an old rocker printing press which I discovered in the basement. I obtained permission to equip and use it for church notices and publicity. Type, new rollers, ink and paper were purchased and I was in business. I had jumped from an ancient mimeograph to an ancient treadle press with type and linoleum block carvings and turned out some credible products with it.

When we graduated, the press went to Rev. Paul Young, a missionary of Latin America, who found personal soul-winning the most natural thing in the world. A stop at a gas station turned into a time of salvation for the proprietor. Paul had taken Thelma and me into the Spanish section of New York City on many Saturdays. He had a little C&MA chapel there and we helped with his street ministry. Thelma had bought an old accordion and played it well. I did object lessons.

One day I had a cup in my hand to use in an object lesson. We all stood together on a corner singing our hearts out and an old, bent woman covered in black cloth came by and dropped a dime in my cup. My first reaction was to run after the lady and explain that we were not beggars! But it seemed better to put the dime in the offering later.

Rev. Young had us participate one summer in a Spanish vacation Bible school in the city. We were quite convinced that the Lord was equipping us for an assignment to South America. When we applied to the Foreign Department we explained that we spoke some Spanish and had experience in the Spanish community, so they assigned us to Belgian Congo, a French-speaking African nation of which we knew nothing. They had to feel very queer about that. But we never doubted that the Lord prevailed in their decision. Somehow, we have fitted Africa just right over 53 years.

After graduating from Nyack we were assigned to a year of French study. The mission created a French school in downtown New York and we were among its dozens of students. Head of the school was a French woman who thought she was a marine drill sergeant. She could be nasty! And she frequently was, reducing pastors of the living God to cringing globs of misery in one conjugation. She had all the natural qualifications to play the witch in Hansel and Gretel - full time. Mademoiselle Thorel was the terror of the campus.

Mademoiselle

But on Sunday she dolled up and rouged up and became a charming Parisian lady who pointed out to us that we were honored clergymen. That was on Sundays. The problem is that there were five days each week when we were mere students of a harsh taskmaster.

During the year of French study the old itch to make money returned. On Saturdays I designed a new kind of belt with little dogs running around it. A dear friend pastored a C&MA church in Port Washington and we made the belts up there. The venture used up the last of our money but we expected to get it all back and have a sizable amount for each of our mothers.

God didn't see it our way. J. C. Penney had us send out samples to its stores but few orders came in and again we had a pile of unsold belts. We concluded that the Lord was weaning us away from commerce for our own good. He didn't want two-minded servants.

About that time, Paul Freed's sister Ruth married Ben Armstrong, son of a C&MA district superintendent. They needed money and asked to buy our silk screens. That was fine with us. We were finished with belts. Ben Armstrong went on to found Religious Broadcasters Association and sat with a series of United States presidents at his annual conventions. Meanwhile, our Wheaton schoolmate Billy Graham and his young wife Ruth were making headlines in the nation's papers. "There were giants in the land in those days."

French was a tough language for me. I began constructing simple sentences, however, and that was encouraging. New York had a chain of restaurants called Horn and Hardart. Its claim to fame was its little cubicles with food in them and a price posted on each. If you saw a piece of coconut cream pie you simply couldn't live without you inserted a quarter, opened the glass door and took out your pie. It was the same for salads, drinks, vegetables, et al. When you had everything you wanted on a tray, you sat in whatever empty seat you could find, often sharing the table with others.

We ate often at H. & H. and enjoyed the food and the ambiance. On one day, we sat at a small table where a little lady was eating. She wore a pill-box hat with fur around the edge. Not wanting to talk in English with this stranger so near, I began stumbling through French sentences. Lacking originality, I tackled what was nearest to us. "The woman has a nice hat," I remarked, and added with some uncertainty, "The fur is rabbit." It was quite an achievement. I went on to other sophisticated French constructions at a level a notch below "Look, Jane. Look at Dick. Dick is a boy. Look, Jane, look." About then the lady with the hat finished her meal, rose and said in beautiful clarity, "Bon jour Madame, Monsieur," and swept away. Look, Dick, look...

At last it was over and we scraped together our outfit. It included two camp cots and camping mattresses, mosquito nets and a brown and white cork and canvas helmet for each from Abercrombie and Fitch in Philadelphia. All we owned went to Africa in about four drums. We had no radio or refrigerator or washer or vehicle. But we had big bottles of vitamins the foreign secretary insisted we buy. I took a few and discovered side effects I didn't need. We gave the vitamins to skinny Africans for years.

There were times while packing those drums that the memory of the Spanish classes we had taken rose up to mystify us. We had been so sure for so long a time that we would go as missionaries to a country in South America and now we were printing a Belgian Congo address on those drums.

One of our African friends voiced one explanation near the end of our first term on the field. "Tata Braun has a white skin," he said. "But he has a very black heart."

We thanked the dear brother for this accolade and realized anew that in singing the hymn of consecration, "Where He leads me, I will follow," we needed no fear or even hesitation. God's wisdom is perfect. In His will Africa became our home, a dearly beloved home.

SECTION THREE

MISSIONS

14

MISSIONARIES AT LAST

Our first trip to Belgian Congo was made during the later days of World War II. German U-boats were sinking ships all over the Atlantic so our ship stayed close to the US coast, going south rather than heading southeast on a direct line to the mouth of the Congo River. One day away from New York we ran into a hurricane. The vessel was one of the Liberty ships built in an upside-down position as part of the war effort. Some had cracked in half in high seas when straddling giant waves unsupported in the middle.

The passengers had been instructed to bring a lawn chair on board to sit on as this was a freighter, not a passenger ship. Few ships had sailed to Africa in the war years and orders for heavy machinery had piled up in America. Almost every foot of the deck was covered with earth movers and other huge machines, and the ship rode low in the water. Its slow roll was pleasant as we sat reading on deck in the soft summer afternoon sun. But as winds developed the deck slanted more and more.

The captain of the S. S. Alma White asked us to bring our chairs up on his cabin's deck when the roll brought the side of the ship down to the ocean's surface. He didn't want us washed overboard. But as the incline steepened, our chairs went sliding down toward the sea at a fearsome rate, to be stopped only as the deck flattened and tipped the other way. It was a thought-provoking experience and the captain decided it was time to crowd into his cabin where we watched keys on pegs swing from right to left and back on a wide arc.

It was night now and floodlights illuminated the aft part of the ship. As I looked back I could see waves cover the entire aft area. One saw only the sea in those minutes, then we would emerge like a submarine from the waters. A gang of men roped together worked the deck, releasing 20-ton machines to plunge into the depths to lighten the ship as its holds took on water. In the morning there was nothing left, not even the navy life-saving rafts or lifeboats.

Yet the waves were mountainous. We lumbered through canyons of water and had waves crash over the prow, completely submerging the forepart of the ship. This went on hour after hour through the morning until we entered the calmer eye of the hurricane for an hour and then advanced into the full blast again. Our goal was the island of Trinidad where the holds could be pumped out and the lifeboats replaced. By evening we had outridden the storm and the seas flattened somewhat. The ship's deck was about two feet above water and the crew was largely in bunks seasick.

It amazed me that while hardened seamen were incapacitated, Thelma and I had good appetites and were completely comfortable the whole 35 days of that voyage. When the danger passed, it all seemed like high adventure. The captain observed that in 25 years at sea he had never seen a storm the equal of that one and never expected to see another.

After the violence of the storm the air seemed purified and charged. The sunset was vivid with lavish color, a massive sea-scape across the western horizon. We returned to our wee cabins on the fantail where the rattle of heavy chains moved the giant rudder to change our heading through the night. In the morning I got a large bucket and collected about twenty flying fish from both the main and upper deck. Gusting winds combined with the low decks had caused them to be stranded on the iron. We had seen endless schools of these fish shoot out of the sea and soar low for a hundred feet before gravity pulled them back into the sea. They were torpedo-shaped, silvery white and about a foot long.

Anchored at Trinidad for a day to be pumped out and re-outfitted with lifeboats added its own experiences. We were taken ashore in lifeboats and the sailors, navy men, got noisily drunk. One fell off the wharf into the ocean but was dragged out. The island offered green coconuts from which to drink the juice, cow-horn roosters and hens, colored rubber sets of toy huts and palm trees - and chocolate sundaes, a life-long favorite of ours.

Back on deck I obtained a hook four inches long and a fist-sized chunk of beef, substituted the hook and beef for the speed gauge on a long rope which trailed aft and threw it out into the water. Hours passed with nothing taking the bait, but at last a shark grabbed it and I pulled it toward the boat. Some sailors joined in and we horsed a thrashing five- or six-foot fellow up to the deck. Just as we were about to get him on deck he gave a mighty jerk and the metal cable which held the hook simply untwisted, knots and all, and the fish fell back into the sea. At that time, all sharks were man-eaters, as far as I knew. We are smarter now.

The pumping ship which tied up to ours to draw out the water taken into the holds in the storm somehow got a large fish wedged in between us. The sailors gaffed it and reported it as weighing about 200 pounds. We ate a lot of excellent fish after that.

On Sundays I was asked to preach to passengers and crew. There was a palpable reverence for God the Sunday after the storm. Everyone aboard realized that we had been together in the valley of the shadow of death.

Weeks passed without sight of land. We crossed from the Brazil coast over the equator to the southwest Africa coast and down to Cape Town without incident. The equatorial heat, oppressive for us because of the constant heat of the engine room felt in our airless rooms, changed to a chill as we reached South Africa in its winter season.

AFRICA AT LAST

The mission had arranged for our C&MA party of four to stay in a lovely hotel until we could book a train north. Booking required sitting in an elegant office sipping tea while dates and seats were worked out.

I recall a cultural oddity at the hotel. One evening we passed a large drawing room crowded with people listening to a radio program with a South African comedian. We joined them and listened. There was a mass hysteria of laughter. I gave full attention to this master funnyman who was convulsing his countrymen and never heard one line that even made me smile. To our group the man was talking gibberish. To his people he was a hilarious genius. If beauty is in the eyes of the beholder, funniness is in the ears of the listeners.

Finally we were booked and left the Cape to go by rail through the Kalahari Desert and up to Johannesburg and then to southern Rhodesia, a long ride. The Victoria Falls area was spectacular and we were there most of a week. Leopard furs were abundant at that time and I bought a small piece of fur to make a hat for Thelma. I did make it later but she felt uncomfortable wearing it. But I had the fun of making it. I found it fashionable and beautiful until the day we tossed it out. Love's labors lost . . .

Victoria Falls has a long, high railroad bridge over it and Thelma and I decided to walk across it one day. About halfway across, a family of very large baboons came across from the other side. I realized they could push us over the edge if they wished. I pulled out my pocket knife, opened it and put Thelma behind me as they advanced. What a relief when they crowded over to their side of the bridge and passed by. They obviously were accustomed to living with people.

We took some close-up pictures of animals there and bought a copper knife with a wood handle covered in a metal design, some raffia cloth and other curios. The train took us to Elizabethville in southern Belgian Congo. The city is named Lubumbashi now. We stayed in a Methodist guest house where a single man missionary welcomed us with fervor. After an evening meal he taught us a game to play. He sanctified it with a different name but it was simply poker. I think the three women in our party never suspected. And it was fun for an evening in the heart of Africa. On Sunday an older missionary took us to a village and I preached my first African sermon in English, which he translated into Swahili. It was our first close contact with Africans in their own setting and it was a good feeling to have at last reached them.

One last train took our foursome up to Port Franqui on the Kasai River. I cannot recall whether it was there or in Elizabethville where I had my early August birthday and was given a gorgeous liver-and-white pointer pup. He was a sweet crank and we named him Grumpy. How so fine a breed came to Africa I never learned, but the Belgians loved dogs and excellent thoroughbreds were brought to Congo by them. Grumpy was a champ. We kept him fed and growing on a long boat trip down the Kasai to the Congo River and to the capital of Leopoldville. He was fun.

In 1945 Leopoldville had about 300,000 of the Congo's 13,000,000 people. Two missions worked there, the British Baptist and the American Baptist. Each had one or two congregations and primary schools. The war had reduced the number of missionaries and advances were few and slow. The first planes were flying into Leopoldville by then and we saw C&MA missionary children, Joe and Dorothy Nicholson, off to America. Joe would marry Betty Miner, one of our Old Stone Church Sunday school girls, and return to a lifetime of mission service. Esther Galbraith, who later became Mrs. Dean Kroh, a Nyack friend and a nurse, flew in at that time, saving two months of travel. A largely empty British Baptist Church for English speakers was located next to the guest house. It was "high church" Baptist - to us almost Anglican in liturgy at the time. We could not have imagined the changes which would envelop this collection of buildings, changes in which we were to play some major roles.

Willys' sketch of Grumpy, an embryonic bird dog

A further train ride took us from the capital to Matadi, the major port, 125 miles inland from the Atlantic. Ocean freighters could sail up to Matadi on the Congo and disgorge their cargoes. Matadi, in the local language, means rocks and the city is well named. Between the high plateau on which Leopoldville is situated, the vast river rushed over enormous rock, through canyons which divert its waters willy-nilly for hundreds of miles, all the way to Matadi. For those miles the Congo is not navigable for ships. The railroad was the link between port and capital.

At Matadi we stayed at the Swedish mission guest house, a clean, well-run oasis of peace in a seemingly endless land of villages. A river boat to Boma took us to the C&MA field at long last. Grumpy could finally run free. He did just that, an embryonic bird dog who spotted a duckling waddling along and who knew instinctively what a good bird dog should do. He sank his teeth into the soft body and when we attempted to open his jaws to retrieve the wee bird, he growled ferociously.

It was a very unpromising way to begin a new relationship with Miss Frances Eisensmith, the missionary in charge. But she was forgiving and gracious about the loss of her duckling. I learned through decades of wretched luck with chickens and ducks that on the average, one might expect to get one adult chicken out of ten eggs set and six eggs hatched. I think Miss Eisensmith had long ago stopped counting her chickens and ducks before they were full-sized. And even then hawks, snakes and disease took a large share of them. I came to the opinion that the only sure chicken was the one served for dinner.

We began to learn Kikongo during a pleasant month in Boma. Boma had been the early capital of Belgian Congo and the mission had bought the Dutch embassy building when the officials moved to Leopoldville. It was built on iron pylons three feet above the ground, probably as protection against termites, driver ants, snakes, mice and cockroaches. Broad verandahs surrounded it on all sides for coolness. The building was of imported lumber and had high ceilings. An eight-foot-high grandfather's clock was left behind by the Dutch, and scores of pigeons lived in a cote nearby.

Miss Eisensmith had a talking gray parrot which she was trying to teach to say "Three cheers for Vungu." The bird already said many other things but it seemed immune to the new phrase. Vungu was where we were to be stationed. A veteran lady missionary whose husband had died was to have been at Vungu to oversee the four new missionaries assigned there, but she had decided she wasn't up to that and went back to America. Vungu had no missionary.

Never mind, the chairman decided the Brauns should go up and see the place. We were given a pick-up and drove four hours north to the mountain road leading up to the station. It was steep, too steep and too slippery for traction. With the truck in second gear forward we found ourselves going backward and stopped at the brink of a small cliff. Congolese villagers from the village helped us get up the hill at last and we saw Vungu for the first time. It was the oldest of the field's stations on a mountain top surrounded by jungle-clad mountains as far as the eye could see.

There were a church, two schools, a big, ancient house, a small bungalow and an overflowing mission cemetery. The most recent grave was that of "Baby Jim" Loucks who died in his mother's arms in the cab of a lumber truck, bouncing slowly toward Boma, still hours away. Baby Jim was the last American to be buried at Vungu, though in our 30 years in Congo, James Macaw, son of the widow who left Vungu, and Joseph Nicholson, Sr. died on the field later.

Vungu station had two small villages on its border. Its schools brought teachers and students to it from afar. Apart from them, the church would have had few attendees. But the district superintendent lived there as well. With the missionaries, this made up the headquarters of a very large but sparsely settled area extending north, south, east and west, bounded by other districts, the river near Matadi and the frontier with the Swedish mission.

Having seen the station and pastor, we drove back to Boma. That morning, before our arrival, the parrot had said, "Three cheers for Vungu" and promptly died. Miss Eisensmith felt it was the bird's conscience. No honest person would say three cheers for that isolated remnant of early missions. The C&MA had three other stations near the railroad which tied Boma to the lumber-filled area north of it. The mission chairman, Rev. Clarence Birkey, decided that we should see Kinkonzi, Maduda and Kwimba stations before being banished to Vungu.

We went by train to Tshela. I recall seeing two kayi antelope prancing on a hillside. A missionary met us and drove us to Kinkonzi, the main station where the field chairman and his sweet wife lived. Next we went to Maduda which had a normal school and exceptionally high morale. The Nathan Tylers were in charge there. We then drove to Kwimba where the Ray Florences and Miss Ethel Mason lived. She invited us for a meal and served us soup and crackers. Several times she offered more crackers and I didn't take them, preferring to wait for the food still to come. To my chagrin, there was no more to come. I should have filled up on crackers when I had the chance.

Miss Mason was assigned to Vungu as senior missionary. Thelma and I would have three months alone there before she arrived. We had no health insurance, no vehicle, no refrigerator, no radio, no running water, plumbing or electricity. There wasn't a butcher shop within 80 miles. My gun was our meat supplier. We had no functional garden. A few Africans brought occasional carrots, bitter tomatoes or tiny potatoes for sale. We kept chickens for eggs and meat and there were bananas and citrus fruits in season and canned powdered milk.

A truck with 75 men's loads stopped on the state road about three miles from our post. Miss Mason, Jean Robson and Edith Gant came through the jungle to Vungu and, after them, 75 carriers. Miss Mason was a flannelgraph expert. She had hundreds of big envelopes labeled "hands, feet, boys, girls" - ad infinitum. We guess-timated that half of the 75 boxes might be big envelopes, but couldn't confirm it. Miss Mason also had a surly, arrogant dog who assumed the right to go into our chicken house and eat our eggs. Chasing him ended in a ferocious growl and bared fangs. He understood clearly that being the dog of the senior missionary had its perks.

Miss Mason was a tall, rangy woman who resembled Whistler's mother. She was kindly and fun and was our Kikongo teacher. She didn't complain when one day an antelope ran right toward our house and I bolted class for my shotgun. I think she got a bit bored with all those pronouns and suffixes. I believe we learned as much Kikongo out in the jungle with hunters or in the kitchen with a helper. That's where fine distinctions were learned.

For example, we learned from Davidi that we were in the dry season, the sivu, now but that soon the rain would come, the mvula. A week later a drizzle sifted down and Thelma said, "Tata Davidi, mvula."

"Nana, Mama," he laughed, "diadi i disala," - this is disala. So a drizzle was disala. The drizzle turned to a spring rain.

Thelma said, "Mvula, Tata."

Another loud "Nana," no, was his response. He added that when the mvula came we would know it. How right he was. One day the wind blew up, the trees bent, the sky grew black, rent by jagged lightning and thunder crashing all around. Rain pounded down on our house's tin roof for a violent hour. Davidi came in and shouted above the din, "Mama, yayi i mvula." This is rain. One remembers that kind of vocabulary definition.

Tata Davidi explained types of rain

Along with two years of Kikongo language study my assignment was to build a road with a more gradual ascent. This I enjoyed. It would begin in flat grassland, cross a marsh and mount the mountain. The grassland part was easy. The marsh required a raised roadbed and four small bridges of heavy beams. That took some time. To cut the degree of rise to 10 degrees we had to spiral up a rather steep mountain. I improvised a two-legged board with a level on it and cut one leg shorter than the other so that when both rested on the ground and the level bubble was centered, we knew the short leg was on ground 10 degrees higher than the long one. With this simple device we pegged a 10-degree rise from the bottom to the top of the mountain and came out nicely near the station.

Working with about ten men I soon learned how Africans work best. They definitely disdained an eight-hour day and did little work in it. What they liked was what they called an mfienda - an assigned piece of work. They worked like madmen to finish, then left, proud to be free men again. Most finished before lunch time.

There was fun with these men. One day I felt one of them was doing poor work cutting down a tree. I took the ax and showed him how to do it. He was dripping with appreciation and admiration as I continued to show him. Then I recognized that the rascal was conning me into doing his work. Chagrined, I handed back the ax and everybody roared with laughter. Clever.

Another day I asked, "Does anyone have a knife? - I need to cut this thing." Nlenzo, a macho type, offered me his with the dry observation that "a man's not a man if he has no knife." Oh!

Nlenzo was to be married soon and was very happy about it. I asked him, "How old is your wife, Nlenzo?" He made two cups with his hands and put them out a distance from his chest. I gathered she was old enough.

I faced a real problem climbing the mountain for lunch. My legs lost their strength and I could hardly climb. I arrived home weary beyond telling, ate and took my daily dose of quinine. After that my strength returned. After awhile it came to me that if I took quinine at night or in the morning I might avoid the daily low at noon. That worked better.

We had attacks of malaria, I far more than Thelma. Probably my bursts of heavy labor caused them. For days I had abundant energy and worked long and hard, only to be zapped by an attack that would put me in bed for three or four miserable days of sweats and chills and a stomach which refused both food and water.

One observation I made is that I could get up at four a.m. - the "first chicken," and hunt all day till dark, walking many miles, and never have an attack. But more than once, a walk to a distant village to preach would bring me down – perhaps this was the enemy's strike.

We went on many preaching trips. On some jungle trips we had to cross streams and we would be carried over by two men who crossed hands, creating a "seat." Sometimes the men took carrying chairs. I didn't like having men carry me so I walked, but it seemed wise to have Thelma use the chair where possible. On some mountainsides the steepness and slippery mud forced her to climb up handhold by handhold.

On our very first trip we reached a large village and were given a hut in which to put our cots and mosquito nets. Davidi was our translator and cook. To our delight, the chief of the town brought us some eggs as a gift. We received them with profuse thanks, as if they were rubies and diamonds. Davidi came and took them, looking very sour. We chatted with the chief. Davidi poured a bowl of water and put the eggs in it. They all floated jauntily to the top. He picked up the eggs and charged out to the chief.

"These eggs are no good," he shouted and put his arm up, ready to throw them out into the jungle.

"Stop," shrieked the chief, "they are good for gifts." Ah, so they were. Brown, stained with age, they were good for gifts.

I had done chalk-talks in the States, copying the example of Phil Saint, and did the same in some Congo services. And people were converted. Vungu had had no man missionary for some years and the pastors were happy to have a "mundele" - white man - visit their villages. Wherever we went we found unburned brick churches with leaky roofs. Rain dripping down dissolved bricks and cut walls. Without prompt repairs to the roof and the wall, the church would fall in before long.

In Nyack a teacher spoke of a wealthy eastern European who was converted and sent out masons and carpenters to repair churches of his nation. At Vungu we copied his example and sent out a carpenter and mason with funds to buy wood and bricks to repair village churches. The large district was encouraged by this and many new churches were built in those years.

The week before Easter we went to a large, distant village, Nzanza Mputu. Each day we researched our Thompson Chain Reference Bible to learn what the Lord did that day and preached about it with love and a yearning for souls. Many young men came to Christ that very precious week. We were to preach in many places after that during the week before Easter and Dr. Makanzu would write a book on that passionate, wonderful week. The whole nation of Zaire would one day be challenged to preach in that week in 17,000 villages.

The chief of the village had had many wives and dozens of children. But now, we were told, he was dying. Would we go preach Christ to him? We were led at night to a hut with a small fire as its only light. A few old crones sat on the floor near a living skeleton lying on a blanket. I crouched down by him and told him of the great God who sent His Son, Jesus, to pay for our sins. In the name of this God who called me, I told him of the offer of salvation and eternal life. I told him that many of his sons had taken the gift of forgiveness from this loving God and I asked him to do the same. He indicated that, yes, he would.

We celebrated the resurrected Christ on Easter and the newly redeemed were full of praise. A good number of those men came to our Bible school to study for the ministry. It was an excellent school and revival was in the air. But the old chief, after we left, called his sons together and told them, "I fooled the mundele, telling him I wanted to become a Christian. I do not. I will die as my ancestors did. Now go out and cut down every fruit tree I planted and dig my grave extra deep to hold all my bolts of cloth, all my tools and all my wealth. All must go with me as I go to the ancestors." So it was. All he had was lost to his many wives and children. He left them only the memory of a mean, heathen skeleton, a hateful, lost soul who had a glimpse of heaven and turned away. Our hearts were broken.

Our first term was a very busy one. I saw that our preachers wanted to dress in white duck suits but tailors charged an abominably high price to make a suit. We had a man who loved to travel so we engaged him to walk the two days to Matadi and purchase bolts of white duck and white thread. When he returned, we hired a tailor to cut and sew a coat and pair of pants each day. We made small, medium

Bycanistes sharpii, one of a hundred water color paintings by Willys of Congo's birds

and large suits and sold them only to preachers at cost. They came from far and near to buy these suits and Vungu pastors were the best dressed crowd in Belgian Congo.

Too, we hired a local carpenter and metal worker to make tools. These men could fashion a whole gun, given a length of ¾-inch pipe and a junk pile of metal. Now they made masons' trowels, levels, drills, bits and metal saws. All were sold at cost to fellow believers, to enable them to build brick houses and furniture. Tools make so many improvements possible.

On the Kasai River boat trip I had met a Belgian ornithologist who was collecting bird skins of Congo for his museum He told me that the greatest collection was in the American Museum of Natural History, in New York City, and gave me the name and address of its curator, Dr. Donald Chapin. I wrote to him and he sent directions on the preservation of bird skins.

The jungle swarmed with many species of birds. I found village boys who trapped birds for food and arranged to buy the birds they caught in their baited snares. I held many, dead or alive, in one hand and drew and painted water color pictures of them which we still have. About 100 different species were skinned and preserved and taken to Dr. Chapin in 1950 for his museum. In appreciation he sent me two-inch-thick manuals of the birds of Congo. Later ones included our name in the text.

Arsenic in powdered and soap-like form were the preservatives used. They were deadly poisons so when the time came to leave Vungu I had a man dig down eight feet and buried both underground. Congolese, by the way, are skilled users of poison to exterminate people they dislike. The poison cup ritual existed everywhere, governed by witch doctors. But any wife or husband knows poisons which, put in food, kill swiftly. Perhaps this fear of retribution lies at the bottom of the Africans' great concern not to leave a person enraged. A man will steal, cheat and plunder another gladly, but having done so, he does his best to restore peace to his victim's heart. He dreads hatred toward him.

I have had a dismissed worker go to the government labor office and file claims for thousands of dollars of the most whimsical reparations. The officer came to our station and spread out the worker's claims. I produced accounts showing we had paid every legal amount and more in salary, rent, transport, medical help, vacations and seasonal gifts. "Yes," he said, "but this citizen of Congo is not happy. He needs to be made happy." At that point, he instructed the worker to leave and then said, "His charges are unfounded but we must give him a token. I demand $10 for him and $30 for my intervention." I gave the money to him.

The worker was brought back and given $10. He was vindicated. Now both Africans shifted into a totally new role, that of appeaser. They joked, they laughed, they flattered me. When they saw I was relaxed, they left. In their culture, an angry person is a vindictive, dangerous person. Instinctively or calculatedly, they strive for peace in the end.

Thelma was a city girl but she took to this rural life with dignity and pleasure. We lived in a two-room house with office and kitchen added. Vungu furniture was simple but adequate, except for our beds. Our mattress was made of horsehair - in a land without horses. How it got there I cannot imagine. Why it stayed, I cannot imagine. The hairs were slippery. Turning over in bed caused those underneath you to slide away toward the edge or center of the mattress. After a week, man and wife slept in two troughs through which the hard slats of the bed's platform could be felt. Shaking the mattress made it a giant formless bag of hair once more and the process began again. No one of the mission but the Brauns lacked Simmons innerspring mattresses. After three years, two days before we left Vungu, the mission sent up mattresses like those everyone else had had for years. The squeaky wheel gets the oil. We hadn't squeaked.

Vungu had no refrigerator. One Christmas our delightful friends, Nate and Helen Ost, came to Vungu from Boma. They brought a block of ice and we concocted an ice-cream freezer with a bucket and a five-pound KLIM tin. KLIM is MILK spelled backwards, a Dutch product of powdered whole milk. Ice cream made with KLIM was rich, smooth and marvelously cold. The ice cream was put in the KLIM tin and the tin put in the bucket and packed with salted ice. When it began to gel, it was stirred thoroughly, then permitted to freeze. Wow! Fit for a king, it was, with jam or syrup on the top.

*Christmas with the Osts was
a happy time.*

The Osts had a genius for doing happy things. They were assigned to build a vacation house on the ocean for C&MA missionaries. During construction they lived in a long hut with reed walls, a sand floor and a thatched roof - a kind of Robinson Crusoe set-up. We visited them there often. Nate was a skilled rifleman and I had a single-shot, 12-gauge shotgun. More important was Nate's Jeep.

The ocean had once covered a vast area and as it receded it left a desert-like plateau, flat as a highway. Bustards fed in the grass of that wasteland and so did small antelope. At dawn, both could be found. There were two sizes of bustards. Both had ostrich-like heads, necks and legs, but one had a body weight like a small chicken, the other like a goose. The small ones felt safe in the grass when a car drove up by them. The larger flew off before a car came within shotgun range. So Nate shot the big ones with his 270 rifle and I shot the small ones with my 12 gauge.

Antelope were another story. They ran early and ducked and dodged like a rodeo cow. The only way to shoot one was from the front seat of the twisting, jumping, rolling Jeep. It took me nine shots to hit my first one. One day we shot four of them and salted down the meat for students of the Bible school. Our hunting was for food for the table. There were no butcher shops in the villages. Canned meat was boring and very expensive. Nate and I both grew up with hunting. We simply used our skills to feed our families.

The tribe along the ocean front spoke a different language from our Kikongo. They held on to their pagan practices as well. Near the mission vacation house was the chief of Vista town. When Protestant missionaries came, he attended the services and came forward at an invitation. When the Catholic priest came, he was a devout Catholic. But when he was dying, he howled with anguish that the devils had come to take him. A full witch-doctor's suit was found in his house.

Vista town has a kumbi, a kind of jungle finishing school for girls of marriageable age. Matrons chaperoned these girls for roughly a year, preparing them for marriage. During a vacation we were permitted to visit their dormitory. Carved on their beds were male organs in profusion. What all they taught these girls I can't know but one day we drove through the village and three bare-breasted girls were walking up the road with missile-shaped breasts pointing straight out like rifles. Weird. No statue or painting of a nude in our culture ever looked anything like that. When the kumbi girls graduated, they dressed nicely and jiggled around in a lengthy, quiet dance. Young men came up and tucked bills into their cloth, large ones. The longer the girls jiggled, the more money they collected. We never learned what happened after they graduated, but no doubt each was considered to be quite a catch for men looking for a wife.

In 59 years our missionaries never made real headway with the Oyo tribe of Vista, but Nate and Helen Ost did. Their sincerity and obvious concern for the people won some to faith in Christ. Sunday schools were started and then a primary school. The Osts wanted to stay on at Vista to consolidate and expand these gains but once the vacation house was finished they were moved to Boma and then Banga to build impressive, large churches.

The two had been married seven years and had no children. At Vista, Helen and Nate lived in a tropical paradise, swimming each day in the ocean and living simply and happily. Helen became pregnant there and had a large golden-haired son whom Nate quickly made into a little muscle man. He had a curtain rod at the top of the door and would hold Sonny up to grab it in his infant hands. Nate then walked away, turning his back on his son, seemingly forever. The boy held tight until lifted down. He was to become what people today call a hunk. Handsome, big and strong, he is also a remarkable supporter of ER ministries.

A globally famous literacy proponent named Frank Laubach and his son came to Kinshasa and asked each mission to send two delegates to his seminar on the methodology which he had developed. Thelma and I were sent to the capital for this. President of the Congo Protestant Council at the time was Rev. Ohrneman, our good friend who long headed our neighbor mission in Matadi. We often stayed in their guest house and had long, far-ranging conversations. When the Ohrnemans heard we were coming to Leopoldville for the seminar he insisted that we stay with them in the handsome, large house in which they lived.

The Laubach system used drawings of objects that had names beginning with that letter. My experience with drawing was quickly put to use drawing letter symbols for the whole alphabet for Kikongo. The tribe had no R sound. When they said our name, the R became an L sound. Each consonant was followed by a vowel sound, so BRAUN became Ba-Lo-Nee. To them, that series of sounds had no other meaning than our name. Back home, baloney brought up other connotations.

We met many young churchmen in those few days in the capital and left, little imagining that we would soon return. Our first term was almost up and we were planning to go on furlough.

Dr. Frank Laubach,
globally renowned literacy
proponent

111

LECO-
LA LIBRAIRIE EVANGELIQUE
DU CONGO

*LECO, Congo's multi-mission
publishing house*

A large, modern, multi-mission publishing house was being finished off near the guest house. Its builder, Dr. George Carpenter, was due for furlough and needed a replacement to administer the very large business. A Belgian businessman was named to the job, but when he examined the books he threw up his hands in horror and quit. We were the next choice. We agreed to stay on an extra year to head this enterprise. We left Vungu and spent a month getting acquainted with the stock and the books. Until the director left there was no apartment open for us. We stayed in the guest house, meeting exciting missionaries from all over Congo at the guest house meals.

Thelma became pregnant in that month, seven years after our wedding. We worked hard filling orders for half a million students in every part of Congo. For six months we kept up with orders, then our stock ran out on some articles. Whatever LECO lacked I purchased in town. However, the mission in America which paid for LECO purchases had been carrying nearly a hundred thousand dollars credit. At a certain point it stopped paying for LECO supplies. This was a crisis affecting every mission in Congo.

We called the LECO board members together. Apprised of the problem, they were shocked and one mission offered to put up needed capital if ownership was transferred 100% to them. That was unacceptable. LECO's problems were ironed out and a few months later when the director returned we were free to return to America for our first furlough. LECO not only survived but prospered for twenty years when missions turned over leadership to African staff.

We had entertained the C&MA chairman at supper the night of that meeting. Thelma bustled around, seven months pregnant, but our guest never guessed. Early in the morning her birth pains began and Chris was born later in the day.

FURLOUGH NO. 1

Four months after Chris' birth we went home by freighter and a little Belgian boy visited Chris often on the ship. Eagerly, the little eyes followed his every movement. He clearly recognized his own generation. Chris charmed our American friends. They clamored to hold him in church and Chris was as happy with them as with us. He was a people baby, tiny as a doll but with a merry smile and bright eyes.

When we reached America our ship harbored at Philadelphia. Our friends, Phil and Dottie Worth, picked us up and after a delightful visit we were driven to Elizabeth, New Jersey, to visit the Willard Crunkiltons. Thelma and Willard had been friends for a decade in Mansfield and he had visited us in Nyack eleven years earlier.

We needed a car and one of Willard's church members had a handsome old Hudson for sale for about $15. It needed tires. We

Baby Chris and his parents leave the freighter.

bought four new ones. And, we were told, it guzzled oil. Little did we know how much oil. We began our trip west in early morning and before we had driven 200 miles there was a banging and a clatter to jar your eye-teeth – and no power. I pulled off the road and called a wrecker. He looked at it and told us the motor was now junk. He gave us a bit for the new tires and delivered us to a motel.

At that time I was unaware of the Amish people. There was a family of them at the motel and we chatted about Congo and our ministries. When we woke up the next morning they had gone, but there was a twenty-dollar bill stuck under the door to remind us that though it looked for all the world that we were alone on this highway, we were not forgotten. Nzambi Mpungu – God Almighty! - won't forget! We picked up a used car that day at a price which worried us, but someone sent us a $400 check in the mail and restored our cash on hand. We drove to Mansfield, a very happy family.

Thelma's many friends in her home town received us with open arms. For a month we visited with Mother Still, then settled in a cottage at Beulah Beach, a C&MA campground on Lake Erie.

I went away on tour in western Pennsylvania, then in western Canada with a senior missionary from West Africa, Leroy Kennedy. Days dragged by. Waiting 23 1/2 hours to speak of the work in Congo seemed an awful waste of time. And I missed my loved ones painfully. But Leroy saved me from total depravity by telling jokes. I listed dozens of them under various headings so I could share them with Thelma when - if ever - I could return home. Tour lasted two months and each missionary was given a dollar a day extra and sent home by train.

Earlier I had noticed a large, round, clear glass window in the wall behind the pulpit of the Mansfield church and decided to improve on it. It measured six feet in diameter. I made a circular frame with inverted scallops, cut thin pebble-grained glass to fit the frame, then began painting a flaming torch between two hemispheres of earth. It was a missionary theme. We carried it down to Mansfield in our delivery truck and, with approval, installed it in front of the clear glass circle. The light shone through the colors beautifully. Everyone liked it and, when a newer, larger church was built years later, the window was the only item of the old church used in its specially designed circular window at the back of the sanctuary.

Visiting Allliance churches made me want to help them. One in Pennsylvania had a miserable sign that looked as old as the church. I bought paint and covered it and re-did its black letters. In New Jersey a church had no board at all, so I built one for them. It used movable letters. In other cities I painted soiled boards to pass the time and at the famous Old Orchard campgrounds, so beloved by Dr. A. B. Simpson, I cut out large cardboard silhouettes of profiles of different races and tacked them high on the rough tabernacle wall. Thelma put up with all of these irregular activities, using her time well in crafting the future seminary professor we called Chrissie.

Spring took me on a tour of nearly three months in Texas. It was warm and exciting to explore this huge state. My partner missionary was a veteran from Tibet and she was desolate because of China's invasion of her field. But she was a saint, a godly woman with an oriental mystique about her. Mrs. Griebenow was good for me.

When the tour ended I suggested to Thelma that she drive down to Texas to meet me. With Chris in the back, she made the long trip from the northern border of the US to its southern border and, together, we re-did the highlights of the Lone Star State. Only young marrieds can experience such excitement as we knew, carefree and thrilled with our great southwest.

Furlough included preaching in many Ohio churches as well as those on tour, and in Toronto we had an oh-so-happy week with the Don Shepsons. Unknown to us, some Toronto Christians covenanted with the Shepsons to contribute to a fund which would one day enable us to buy a house. That is described in a later chapter.

That first term of missionary life had its joys and its sorrows, but God had worked in a wonderful way. Sharing the evidences of His presence and power, displayed so vividly both at the primitive jungle station and for the last year in the nation's capital, filled the furlough year with thanksgiving and a desire to return quickly to the field.

Chris enjoys America.

15

KINKONZI MINISTRIES

BACK TO AFRICA

At the C&MA annual conference Dr. Snead, the foreign secretary, took us aside to tell us we had been assigned to Kinkonzi station to direct the Bible Institute. I was deeply saddened not to be going back to Vungu where we had so many friends. There were four married couples and three single lady missionaries at Kinkonzi. Of these eleven, eight had seniority over us and I wondered what mission life would be like under these circumstances. But I found that it was good to have old hands seeing that everything kept running on schedule and soon our helpers decided we knew the ropes well enough to lead and we began to shape the school into a new image.

There were only 17 students in this highest of pastor-training schools. We were told that the stations had scoured the country to find men who could pass the entrance test. We would have to teach only these men for three years because there were no others available.

Thelma trained the men of the school to sing some rousing Christian songs in French. We took them to major services and everywhere their singing created great excitement. We held gospel rallies and had weeks of evangelism, and the men looked great and sounded greater. When the school year ended we had so many fine new men wanting to take the entrance exam that it was easy to take on a second class and a third and fourth, for we added a fourth year to the course.

That second term was the best of times for missions. We reaped ripe fruit from the plantings of decades of drought and stony ground. Across the board, Congolese had concluded that the white man's God was powerful and they wanted Him to bless them as He blessed us. They changed many long-established habits to please Him. If He hated stealing, they would stop stealing. If He hated drunkenness, they would leave palm wine alone. If He hated the immoral dances which ended in sexual debauchery, they could live without that too. Dishonesty and lying could go as well. If they borrowed money and promised to repay it month by month, they did it as indicated. Violence too was ended. The one thing few men could stop was adultery.

The government required that all preachers, ordained or laymen, be registered on 5"x7" cards. These showed their family names, village of birth, date of birth, education, children, etc. The mission added two questions of its own: "Since you became a Christian, were you ever disciplined by the church? If so, for what?" I don't think there was one preacher in forty who did not write "Yes" to the first question and "Adultery" to the second. One man philosophically advised me, "There is only one sin, Tata." And that, for the Congo of the early 1950s, was largely true. A cultural transformation had occurred out of a very healthy fear of God.

Consider that in those halcyon days we could leave tricycles, toys, bicycles, lumber, tools, cement and roof tins outside night after night. Our front door was never locked night or day. The little hook on the screen doors, if hooked at all, would conveniently bounce open with a light tap from the outside. Women missionaries frequently walked jungle paths at night to hold meetings with the women of nearby villages.

There was a popular song in that era that went like this, "Oh, bongo, bongo, bongo, I don't want to leave the Congo, Oh, no-o-o-o-oh. Bingle, bangle, bungle, I'm so happy in the jungle, I refuse to go." We all sang it. We all agreed. We had so much to give to this receptive people and they were so pleasant and so grateful that life was about as good as it can get. It would change in 1959, but we had no indication of that change until it came.

We were too busy doing good unto others to anticipate trouble. More students required more student housing. We had to make and burn the bricks, pit-saw lumber, level sites, build foundations, walls, roofs and roads. The old student houses built over 25 earlier years were cracking badly up on Mankundi - Friendship Mountain - because rains had washed away supportive soil around foundations. We began at the top of this ravine-tortured area, restored land to each foundation

118

and planted a strong, deep-rooted grass to hold it forever. Stones carried up from the stream were built into retainer walls. The camp was indeed handsome when all was done.

Hundreds of fruit trees were planted, a little stream was dammed to create a lake stocked with tilapia, a vegetarian fish. The large stream that flowed through the valley was bridged so trucks could arrive at the camp. Roads were built. The Bible Institute camp grew to about 500 people (93 students). A day care camp was built for babies so mothers could attend their own school. The primary schools of six grades had over 400 students, and people by the hundreds flocked to the hospital every day. Workers, over 100 in the building season, swarmed on the station. We were actively helping over a thousand people every day in our schools and hospital and church.

A nice crop of missionary children needed schooling. Their school was built on Kinkonzi station. On weekends a good number of parents might come to spend time with their youngsters. Their teacher, Miss Mildred Gresham, taught them well in her two-room school and founded them solidly on God's Word. All was well in that quaint but very satisfactory institution. It was when the children went away to the high school in the capital, away from their parents, that so many turned away from the Lord. Our boys had an advantage. We had moved to Kinshasa at the time Chris was high school age. He and Paul and Phil always lived at home. Perhaps that is why each followed his Lord.

Radios were still using expensive tubes in those days and were out of reach for Africans. It was the time-slot for the ubiquitous phonograph. I met a layman built for basketball in the guest house in the capital who was recording languages for Joy Ridderhoff of Gospel Recordings. I invited him to Kinkonzi to record Kikongo songs and messages. He came and brightened the lives of our single ladies. To the disappointment of all, he didn't seem to be looking for anything but Kikongo recordings.

I still recall the mellifluous voice of Tata Alibeti Paku, later Bishop Albert Paku by virtue of the fact that in a sermon, Bishop Bokeleale pointed his finger at old president Paku and said impromptu, "Why, this man is a bishop." Since that day, Rev. Paku has proudly carried the title of bishop, the only one in the dozens of nations where the C&MA has churches. And, by the way, the finger-pointer himself is the only bishop of the Disciples of Christ worldwide. Congo shows the way!

On the first record received from Gospel Recordings there is a bit of music and then, startlingly clear comes the young voice, "Tombe kiamana bwa mu nsi a Isaeli." Darkness had fallen in the country of Israel. It never failed to get attention. Darkness is a time when ghosts move through the land. In fact, the basic ultimate reality of Congo life is the belief that all sickness and death come from the eating of the life force by bandoki - evil spirits. Discovering whose spirit is doing it to a dying person as early as possible is obviously of greatest importance. And it takes a witch doctor to identify the culprit. That is doubly difficult since the ndoki person won't even suspect he is ndoki, because spirits do their evil when humans sleep.

In the old days, the conclusive test was by poison. If the person died, it was because of his guilt. If he lived, it was because he was innocent. Sorry for the inconvenience. Next drinker.

While India was pressing on toward a population of 700,000,000, Congo, which is almost as large geographically, hardly reached 13,000,000 over millennia of years. It's not difficult to understand why. Everyone has sick days. Everyone eventually dies in India or Congo. But in Congo when a person became ill, the witch doctor killed the ndoki. How many times would a person be sick in his life? How many bandoki would die to protect him? Populations don't grow very fast with this kind of health care.

I was invited on one furlough tour in America to be the guest on a radio talk show. The interviewer was an arrogant type. He sized me up with a scowl and asked, "Why did you go to a happy, successful African society to ruin it and visit upon it the ailments of our society?" Why indeed? I had answers. Lots of them. And they all pointed to Jesus, the Savior of individuals and of races and cultures. Congo needed Jesus above all else. And Jesus' servants were helping move Congo out of darkness to light.

Back to the records. We sold 17,000 of them and I suppose over half the populace of our field heard all eight sides. We bought 70 phonographs and sold them at cost, but the low-cost transistor radio appeared on store shelves at that time and phonographs plunged in demand.

And what of the Gospel Recordings worker? While he was with us he spoke much of wanting to start a radio station in Europe to beam the gospel to Africa. I urged him strongly to go to ELWA radio station in Liberia. I was to learn later that he traveled widely in Europe seeking for a good site but found none. So he flew to Liberia's capital, Monrovia, where ELWA was established and, acting like a tourist, spied out the land. After a week he asked, "I wonder how much a transmitter beamed to the south would cost? I have a friend who might give up to $15,000 toward one." Several weeks later he gave a check, I believe for $200,000, part of an inheritance. As a result of our involvement ELWA would broadcast hundreds of Kikongo daily programs prepared by us in our old hen house absolutely free.

At Vungu I had obtained copies of all the C&MA books published in Kikongo in 60 years. They took two inches on a shelf - an inch every 30 years. Clearly we didn't have much to say to the tribe in those years. In our second term we hit our stride publishing many Christian books, mostly Bible studies. Thelma translated Newell's *Revelation* and *Romans*, Rev. Hess did *Torrey's Topical Textbook* and others pitched in. We did more than an inch a year of new titles and the C&MA had more Kikongo books than all other missions combined.

In America, with our hundreds of millions of readers, many books have only one or two thousand copies printed - and many of them don't sell. In our small area, 100 miles square, 3000 books could be rapidly sold. Congolese wanted to know more about the white man's God! Colporteurs could sell a suitcase of books on a Saturday. I sold 1000 Bibles one weekend. And since the franc was steady, a small profit helped to build up stock and pay salaries.

We had a small offset press but our newsprint paper absorbed moisture from the jungle dampness, causing it to cling to the rubber printing blanket and jam. That machine was a nightmare but we managed to get some nice chorus books out of it and other useful pieces. At the end of the term I took it back to America and sold it. In a drier atmosphere and with the right paper it would do a good job.

Music played an unusually big part in our lives. Thelma played daily for her and my enjoyment, hymns, classical music and cute little ditties. With some she sang the words. I recall one that went like this, "Man's life's a vapor, full of woes. He cuts a caper; down he goes. Down he, down he, down he, down he - Down he goes." It was a sober reminder throughout my young years. I stringently avoided cutting capers. I knew the consequences.

She played the accordion in services away from home and was very skillful. After awhile almost every missionary wife had an accordion. One happy evening in an annual conference, all the wives with accordions played together for one or two numbers. The church was full of Africans and they shouted their approval of this powerful new sound.

We drove Thelma's quartets all over the field and I don't doubt that hundreds of men in ministry today first heard God's call listening to the booming bass voice of Aloni Mabiala singing, "Nkento lenda vilakana mwan'andi wanswa. Kansi Nzambi Mpungu kana vilakana ko." A woman is able to forget her tiny baby, but Almighty God will never forget us.

By the way, Nzambi is the Kikongo word for the Creator God. The African view of God as Nzambi Mpungu is understood better when the word mpungu is identified. It means gorilla, the giant man-like creature that pounds his chest with mighty arms that can toss a man like a doll; an inscrutable, menacing presence from which one cowers, eyes downcast in submission. To stare at it is insolence leading to attack. To run from it is to be bitten severely on the bottom. Every child learned that faced by an mpungu, man humbles himself, but must not flee. And God was "mpungu a tulendo" - the Almighty power.

The song revealed another side of this God - He loves beyond the love a mother has for her baby. A mother might forsake or forget her infant, but Almighty God cannot forget us. It is part of His nature to love us and He cannot change. In a world where mothers became the prime suspects of being soul-eaters when their own daughters' babies became ill, it was highly important for older women to know God loved them, even in the clamor of witch doctors and poison cups. Their ancestral cults might expel them from this world, but a

122

loving God who cannot forget awaited them in the next - if they had made Him theirs in life.

There was back in 1957 a *Sunday Magazine* that was proudly displayed in Christian bookstores as a new genre of Christian publications. Denominations and missions had publications for their people, mostly printed on yellowish newsprint with no color. *Sunday Magazine* was printed on shiny white paper, used color and was young, bright and ahead of its time as an interdenominational periodical.

Somewhat earlier for devotions I had begun writing out in my vocabulary a parallel translation of Scriptures. It made the verses take on new life for me. It occurred to me that others might like to do that for their own inspiration so I sent an article to *Sunday Magazine*. It bounced right back with a note implying that this was sacrilege. Oddly, a few miles away a man boarded the train each morning writing the Bible in his own words as he went. His name was Ken Taylor and his *Living Bible* covered the globe.

Robert Walker became the editor and changed the magazine's name to *Christian Life*. He was a man with a purpose to strengthen Sunday schools by challenging all of them to compete in an annual Sunday school growth contest. There were, I believe, four categories, such as: 1. Sunday schools with fewer than 50; 2. From 51 to 100, etc. The number referred to the average number of students the past year. There were fine prizes for winners in each category. We received *Christian Life* and it convinced me to get our Kinkonzi Sunday school in the competition.

I learned that our last year's average was 168. I believe that was Category Three. The contest was for six specific Sundays. We set to work, doubling, tripling our staff of teachers, planning vivid object lessons for each Sunday, using special music, the p. a. system and lots of extra attractions. We asked the preachers of 13 surrounding villages which regarded Kinkonzi's church as their Sunday morning place of worship to meet together. We gave each a measure of gunpowder to be distributed to any man in their village who had a gun. At seven p.m. on Saturday, all the men would raise their guns skyward and blast off. Then the big tree-trunk drums would begin to beat in all the villages. We gave each village a handful of pictures

Kinkonzi Sunday School contest

from Christmas cards. Christian women were to go to every hut, give a picture and announce the Sunday school contest the next day.

That population had never heard so much shooting, shouting and drumming. Something momentous was going to happen at Kinkonzi and they all wanted to witness it for themselves. For six weeks the whole area was caught up in the Sunday school contest. We invited the territorial head of the Belgian government to come and greet the people. That Sunday over 2000 people came. Over six Sundays we averaged more than 1300 - up from 168 per week.

Mail was very slow between Belgian Congo's interior and Illinois so by the time our report reached *Christian Life* the prizes had been awarded. But Mr. Walker sent us $200 as a consolation prize. I was to meet him in Berlin at the first World Congress on Evangelism. In a conference for Christian publishers he proposed that a new sheet on mission activities was needed. He never started one, but *Pulse* answers that need very well these days.

When the next annual conference for our field rolled around the old president, a taciturn chieftain, muttered out of context, "Tata Braun, you are a strange kind of person." It was a criticism, but I had no idea of what. I asked. Laconically, he opined, "You have a contest for your station, but what about the rest of us?" Aha! Now I knew what to do. I offered to prepare a contest for all the churches. The old man was satisfied and so was his whole executive committee.

It was a big job. We announced four categories with five prizes for each. We sent out hundreds of entrance sheets asking village lay pastors to write their average attendance the past year. No problem. They kept records. There were six dates with a square for each date in which the attendance was to be written. Lines for the name of the village and the name of the preacher were all to be filled in, then sent back to us. There were descriptions of what Kinkonzi had done to increase attendance, included with the entrance sheets, and thousands of pictures from Christmas cards were distributed.

Over 300 Sunday schools sent in reports of fabulous increases. Maduda station had over 900 new people to seat beyond their capacity. They built a large new wing on the momentum of the contest. Overall increase averaged about 300 percent. I am confident that church attendance for the entire field had never been so large, and probably would never be again, as in those six Sundays.

The next step was obvious. Why not a Sunday school contest for all denominations of all Congo? I was present in Leopoldville when the Congo Protestant Council met and broached the idea. They voted approval and I returned to Kinkonzi to print announcements in six languages and sent them out to all denominations. The dates of the contest passed and some reports came back. Some said, "Sorry, we have no Sunday schools." One lady, a missionary of a major mission, complained, "We have too many people coming now and don't want more."

I got a strong impression that the C&MA was miles ahead of most missions with its Sunday schools. We tried to encourage others seven years later as part of the Christ for All national movement, but I have no accurate reports on progress made.

In that same term, Evangelist Oliver Greene came to preach in the C&MA field in Congo. He had a highly visible tent ministry in America in those days, using a huge circus-type tent of many poles. Thousands attended his meetings. Evangelist Greene lived in Greenville, North Carolina - where else? He had a Bible teaching ministry comparable to that of J. Vernon Magee. Both men have been long gone to their reward, but their voices still ring with conviction on regular radio programs and listeners are instructed to mail their gifts to Oliver Greene or J. Vernon Magee.

Oliver loved to preach. When he reached our area we had about a thousand people out to hear him. The next day we drove to Yema where he preached to another thousand. It was fun translating for him. He was a dynamic, muscular orator and I got my exercise trying to translate his gestures, voice qualities and words as well for his Bantu audience. Inevitably, many came forward at the invitation. We counseled and prayed with these seekers and left Yema for Banga, the railhead where our visitor would get the train to Boma.

At Banga, sitting in a tiny mission bungalow-guesthouse, munching Thelma's tasty sandwiches, we had our last conversation together. It was then that our visitor made his most important observation of the trip. "Brother Braun," he said, "you need a gospel tent." It was a totally new thought and eventually it would take me all over Africa, offering gospel tents to big-city churchmen.

At the time, we could get large crowds together in other ways. Besides, I had no notion of how tent evangelism worked. But accepting this evangelist's analysis of our need, I simply assured him that if he sent us one we would use it well.

It took a year between his promise and the actual arrival of the tent. It came in three heavy bags with no instructions at all. We peeled the sacks off of the three sections of the tent, spread them out, arranged them in proper sequence and figured out how they could be laced together. Helpers chopped two trees for center poles and attached the ropes and pulleys to raise the tent. The poles turned out to be far too high so, by trial and error, we shortened them until it looked right. There were ropes around the edge so we drove a strong ironwood peg into the ground for each rope and stretched the tent out. Ah, but the edge of the canvas was so low we had to

Congo tent where 40,000 made public decisions to follow Christ

crawl under it to get into the tent. A stroke of genius led to cutting five-foot poles to raise the edge. Wonderful! All this detail sounds trivial now, but if you have never put up a tent it can be quite a conundrum.

Over 40,000 people made public decisions to follow Christ under or around that tent. It seated 900 crammed-in people. Often 3000 would surround it, listening to the large public address system's powerful call to salvation. One Sunday over 10,000 people swarmed around it. The mass divided up into ten crowds listening to ten evangelists declaring the love and salvation of Jesus Christ.

After the tent's first year, the Congo field reported over 5000 people baptized. All overseas C&MA fields reported a total of about 10,000 baptisms. Little Congo had half the worldwide total for one whole year, and it was the tent that accounted for about 3000 of them.

The tent went from victory to victory. At Vungu, our first station, it brought incredible revival. Giving was phenomenal. With the funds contributed there a brick machine was purchased and many new brick churches were built in revived villages of this huge district.

This first tent was the most effective tool of evangelism in the C&MA field for five years. It was replaced by others, and another was purchased for Kinshasa which traveled to major cities and was instrumental in bringing masses of people to Christ. Two tents were sent to eastern Zaire in the '60s, and in 1976 ER began sending out tents to major cities of Africa. A total of 23 were provided by ER in its early years.

It is impossible to say how many people will be in heaven because of these tents – 30 in all -, but in view of over 30,000 reported converts from the first, the total number of professions of salvation could approach a million.

The most significant fruit of tent evangelism was that in great cities where evangelism was a forgotten ministry, these tents restored the gospel message to its biblical role of preeminence. Kinshasa's denominations, pastors and churches relearned the doctrine and the power of the Word of salvation, of repentance and of personal faith in Jesus' cross and empty tomb. Tens of thousands were truly born anew and revival spread far and wide. It was no small gift the tents gave to the Church in Africa.

Baby Paul was born at Kinkonzi in our second term and the Braun family went home for its second furlough with two blond boys and a thrilling repertoire of victories to report to congregations of Canada and the United States.

FURLOUGH NO. 2

We went on furlough in 1954. We had added one extra year to our first term and would add two years to term three, five to our fourth term and then serve two and one-half years of service at home. We had four furloughs instead of the normal six for our thirty years as Alliance missionaries.

It was not that the Brauns liked furloughs less than other families but that God gave us compelling reasons to stay on the job. Dr. V. Raymond Edman, prexy of Wheaton College in our time there, was fond of saying to the student body, "It's always too soon to quit." I suppose we over-learned that one.

An interesting and humbling experience was ours in the large mission guest building in New York City. Thelma and I were in the sitting room area when the door banged open and a leader of the

Chris and Paul meet America on Braun furlough No. 2.

denomination barged in. I broke into a big welcoming smile, ready to share our harvests on the field with this great man of missions. However, his focus at the moment was not on harvests or missions. Plainly displeased he called out, "Who left the street door unlocked?" A severe penalty was intimated for the guilty one!

He seemed to recognize our innocence and explained in a somewhat subdued voice that in Times Square the street door HAD to be locked every time it was used because of the prevalence of professional thieves. Having made his point, he left. Missionary heroes would have to wait for heaven to get any recognition they may have deserved.

Furlough year was wonderful indeed. It was largely spent in Mansfield in the large home of Clyde and Vivian Garn. Clyde was the oldest of Thelma's four half-brothers. Never were there more gracious people. There were actually three families living in the house - an expanded family unlike any I had known before, enjoying each other, respecting each other, liking the situation.

The mission assigned me to the usual tours - one in East Canada, one in California as I recall. Mother Still was in heaven now. My mother was with Dorothy, now Dr. Dorothy Braun, professor at King's College. I recall a picnic with them in a park with a lake. A big bullfrog was baroomping away in the distance as evening fell. Six-year-old Chris slipped away after the meal and came back with a giant frog squeezed determinedly around the waist by his straining fingers. We took it home and, for want of a better place, put him in the bathtub. Throughout the night he serenaded the household. It is surprising how a bathtub in a bare-walled room can magnify sound. The next morning Chris agreed to return him to his wife and children in the park. But I had to admire his spunk in scouting an unknown shore until he zeroed in on the frog's location, then stalking it and inching close enough for his short arm to strike out like a snake and grab the slippery reptile - and hold on until he got him to his folks. Bravo, Chris!

Thelma enjoyed a very busy furlough. She was an outstanding speaker and two terms provided much sermon material. She was the woman speaker at the annual council that year and was invited to many of the major congregations of the denomination all year long. It is nice being married to a celebrity when she is home. Otherwise it can be very lonesome. Being away on preaching tours five months of the year was tough. Having more weeks alone when I returned was no less so. I wished for Congo where we were all together. The months churned by.

That year in America, the old crank phones were replaced by dial phones and we got hold of six of the old timers and installed them in five missionary houses and in a distant pastor's house. That gave us a party line with a short ring for house number 1, two rings for house number two, etc.

We bought a ton of rolls of tarpaper roofing as well for buildings in the Congo. It ended up on a church, the only one of its kind in Congo, I suspect. Needless to say, we traveled back to Congo by ship and freight was no problem. When we arrived in Congo we went to our old home at Kinkonzi and began the new school year. The wire fence was put up around the entire station, an area of about 60 acres. A cattle-stopping grill replaced the old gate and a large concrete sign was erected at the entrance. Proudly it announced to the many trucks and cars going by that this was Kinkonzi.

On furlough we had preached in a missions conference in Indianapolis where Rev. Russell Kauffman was pastor. He had a unique gift of love from God. He didn't have to work at it. It was in his eyes, his voice, his body language. That love was for all men and always it revealed Jesus. I sat in a barbershop while he got a trim. Barbers are inveterate conversationalists on any subject. Clowning with customers is their first profession. Cutting hair is secondary. With Russ, in two minutes the barber knew he had a man in his chair sent to him from God. I think he was as close as a man can get to a human rendition of the first part of John 3:16. Russ loved the world of people with God's love.

His church filled up with doctors, lawyers, bankers and professors – all to hear a man who had only three years of the Missionary Training Institute. But they could all testify that few men spoke as this man. Six thousand miles away from him, his recorded tapes could thrill your soul.

Russ had a special love for missions. In a time when the average church gave $10,000 for missions and the Ockenga superchurch gave $250,000, the highest in America, Russ's people gave $125,000, comparable to the giving of Oswald J. Smith's Toronto congregation. Russ was tops in mission giving in the Alliance that year and was invited to other churches' mission programs to breathe life into them. Often giving doubled or tripled where he was a speaker.

In our week there Russ mentioned that he had a week of evangelistic meetings in his church every year at which he was the speaker. It was preceded by a week of prayer and God faithfully blessed it. I jotted down the pertinent details with the intent to do something like it at Kinkonzi.

TERM NO. 3

After settling in for our third term, I spoke with our district superintendent about the idea and added a new wrinkle: A Ten Friends Campaign. After prayer the idea came to have every Christian choose ten unbelievers, five of his village and five of other villages, to pray for three times a day and to actively work for their salvation. To get the thing rolling we sent invitations to four district superintendents, asking them to bring their village lay pastors to the station three nights in a row for a joint pastors' meeting. They came from miles around with no idea what to expect. That first evening the theme was the mighty sovereignty, love and holiness of God. An hour of prayers of praise followed and the men went home jubilant in spirit.

The next day there was a "woman rain", the kind that goes on and on quietly for hours. Would the men come in the rain? They would. That second evening the theme was man and his sinfulness, his waywardness, his lostness apart from Christ. That was followed by an hour of prayers of repentance, calling on the Holy One to cleanse and show mercy. The men walked out deeply thoughtful.

They came back for the third service and the focus was on the lost all about us: friends, relatives, neighbors - far from God, far from hope of heaven. At the end, a table was brought in loaded with printed folders, the Ten Friends Campaign folders. A pastor said to the men, "Count up the number of church members in your village, then come and tell us the number." They came one by one and each received a folder for each of his church members. "Now," said the pastor, "write down the names on one folder of five unbelievers in your village and five unbelievers in other villages for whose salvation you will work and pray." They did it.

To conclude, the pastor said, "Please go back to your villages and preach three sermons like the three you heard here on God, man, and the lost to your members. After the third sermon, give each member one of these folders and have each write whatever names of unsaved people they choose to pray for, five in your village, five in other villages. Three times a day the village drum will be beaten to remind you. When you hear it, drop to your knees and pray for your own ten friends."

So it was, a month of prayer was begun in four districts to be followed by a month of evangelism in all the villages. Near the station we had two weeks of tent meetings. Next, we began our week of evangelism in the station church. I have forgotten who preached, but the church was packed with people looking in at windows and doors. So many were saved. About 120 were baptized on one Sunday and we had to tear off the front of the church and extend it about fifty feet. A tower was added to the new construction.

We learn so much from each other. Bless Russ Kauffman's heart, his personal method of winning people to Christ with an annual week of evangelism transplanted so well in Congo! It brought salvation and revival to many congregations that first time. Later the folder was changed from Ten Friends to Three Friends and was used nationwide in Congo and in other African nations and in the USA and Canada as well.

Ideas in the hand of God become powerful, to the pulling down of the enemy's strongholds. I confess that I am constantly looking for new ways by which God is blessing His Church. They show up in the most unexpected times and places and they are almost always transferable to other cultures.

The children of men are wiser than the children of God in this regard. For generations they have scoured the world for new plants, new birds, new animals, reptiles and fish, including the glaciers and the deepest sea. They have identified hundreds of thousands of species both helpful and harmful to men. Billions of dollars are made by businesses springing out of this ceaseless gathering of knowledge.

But the mighty works of God can go on unnoticed, unreported, flowers born to blush unseen upon the desert air. It cannot be doubted that the Holy Spirit is constantly guiding eager servants around the world to fresh ways to bring His Church up to the state of holiness, revival and power set forth in Scripture. But few indeed are the observers and recorders of the acts of the Holy Spirit in our day. There is no organism of the Church which effectively combs the world to find and describe what, where, how, when and why the Spirit is working in power in His global Church. So much is lost to the Body by this near vacuum in our generation.

In this third term a fourth year was added to the Bible Institute. Two of its graduates with only six grades of elementary school before coming to the BI and no high school at all made passing grades in an American college for two years – because we had taught them English in the fourth year. Students increased to 93 in those years and we recognized the importance of training these men in trades so they could earn enough in fewer hours and have time for the ministries they were equipped to conduct. Tailoring, masonry, carpentry, wood carving and car repair were taught, for most would be self-supporting lifelong. At the time there were only thirteen ordained pastors in the whole denomination. In our time in the B.I. we trained over 200 men qualified for ordination, but only a few would be ordained for financial reasons.

A high point of this term was the recording of daily radio programs in Kikongo to be broadcast from ELWA in Monrovia, Liberia. The programs called upon pastors, students, singers, women and youth to participate in radio programs – a wonderful experience. Thelma's electric organ, set up in our chicken house, and a tape recorder operated by a student made hundreds of excellent programs possible.

It was a time of much building of houses for teachers and dozens of student families. In vacation months we had a hundred brick makers, foundation diggers, brick layers, carpenters, cement workers, lumber sawyers and kindling cutters at work putting up new buildings, a two-arch bridge, a nursery building, a two-story school building and a two-room Bible school.

One of the delights of ministering to a jungle tribe unacquainted with our modern life is introducing new activities to them. Thelma listened to each of our pastor students sing and chose four of them to learn four-part harmony – a new thing in their experience. She had a small piano in the house and after classes ended at noon the four men came to learn their four separate parts. It often took a full month for them to get it right for one song. When they sang their song in church the congregation was amazed, excited, buzzing with comments. They had never imagined that their voices could sound so beautiful.

We had a station wagon and were able to squeeze the quartet into it and carry them to large churches near and far. People loved them. They were the "pop stars" of the countryside and I do not doubt that many men came to study to be pastors because they were so blessed, so thrilled by the songs of these four men. I recall one service where the men were singing and one middle-aged woman couldn't constrain herself. She stood up during a song and began waving her arms like a song leader. No one thought this odd. She was just doing what all of their hearts were doing.

These four "stars" were widely imitated and influenced choral groups everywhere. Four decades later choirs are a major part of every congregation and have played a remarkable role in preserving the Church.

In the 1970s President Mobutu began to oppress the Church. He made a law banning all Bible names in Zaire. John, Mary, Joseph, Elizabeth, Peter, Sarah – all had to be dropped and be replaced by tribal names. He demanded that Sundays be used for civic duty (cutting weeds, sweeping roads). He abolished all church youth groups, wanting to discourage youth from attending church. The churches complied, but brought youth into choirs.

The president didn't try to abolish singing. But churches grew wonderfully with multiple choirs performing in every service. And they didn't just sing. They dressed in spectacular robes, dresses or suits: men's choirs, women's choirs, youth choirs, children's choirs with loud, clear voices and motions and emotion.

Music, for Africans, is soul food. Every choir had a tape recorder and recorded the songs of other choirs. They worked hard to create new songs, hundreds of them, and to dramatize them with actions and powerful bass or keening tenor.

The studio we built at the Center of Evangelism was busy night and day recording choirs from the hundreds of city churches. Once recorded, copies were made by the thousands and sold all over the country. The library of these choirs contributes enormously to the popularity of the daylong broadcasts of Sango Malamu, prepared in our ER studios. All over the city store owners blast these songs out on powerful public address systems, both in Kinshasa and across the river in Brazzaville, the capital city of Congo.

Thelma's quartets of the 1960s were so popular that they were invited to sing in Leopoldville (the name of the capital at that time). We lived about 300 dirt-road miles away but one Friday we crowded into our long-suffering station wagon and drove twelve hours to the capital. On the way, we had an accident. The dirt road narrowed to a single car width for a small bridge on a curving stretch. We reached the bridge at the same time as a Belgian geologist's car and neither driver could see the other car soon enough to stop completely. The contact caused little damage and both vehicles continued on their way.

The quartet was roundly applauded in the churches of the capital. The men had never seen the city before and they marveled at its grandeur. We returned home after twelve hours of tiring driving, arriving late at night.

Thelma trained all of the students as a choir. We had to rent a truck to haul them to services. It cost us a princely sum to do so but it added a new dimension to their lives. Students came from small villages with a few church members in tiny chapels. It was a horizon-expanding experience for them to go to large churches filled with villagers who came long distances for quarterly meetings where new believers were baptized, young people were married, communion was served, the gospel was preached and more people were saved.

For the students to stand together in the front of the church, looking at hundreds of expectant, happy faces and singing their well-practiced songs, was sensational. And for young men in the audience who heard them sing a new door opened – one that led to their entry into school a year later, and to a life of service to God.

Remember? There were only 17 qualified applicants for the school in the whole area that first year. In our time in the school over 200 graduated. From reports we have heard in the 32 years since we left, well over 600 more have finished the school. School choirs and quartets, begun by Thelma in the 1950s, deserve much of the credit for the growth of the student body. New facilities, new courses and a fourth year followed logically as the school became the spiritual engine of the churches of the entire field.

We bought used trumpets, trombones, clarinets, guitars and accordions for the students to learn on. They played them with fervor. What was it, lying dormant for centuries, that sprang to life in these jungle people when music became possible to them? In the cities, Belgians were training them for jazz. Song writing began to flourish in the church and in bars. Congo songs were recorded and sold all over Africa.

Not every nation of the continent has come to sing like ours. Not all had a Thelma. Fifteen years after her early beginnings, every urban congregation had not one but three or four large choirs which included almost every adult in fellowship as well as some budding youngsters. Congolese must sing. If choirs were outlawed in churches, churches would empty out. But the singing would go on, under backyard mango trees, out in the jungle, on a distant hilltop. The people will always sing and Nzambi Mpungu will be their theme.

Thelma and I provided phones, toilets and running water for six houses on the station about four years before independence in 1960. "Civilization" had come at last! But it was not to last. Political chaos had already set in and the population had forsaken the Lord in favor of a violent grabbing of freedom, power and wealth which led inevitably to war and impoverishment.

In these years a first African pseudo-Christian cult called Makukusa was reported in some villages. Its main attraction was its all-night dances. Pagan dances had been preludes to free sex orgies. The African church had abolished them. Now, in the name of God, the dances came back independent of the church. We published tracts declaring this a false and sinful cult. It didn't gain much ground for a more attractive cult was sweeping through large areas.

Kimbanguism called itself the "Independence Church". As the fervor for independence flamed high, Congolese turned against all white people alike as enemies of their freedom. Even pastors were called flunkies of the missionaries. So an independent African church seemed to be the logical accompaniment of independence.

Kimbangu was a kindly old Baptist lay preacher like hundreds of others. But he had a reputation as a healer of the sick and made trips to hospital areas where all the patients left to hear this man and to be healed.

Like an Old Testament prophet he walked far and wide, the crowds following him and the stories about him growing wildly as they passed from mouth to mouth. The colonial government grew fearful and arrested him. He was sent hundreds of miles away as a prisoner. And it all happened again! The Belgians sent him a thousand miles to the southeast and, in a major jail complex, he spent his last days, a hero beloved of his people.

The sons of Kimbangu were educated government employees and when the cry for independence rose to a nationwide din, they created a national freedom religion of their father's reputation. I first heard of Kimbangu in the mid-forties. "He flies anywhere. He could be right here. He lives in a house with a door too small for a chicken to enter. All of his goats have two or three kids at a birthing. He meets with his people in the deep jungle and they walk on fiery, red coals and their feet are never burned."

Kinkela, our oldest pastor. Sand in his eyes was no cure.

There was an old African healer in the late fifties not far from Kimpese. His reputation was gossiped everywhere. He lived near a shallow pond with a black sand bottom. One of our oldest pastors was almost blind. His sons trucked him up to the healer's village and there the famous man walked Rev. Kinkela into his little pond and rubbed sand into his eyes. They were not healed. He died with infected, painful eyes. Families rented trucks to drive dead relatives hundreds of miles to the healer, for he had the reputation of resurrecting the dead. The trucks returned with evil smelling corpses.

The stories of the healer's prowess grew until every sick person wanted to go to him. At last I sent a strong Christian schoolteacher to the man's village about 150 miles away. He spent several days watching everything, then came back and reported. He told us there was a long fence of walking sticks that reportedly were left when crippled people were healed. He saw hundreds prayed for, including corpses. But he saw no one healed. He spoke of this in the local church and people stopped sending their blind and crippled to the healer. The stories about him ended.

But it was a time of wild expectations and of other stories – stories of violence to white people, of looting and torture and sudden wealth. "You don't have to wait for the white man's God to get rich. Just go take what you want!" Catsup, it was said, was African blood. Spam was ground-up African children. White people drove through villages at night with open fronted machines that ground up people to be canned and sold. An international race-car meet was cancelled because Congolese dock workers refused to unload the strange looking machines.

This was a period of unlimited dreams, when cooks were to become senators and teachers mayors of cities. It was also a time of fear. A person was taught to hate his white friends, to threaten them, to cheat them. Or worse. "Drive them out and take their cars and houses." And they did. Close Christian friends came to see all the favors given them in the past as trivial, far less than they deserved. Hatred replaced love. Charges were made to the new Congolese government against missionaries who built schools and hospitals and made education available to thousands.

One such man, chairman of our mission, was taken from his home, shoved into the back of a government truck and driven twenty miles to the city of Tshela where his "crimes" were shouted to the people who lived there. Their shouts of hatred and violence followed him to the jail. He was an honored missionary of 20 years, known to all the government leaders. Their underlings had had their fun so the man was quietly returned to his mission station. But he and all the other missionaries recognized that they now lived in a land where law and order had been replaced by kangaroo court justice.

Congo would plunge down, down, down for at least 45 years. Who knows how much longer?

In spite of it all, I requested permission to open a school of theology for graduates of our four-year Bible Institute. Our annual missionary conference voted its permission but the president of the African church, Rev. Thomas Paku, privately refused saying, "My son was not given such higher education and I will not permit anyone to surpass him." All other pastors wanted the school but without the president's approval the school could not open.

For over ten years the mission did not open this school, but eventually it did and Chris was one of its instructors.

Our furlough time had come so we returned to America once more, full of praise to God for the countless miracles He had performed for the salvation of thousands throughout those years. And this time Philip was the new blond Braun baby we introduced to America.

Three blond Braun boys see America.

16

KASA VUBU

In the northwest part of Congo there is a large, flat region covered with ant mounds about six feet high and 25 feet in diameter. The mounds are about 80 feet apart - about as far as a queen ant could fly to start a new colony. Seen from the air, it would resemble an enormous polka-dotted plain.

The vast area of Congo prior to the Belgian colonial period can be best envisioned as an endless tropical jungle with small villages hacked out of its greenery, separated by the distance women could carry home their babies and food from their fields. When villages grew so large that available land for fields was too far for women to travel, a group of distressed wives would insist on beginning a new village with land close to the clearing. Lucky ladies, they would get to their fields in five minutes, put their babies in a safe place and begin digging, planting and weeding much earlier than when their fields were an hour away. And cutting off 55 minutes from the daily trip home with tired babies, heavy tubers and a high load of firewood was an enormous relief. So, as with the ants, the weariness of female members decided how far apart ant colonies or villages would be in Congo.

Congo, in those days, was a land of villages which averaged 300 residents, none of whom could read or write. With the arrival of missionaries, motivation to teach literacy entered Congo, because missionaries were eager to have Congolese Bible readers. Reading God's Word was of primary importance for new converts. So missionaries were the first to begin the process of education. Mark well this fact. All the doctors, lawyers, politicians, judges, pastors, teachers and construction workers of modern Congo are what they are because early missionaries opened the Bible and the world's knowledge to illiterate Africans who could make no sense whatever of the strange marks on the white leaves. History leaped forward through God's Word!

It was a Bible reader, trained by Roman Catholic nuns, who became the first president of Congo. He was taught to be a priest but there were few educated men in Congo when the passion to be independent exploded across the nation, and cooks and nurses and grade school teachers rose up above the crowds to become senators, mayors, cabinet members and ambassadors. A man trained for the priesthood had more awareness of world history and governments than almost any other villager. After all, schools were only offering fifth grade throughout the nation, except for a few high schools just getting started, and there were only twelve university graduates in the whole populace.

But the urge to be independent was one that fired the hopes of the people. At times a little knowledge is a dangerous thing. Perhaps fifth grade knowledge was enough to create wondrous expectations of wealth and power in the hearts of multitudes but not enough to raise the question, "Are we ready for self-government?"

Kasa Vubu was one of a number of leaders flown to Belgium to plan for independence. In a local newspaper in the city of Matadi a paid ad appeared, "Kasa Vubu, we follow you, our eyes closed." And they did. Four hundred school boys on our station enjoyed marching like soldiers, singing songs of independence during recess. Those were glory days. Their teachers were earning a fabulous government-paid salary and all the boys were well-dressed. "Congo dependent, o oh o oho," they shouted, not aware of the implications of the dropped "in" of the word independent.

One student couldn't march but he stood proudly watching the others. He wore a large snail shell on a string around his neck. I hadn't seen that kind of decoration before so I asked him about it. He explained that it was the symbol of independence. Before the Belgians came, he said, his people were free in the forests. But when the whites came the people went back into their shell like the snail. But soon they would be free and come out of their shells.

It was a nice thought and I could have been more enthusiastic if these Protestant school children, many baptized, were not singing, "We'll drive all the whites into the sea without clothes," smiling, teeth gleaming in the sun, as they looked at me. Those were not sugar plums dancing in their minds, those were the five Brauns, the six

Krohs and Miss Fulton running naked into the waves at Vista, disappearing under the water, leaving all our belongings for them.

Miss Fulton, a white-haired veteran near retirement, lived alone in a small guest house. She wore a police whistle on a cord around her neck day and night. Why? She had heard loud-voiced men go under her screened windows saying, "We'll kill Mama Fulton on Independence Day." The whistle and God were her only defense.

I had been a hunter for thirty years. I had a gun and used it well. I also had a wife and three sons. As Congolese became more outspoken in their boasts and threats I could not avoid the question, "Would you kill to protect your family?"

Our firstborn, Chris, rushed into the house one day saying that a big man with a bush knife had run after him and shouted he would kill him. Chris had escaped into the bushes and came home to face a fear he had never known before. Would I kill to protect my family?

Our lives were dedicated to saving men and women. For that we lived in this place. Only for that. When the government forced all whites to turn in their guns, I sold mine to a long-time friend, a Congolese judge who had wanted it for years. That largely answered the question about whether I would kill or not. The Lord answered the rest by putting His angels around us through all the years.

As the weeks of June 1960 passed, we made our usual shopping trip to Tshela to buy soap and flour and whatever was needed. In earlier years Christians would rush up to chat with us happily. It was an honor for them to be seen with missionaries. But for some months we noted that Christians kept their distance from us, not wanting to be harassed by anti-white bullies. However, on this occasion a stranger came up to us and with considerable belligerence demanded money for whiskey for the celebration. Gently I explained that I was a missionary and never gave money for whiskey. Before I could offer him a case of Coca Cola he glared at me and shouted, "We'll cut your throat!" He stamped away enraged.

The drive back to our station gave time to reflect on this man. His conclusion must have been that all whites were hostile to the independence movement. I was not, but he couldn't know that. I decided I had to make a statement publicly. For the next three days I was on my knees painting a 16-foot sign with an 8-foot picture of Kasa Vubu and a 4-foot sentence in large letters, "QUE DIEU BÉNISSE LE CONGO" - May God bless Congo. And though usually I left my writing and art work go unsigned, this time my name appeared conspiculously at the bottom of the sign. It was important for them to see that the white missionary had some part in the celebration of their independence.

Assembling hardwood beams, carpenters and the paintings, I trucked them into Tshela and asked the soon-to-be government leaders for permission to erect the sign at the crossroads where everyone passed. Permission was enthusiastically granted. By the time the holes were dug and the sign put up, the new government had erected flags on both sides of the tall boards and added ferns and flowers. A crowd had gathered to see this obvious salute by a white man to their soon-to-be president and I was told years later that my sign, erected in honor of a day, stayed up several years until the weather destroyed it - and until enthusiasm for independence had largely turned to near-despair.

The new government gladly responded to my appeal for ten of its men to go to our station to protect it against roving gangs. The church people also provided ten men who stood guard day and night at the entrance to make sure bandits did not enter. In the week following Independence Day in which Belgium's King Baudouin declared Congo free, rioting broke out nationwide and city stores were pillaged, plantations plundered and general mayhem spread far and wide.

In that very week, all the missionaries of our C&MA mission were on our station for annual conference and all sheltered under the protection of the men at the entrance. I was told later that all other whites of the whole area had fled their businesses and stations and gone to the army base at Kitona. Terrible atrocities were reported in the region, but the nearest we came to trouble was a gang of men who demanded gasoline and food. Gas was unavailable so I dared not give any of the little we had. We had a fine, large orange tree loaded with fruit and I gave the men liberty to take all they wanted of the oranges. That seemed to satisfy them and they stripped the tree and left. I heard later that in all Congo there was only one other mission which did not evacuate at that time. The picture of Kasa Vubu served us well.

Not long after that our furlough time arrived and I learned that I had to drive to Boma, the leading city of that area, to seek a special letter from the government permitting our family to leave Congo. When I arrived at the government headquarters I was told that President Kasa Vubu was in town and was dining at a hotel. I went over and asked a guard if I could greet the president. I explained that I was the missionary who made the sign board at Tshela.

The guard went to the president's table and chatted with him for a few minutes. When he came back he said, "When the president finishes eating he'll call for you." I waited while the presidential party devoured their main dish (each had a whole chicken) and their dessert. Then I was ushered in. I spoke in the president's Kikongo, telling him that I had enjoyed painting the big sign and attending the Tshela Independence ceremony. He asked if I would make a bust of him and I agreed.

On my way out of town I turned left off the Kalamu Road onto the highway to Tshela as I had done many times. But this time a soldier with a sub-machine gun rushed up shouting wildly. I stopped and looked into drug-crazed eyes hot with anger. "You didn't go around the round point. There, there!," he shouted. I saw a thin branch of a tree stuck in the ground. He had created a "round point" (the then-current term for traffic circle) unmarked in any way and was itching to mow me down for not recognizing the little branch as a traffic circle. I told him I was a friend of President Kasa Vubu so he didn't shoot me, but he looked disappointed at having missed a glorious opportunity.

A few days later our family drove toward the port city of Matadi to board a freight ship for New York. We reached the north bank of the Congo River where we would have to wait for a ferry to take us across. A soldier came up and demanded to see our papers. I presented the Boma paper and he and another shoved guns in my back and pushed me toward a motorboat at the bank of the river. I left Thelma with three wailing boys and was taken across the river and paraded as a prisoner to the Matadi administrator's office. On the way I saw good friends who gasped to see me under the guns of soldiers. None dared intervene because of the guns, but they followed to learn what was happening. I was herded into the administrator's office and my papers were shown to him. He stamped them with his seal and I was free to go. But where were my wife and three sons? I have forgotten how and where we met, but we boarded the ship and sailed to our homeland where sub-machine-gun-toting drug-crazed soldiers are not eagerly shoving the muzzles of their guns into one's back.

Safe in a mission-owned bungalow in Nyack, I soon bought some water-clay, built a metal armature for head, neck and shoulders and set to work modeling a bust of Kasa Vubu. To my delight, Thelma found an article in a New York newspaper reporting the presence of the president in New York. It even told the name of the hotel in which the president's party was staying.

The next day Thelma and I went to the city and visited him. A US state department officer, a Mr. Roberts who had served in the US consulate in Leopoldville (now Kinshasa), was present and welcomed us. He approved our offer to escort the president to places of interest in New York. He confided that Russia's Kruschev had banged the United Nations' table with his shoe and threatened to move the UN out of America if the US continued to play politics with every African president who came to the UN. To calm the situation Kasa Vubu was given no official celebration. He was almost abandoned in his suite of rooms with no one of his party able to speak English to news reporters and other national leaders. For several hours I was pressed into service answering phones for the Congo delegation.

We planned a Saturday outing for the president and his Congolese aide named Luyeye. We were to go to the newspaper which sent the reporter-explorer Stanley to Congo. Next we were to visit the American Museum of Natural History where about one hundred bird skins I had collected and treated for a Dr. Chapin in the late 1940s were part of the world's largest collection of Congo birds. Unfortunately, the ambassador of Ethiopia to the US visited the president for two hours and we had to drop our planned visit to those first two places.

We set off for Macy's on 34th Street in Manhattan. The US government arranged to send an unmarked car ahead of our car and when we turned into 34th, the traffic had been stopped permitting us to go the "wrong way" and make a legal "illegal" U-turn up to Macy's front door, where representatives of Macy's president awaited us, surrounded by plainclothes security men. We were escorted up to the Macy president's office and this gentleman explained that royalty from around the world shopped at Macy's and he would be happy to meet any needs the president's family might have.

He then escorted the party through the world's largest department store. In the sports department he asked if the president had children. Yes, he was told, he had five. In his kindness, Macy's president gave a football to Congo's president. Kasa Vubu was a charmer. With great dignity he thanked his host in flowing words of thanksgiving. Later, walking to another department he confided, "Tata Braun, this ball is sick." It was football season in America and the egg-shaped ball he had received was sick indeed as far as this man's soccer-playing nation was concerned.

Back on the ground floor, our host gave his visitor a five-pound box of chocolates for Mrs. Kasa Vubu and bade us adieu. We were in the women's department and lovely purses were on display. It was a good moment to shop. The president pointed to a purse and the clerk indicated that is cost about $100. That was too much. He pointed to another. It cost about half as much but, no, it was still too high. A third was less than $10 and suited him just right. He pulled out his wallet and I saw about 3/8 of an inch of solid, brand new $100 bills. Gingerly, he handed one to the lady and was surprised at the handful of bills he received in change.

From Macy's we drove to the Empire State Building, then the world's tallest, and again were met by the waiting director of the building who presented the president with a large bronze replica of New York's most famous landmark. Looking down at the ant-sized people below, the president wondered out loud about the size of the bamboo needed as scaffolding by the builders. He knew about scaffolding from the nine-story buildings in Kinshasa and enjoyed the humor in picturing bamboo a thousand feet tall.

We next saw him on the stage of the United Nations dressed as a Roman Catholic priest, thereby gaining the votes of Catholic nations around the world. He made a passionate speech calling for the replacement of Lumumba-appointed Communist delegates to the UN by his own democratic delegates. He won the hearts and the votes of the UN, and the direction of Congo away from Communism was established for at least 36 years.

I had taken several head and shoulder pictures of Kasa Vubu to help me in my sculpture and two months later took my piece into the city for a casting of high density ceramic beautifully finished like old bronze. Seeing it completely convinced me that I had to make a copy. I brushed on liquid rubber until it was 3/8 inch thick, then lowered it into a box and poured plaster of Paris around the rubber mold, being careful to provide a divider to open the casting in two

Bust of Kasa Vubu,
Congo's George Washington

148

halves. It worked! The original bust was unharmed and I packed it carefully in a steel drum and drove it in to the docks of the New York shippers to Congo. When the director learned the content and the address to which the drum would go he insisted there would be no charge. The drum would be delivered to the president's palace with great care.

The next time I saw it was in the Boma family home of the Kasa Vubus. By then the president had been retired by Colonel Mobutu who had taken over in a bloodless coup. The president told me that Mobutu had advised him, "Take a few days off until I can get rid of Prime Minister Tshombe and you will be president again." He added with real appreciation for such clever duplicity, "Of course he never meant it."

I had driven from Kinshasa to visit the president because a distinguished missionary doctor was soon to retire and, as editor of *Congo Mission News*, I wanted a testimonial from the president about Dr. Glenn Tuttle, since he was the president's personal physician. And here is an interesting item. There were hundreds of Roman Catholic doctors from which this Roman Catholic leader might be expected to choose his private physician. But he chose a Protestant, an American who had shown outstanding initiative in building a very large medical facility, the Evangelical Medical Institute at Kimpese, funded and staffed by numerous foreign missions.

In his home, the president seated me in his own favorite chair, next to which was an end table with my bust on it. I enjoyed running my fingers over it once again as I discussed the article on Dr. Tuttle with the George Washington of the Democratic Republic of the Congo. While I waited he wrote, "I join with numerous friends who testify of their gratefulness to you at this time of your retirement.

"The eminent services which you have rendered to the Congo with such devotion, constancy and faithfulness in the accomplishment of your noble mission speak clearly for themselves.

"God bless you during your retiral years and prosper your work in Congo.

With deepest friendship,
J. Kasa-Vubu."

The president also gave me a letter of introduction to the current Minister of Public Health, Dr. Martin Tshishimbe, who added his own words of testimony, including the following, "Your long years of service, crowned by the creation of the Evangelical Medical Institute of Kimpese, provide me with a magnificent memory of a life consecrated to God and my people." *(Congo Mission News*, July 1966, page 10, article "Good Bye, Doctor.")

I never saw the president again, though I visited his home after his death, hoping to see his wife, the bust and an ebony bas-relief carving of the head of Christ on the Cross which I had made and given him on his visit to New York. My copy of the bust rests unseen in the garage, covered with the patina of dust, a near forgotten memory of three decades past of a great man and a fascinated missionary caught up in the hopeful hubris of a generation of Congolese tasting freedom in the modern world for the first time.

Being a missionary in a revolutionary time among a people intoxicated with the thirst to change their country demanded constant wisdom and safety from the God who rules the world. During those years of peril the everlasting arms of that Almighty God proved the stabilizing factor in an otherwise hopelessly dizzying world.

The Psalmist said it well: *In the time of trouble He shall hide me in His pavilion* (Psalm 27:5). In those bloody days when many missionaries were being slaughtered the pavilion in which He hid us was a 16 x 8 foot sign that said *May God bless the Congo*. That was our prayer for the people whom we loved in a time when love had given away to violence in many of their hearts.

17

NKOKOLO

There is a world of difference in Christianity lived in the "fear not, little flock" mentality and that lived in the "When the saints come marching in!" In the pre-Independence period we moved out of the "fear not" zone into that of marching saints, thousands of them. It was a heady experience. The Sunday school contest and the tent did that for us and, one day, we held our first mass open-air crusade.

Mayunda was a small market town where four roads met. Each led to a different church district. By simply writing letters to the four district superintendents announcing that a rally of four districts was to be held on the following Sunday at Mayunda, a huge crowd was assured.

This had never been done before. It never occurred to anyone that it was an option. But the large numbers gathering at Sunday schools and at the tent eventually triggered the idea of a multi-district outdoor mass evangelism rally.

We knew we had to build a wooden platform to be seen. We knew we needed a strong P.A. system. We wanted banners to serve as a backdrop for the platform. And we decided we had better whitewash lines to show the people where to stand, leaving aisles open and a large space for seekers in front of the platform.

By God's grace a nationally famous personage came to visit us a day before the Sunday rally. He was Colonel Nkokolo, second only to Colonel Mobutu in Congo's army.

Colonel Nkokolo had a look of physical power and vitality, lighted by a warm smile of Christ's presence in his life. He told us some of his experiences overseas. He told of a man-eating lion, which was the terror of a village. He was sent by the army to kill this beast, and he did so.

We were enthralled by this incredible brother in Christ and asked if he would speak to the people at the rally. He agreed, and the crowd heard a thrilling testimony from a unique Congolese. There were three services that day and at two of them a call to repentance and salvation brought large numbers of people forward.

When it was all over I rolled up the wires, installed the generator and P.A. system in the back of the car. Everyone had gone home but our family. Weary but extremely happy for all God had done that day, I sat on the big log drum and prayed and praised God in a reverie of worship. How near He seemed. Somehow, I knew that this new experience of creating great gospel rallies would be repeated over and over. What I could never have guessed is that on several occasions 70,000 people would march down the main boulevards of Congo's capital to enter the national stadium, and that some 15,000 would come forward for salvation. "One step at a time, dear Jesus, is all I'm asking of You…" is a good song – and an excellent prayer too.

Colonel Nkokolo went back to the capital. The Ghana embassy was embroiled in a Lumumba-Kasa Vubu contest. Congo's president sent Col. Nkokolo to the Ghana embassy with an order that a certain embassy official should leave the country for engaging in subversive activities. Unarmed, he knocked at the door. Machine gun fire from inside killed him on the spot. How we hated Ghana for this!

But we were to go to Ghana a few years later, over and over, to start churchmen on a national movement of evangelism which was to effectively bless the Church from 1967 to 1990 and continue its Ghana Evangelism Committee into the 2000s when its leader would be Dr. Mathias Forson, who is now ER's director of a School of Evangelism and the executive director of the Africa Decade of Advance, ADA, operating in twenty nations.

Our introduction to Ghana was darkened by the memory of the cruel murder of Congo's honored leader and our beloved friend, but the light of the gospel being proclaimed through the leaders of the evangelism movement won our hearts to a love for the country and its people that continues through the decades.

Colonel Nkokolo left behind a history of valiant heroism in his troubled nation. That record was immeasurably enhanced by the strong testimony he so eloquently gave at little Mayunda about the everlasting life he had received through Jesus Christ. No enemy's bullet could end that – it only opened the way to a new and glorious phase of that life.

18

SWITZERLAND-LUKULA

*Their parents' French studies took the three
Braun boys to Switzerland.*

After Independence Congo moved away from many tribal languages toward a more unifying use of French. As educators in the state of Lower Congo, we had taught in Kikongo for ten years. Our French was fluent but needed improvement. The C&MA, after furlough, sent the five Brauns to Geneva, Switzerland, for a year of study in John Calvin's old University of Geneva, along with a dozen new missionaries. Housing was pre-arranged for the other families but it was left to us to find a dwelling. A very old stone house that had been unused for seven years was available. A gardener and his wife had lived there. One became very ill and both moved to a son's house, leaving unmade beds with unwashed sheets and the odds and ends of a lifetime scattered around. The only heat in winter came from a wood-burning iron range in the kitchen end of the house. We made a deal with the owners to have the rooms rent-free, if we repaired, repainted and re-furnished the place over nine months.

Wood smoke had blackened the walls, so we repainted it all. A trip to Germany provided a used Volkswagon Combi, which we filled with a kerosene furnace, an electric range, a hot water heater and needed linens. After a month it was all installed and the family was quite comfortable for the winter. When we left, a missionary family back from Italy moved in, happy for so nice a home.

Our three boys went in three directions each weekday. Chris attended a junior high school, Paul a French grade school and Philip a French nursery. We dropped Phil off on the way to school each morning and picked him up each evening. The farewell was unvarying, a shout of workers, "Salut, Phillippe!!" And he always looked so pleased, but shy, being the center of such boisterous attention.

It was our only time in Europe with weeks of vacation and we loaded up our Combi with guests and "did" Europe. On one delightful

French study gave opportunity to "do" Europe.

154

occasion Mother and Dorothy visited us in Geneva and we made a long trip together, I think through Germany, Belgium, Denmark and into Sweden. But at that time we knew no relatives. Happily, Europe's prices were very low then.

The longest trip took us to Egypt, Jordan, Syria, Turkey, Lebanon, Greece, Yugoslavia, Italy and France. We could not visit Israel but much of where we were in Jordan is now in Israel. These months in Europe made the extensive travels that would be required of me a few years later far easier to plan and to carry out.

At last the school year ended and we loaded our Combi and family on a ship to Congo. Our appointment was to Lukula, an isolated station where, after Chris and Paul went away to school at Kinkonzi, Phil, Thelma and I were alone. In that year we re-established tent evangelism. It had ceased in our absence. We built two more school rooms and we made trips of evangelism in the district.

A thief entered our house during a heavy rainstorm. We heard nothing, but he stole clothes, a typewriter, a radio, our keys and all our money. In the typewriter was a tract being written. The title was, "Why did he steal?"

Stealing was endemic then. Independence made thieves of almost everyone. The powerful stole from all and all felt they had to steal to get back what was stolen from them. One of the conundrums that emerged from the president's Authenticity Program was: to be authentically African, go back to pre-Christian customs. Having officially rejected the Ten Commandments, the slippery slope led down, down, down. Many civil wars, many ethnic cleansings, whole-city, every-city plundering by the army, gangs that robbed villagers, no roads, dizzying inflation, invading armies from five or more nations, AIDS sweeping through the land, useless roads and bridges, all these are the non-stop wages of a people who until 1958 wanted to please God and were enjoying His peace and prosperity.

During our year at Lukula, we attended a political rally organized by richly dressed officials who arrived in two large limousines. One of their leaders was doing his best to win some applause from the crowd. "We promised you independence, didn't we?," he shouted and paused. Silence. "Well, you have independence, haven't you?," he yelled.

A long silence was finally broken by a lone voice that roared, "You have it! We don't!" That was true.

The early interpretation of the word independence for the average citizen was, "Everyone will be rich, free and proud." The officials glowed with independence. The people they were trying to enthuse had fallen deeper and deeper into poverty, hopelessness and shame.

An invitation was sent to us by LECO to come to Kinshasa and work with a new publication, MOYO, Kikongo word for LIFE. We left Lukula's isolation for the capital and a new life.

19

KINSHASA AGAIN

The move to Kinshasa involved renting a truck to carry our furniture and household goods and also driving our car and family eleven hours to the capital. An African trader sent his brand new truck to pick up our things and we were free for the long drive. The truck would arrive later in the city.

We made the trip, moved into an apartment by the Congo River and settled into our work. News came that the truck had gone out of control going down a mountain and crashed, killing six riders on the freight. We were to drive to a town near the wreck to learn the details. I drove there and was told where the wreck could be found. Villagers had stolen almost everything in the night, ignoring the dead and dying. A few things were picked up and we returned home, only to be sued by our cook for a fat long list of things he said were on the truck. The government agent insisted that since he was in our employment, we had to pay every cent. We did.

The ministry in Kinshasa was most enjoyable. Our first assignment was to work with Mr. André Massaki, editor of *MOYO,* a monthly magazine in the Kikongo language. We were to do page layout, titles and art work. I was also to oversee typesetting, make corrections, obtain and make linoleum block pictures as needed, deliver packages of printed magazines to pastors to retail and to collect sales receipts.

There was no other job in the city that took a missionary to every pastor and every church in the city each month. In a short time I knew every pastor and every congregation. I was invited to preach widely. I had a handle on the presence of the Church in this strategic city of a million people as no one else did. Knowledge is power. Seeing where the Church stood in this population led to new plans,

Mr. André Massaki, editor of MOYO

new initiatives. It was for that that God sent us to Kinshasa in 1963 and kept us there until 1970.

Soon after our arrival we became fast friends of Dr. Pierre Shaumba, the first Congolese president of the Congo Protestant Council. He was a spiritual product of Dr. Alexander Reid, the remarkable veteran missionary of the United Methodist Church in the central part of Congo.

One of the ministries of the Congo Protestant Council was to publish *Congo Mission News* every quarter. It was an English magazine about mission activities. Dr. Shaumba was uncomfortable publishing an English magazine for the 2100 missionaries in Congo at the time. He asked us to do it. We did for five years, always informing him of what articles were to be used so he could add to or subtract from them. He never proposed changes and was always happy with the publication. The times were rife with crises and missionaries subscribed for every issue.

Jottings was begun in *Congo Mission News*. It added missionary-based humor to an otherwise all-work and no-play magazine. It was not really a fun time. Two hundred Catholic and Protestant foreign missionaries were martyred soon after we began editing the publication. Tears flowed. Missionaries abandoned their beloved stations and fled to the safety of the capital. But the meaning of life – their call - was back on those stations. A steady stream of missionary families flowed out of a nation that did not really care. Congolese pastors were ready to move into mission houses, use their equipment and vehicles and assume their authority. With a Congolese president as head of the nation, they concluded that Congolese pastors could serve God as heads of stations. That time had come.

There were, however, many useful things to introduce to this young Church and we set ourselves to do what we could. For example, there was a monthly meeting called the Council of Pastors of Kinshasa,

COPAK. Only three or four pastors of a possible 35 attended because they had no plans, no program. They had devotions, argued over "stolen sheep" (members) and had coffee and cookies. I attended because these were the men of authority who would make decisions when decisions were needed. Through COPAK I introduced a plan to distribute 1,000,000 pieces of evangelical literature to 200,000 homes.

Dr. Pierre Shaumba and his wife asked for editorial help

Protestants are basically isolationists. Each denomination sees itself as the best and wants its members to be loyal, convinced and supportive of it alone. Kinshasa denominations had never attempted a citywide effort of any kind until we proposed this one month of every-Sunday visitation by 1000 members of all denominations. Each of four Sunday afternoons 50,000 homes were visited by Christians, and 250,000 Testaments, tracts and information sheets picturing every congregation, its pastor, address and hours of services, were distributed.

It was one vast learning experience. Protestants were a despised minority by Belgians who were Catholic. Protestants hid in their churches. Protestants had never boldly gone to every house, every family and given every soul a handful of Protestant publications. It changed the way Protestants saw themselves – forever.

Secondly, we bought a gospel tent at the invitation of the COPAK pastors and charged them with setting an annual schedule of the places the tent would be set up. And they had to name the pastor who would preach every night for two weeks. None of them had ever preached every night for two weeks. And none of them had ever given an invitation to sinners to repent and come forward to prove it. That tent taught them evangelism and made evangelists of them all – a profound change for the 35 congregations of the city.

COPAK suddenly found itself doing very important and exciting things. Its theology was coming alive. Hundreds, thousands

In the name of Jesus, 50,000 houses received gospel literature.

of "know-so" believers were going from the tent to the churches to be baptized and join. We didn't have to say a word to convince Kinshasa's pastors that evangelism was a wonderful, new way to serve God and to see the churches grow and come alive. The tent did the convincing, beginning in 1966. Thirty years ago we recorded over 50,000 converts and even more re-dedications in the tent. Stories were confirmed of madmen as well as many others being healed through the ministry of Evangelist Massiala, one of our early students at Kinkonzi. Frankly, as a preacher in his pastoral days, he put entire crowds to sleep from boredom.

It was God's Holy Spirit who changed him into a dynamic soul-winner under the tent. I recall an occasion when after two full weeks of tent ministry near a large church, the pastor of the church begged Rev. Massiala to preach two more weeks in his church. I've rarely heard of any American evangelist being so mightily used of God that a congregation would want four weeks of his preaching. The only cases that come to mind are Billy Graham and the Sutera twins in a flaming revival.

Evangelist Massiala did not preach only in Kinshasa. We trucked the tent to Mbanza Ngunga – City of the Drum – for two weeks and revival came and the meetings went on for a month with many hundreds converted and baptized. One of the born-again was a renowned witch doctor who rushed to the altar with a gunnysack full of the tools of his trade, fetishes of many sorts.

These were displayed in the display windows of a Christian bookstore, which it was my job to decorate each month. I watched crowds of Congolese press up against the glass identifying these powerful fetishes. Each had a dreaded name and function. People on the street could identify them the way our children identify the makes and models of cars speeding by. Obviously the devil's craft had long been standardized over large areas and the population learned of these objects of the black arts from childhood. Incredibly here, in a Christian bookstore, defenseless, robbed of their fearsome powers, not one but an entire arsenal of Satan lay open for all to view. Jesus led captivity captive before the throngs of this mega-city.

Evangelist Massaila, from sleep-inducer to a dynamic preacher

This was the first sack of many to be brought back by our evangelists. And each one left whole areas liberated for a time. Praise God! The final battle had not been fought – yet.

The Church of every decade and every generation must carry the struggle deep into the enemy's territory. We had our time, our window of opportunity, for which we are eternally grateful. But our sons' generation must fight the good fight, and their sons' as well, for the hordes of hell are endlessly active. They cannot win in a battle with Spirit-filled servants of God. But they easily win when God's people quit the fight.

The tent taught a generation of pastors that weeks of evangelism were God's way to bring multitudes to Christ. The tent made evangelists of dozens of pastors in the 1960s and hundreds of pastors in the 1970s and thousands of pastors in the 1980s and 1990s. Oh! Don't you see the magnitude of the teaching of a nation's pastors to go beyond dead preaching of purposeless sermons and to reach out in holy passion to win the lost and dying?

Witch doctors abandoned their fetishes.

So much of Congo was churched by large, rich, liberal denominations that had lost their message of salvation. The capital

161

city's leading pastors had never, ever seen a week of evangelism or an invitation to come to Jesus. Vast areas of Congo lived a churchianity that needed no cross, no tomb, no Savior, no Lord. It was organized, trained, professional, secular, and dead in trespasses and in sin.

The tent was God's tool to turn this church to Him, to the Bible, to salvation and to life. In some denominations 90% of their missionaries, by actual count, were outspoken liberals. The most evangelical of missions' missionaries were 85% assigned to social services and in their annual conferences any proposal that was aimed at evangelism and soul-winning met with strong head-on opposition, whereas any proposal for advancing the educational or medical work passed effortlessly. Said clearly, evangelism was out and social service was in throughout the nation from the mid-forties to the final departure of missions in the nineties. The tent and all its related ministries produced a "counter-culture" to missions in their official programs.

Those years in Kinshasa were golden years for Thelma and me. They were years of health, challenge, family joys and growth in vision and harvest. Chris completed high school and left for Biola College where his grandmother and aunt lived. He gave to them seven years of family life they had largely lacked because of our decades in Africa. Paul was happily active in Kinshasa's American School, as was Philip, five years Paul's junior.

We lived well, worked hard, were surrounded by friends. Thelma had important committee meetings with the International Church board which was building a quadrangular Sunday school of which she was superintendent. There were Sunday school classes to teach, music to plan, birthdays to celebrate, school and sports events to attend, trips to make outside the city and always, always work awaiting.

The prayer on the Kasa Vubu billboard, May God Bless the Congo, was being answered in the salvation of many thousands in those days of outreach and revival.

20

CHRIST FOR ALL

In America national TV, national magazines, local radio programs and local newspapers switch from one concern to another, day by day and week by week. The populace follows their focus, 265,000,000 heads turning like automatons, from yesterday's story to today's.

In Congo, every head had begun to stare at only one story after Independence – the dangers and threats of the civil war. Missionaries were glued to short-wave broadcasts from Voice of America, the British Broadcasting Corporation and whatever Congo stations they could get. When the news ended they huddled together for hours, evaluating every word. Ministry was largely ignored. The war had everyone's full attention. Congolese pastors, village lay preachers and school teachers were equally paralyzed by the news of the war. All of life was bound up in a single concern.

Dr. Shaumba voiced a desperate SOS.

Dr. Pierre Shaumba, head of the Congo Protestant Council, saw this ecclesiastical paralysis and it frightened him. The servants of God were no longer serving Him. They were immobilized. Somehow they had to be freed from this deadening preoccupation. How could a whole nation be re-focused on the sovereign Lord and re-inspired to serve Him fully? The solution had to be national – a movement reaching out powerfully to 17,000 pastors in seven states. It would need to communicate in six languages and be action-oriented. Pleasant platitudes, devotional themes, arguments and condemnation would not do it. What would?

Dr. Shaumba came to me with the problem. He said, "Tata Braun, in three days the annual Congo Protestant Council meets in Matadi (a port city). Will you prepare and present to the delegates a national movement that will free our missionaries and pastors from their near-total inactivation by the war news and get them looking once more to God, whose servants they are?" I had only two days to respond to his request. We discussed options for a time and he left.

Drawing on the splendid Evangelism-in-Depth program of Latin America Mission and from our personal experience, we prepared a 24-month program which challenged every denomination each month to participate in a new outreach project. An organizational plan, with dates for a national conference on evangelism, for a conference in each state and for a conference for each denomination, was also prepared and presented to Dr. Shaumba. He examined it carefully and liked it. We went to the city of Matadi for the CPC meetings. That year only three missionaries were present, the presiding officer, an outspoken liberal and I.

When my turn came to introduce the plan I read both sections and sat down for the inevitable debate. In independent Congo, any discussion by churchmen had unappointed devil's advocates who did their best to defeat the motion. For some time it seemed that the devil's advocates outnumbered any supporters. To my amazement, it was the liberal missionary who rose to speak for the program. Others spoke for it and a vote adopted the first truly nationwide movement of evangelism in Africa.

The details of the monthly plans were worked out over four days in a National Conference of Evangelism whose delegates were seven missionaries and seven Congolese churchmen. They interacted with high enthusiasm, decided on each month's activities, set a two-year calendar, appointed me the national coordinator of evangelism - with no income, of course - , and went home to plan their state conferences on evangelism. Norman Riddle's excellent book, *Zaire: Midday in Missions*, says this about Zaire's national evangelism campaign (pp. 83, 84) "In 1966 the General Assembly of CPC (Congo

164

Protestant Council) voted to inaugurate a national campaign of evangelism entitled *Christ for All*. The delegates did not realize the full impact this campaign would have on the nation. Rev. Willys Braun had the vision for a campaign which would help unify the churches, would galvanize their congregations into action to heal the wounds caused by the rebellion (1963-1965), and would rally Christians around the central purpose of winning people to Christ. The following year at Bukavu the General Assembly voted to open a Department of Evangelism and Life of the Church and to call Rev. M. Makanzu as full-time director. Thereafter he and the Reverend Braun collaborated in a gigantic effort which made a lasting impact on the churches and the nation.

"A national committee was formed and later on provincial ones to set the major plans for the campaign and carry them back to provinces, regions and congregations. Some provincial committees continued on after the end of the campaign in 1969. Norman Riddle was personally associated with the committees in Bas-Zaire and Bandundu provinces, which continued to focus the attention of the churches in those provinces on the Great Commission task of discipling the tribes.

"A veritable flurry of activity spread across the nation. Christians were summoned from the shock of the rebellion to renewal and purposeful service. Many rallies were planned and executed. A series of top evangelists was brought from abroad. Howard Jones and Ralph Bell led off with a rally in a smaller stadium in Kinshasa, followed by meetings in several key congregations. Timothy Dzao of the Spiritual Food Church of Hong Kong was the evangelist the next year in several successful rallies across the city. Barry Reed, a Baptist from New Zealand, ministered to the people, particularly pastors and leaders. Finally, Ford Philpot and his team came for a giant rally in the huge soccer stadium in the heart of the city where over 75,000 assembled and hundreds came forward at the invitation. This climaxed a series of five three-day rallies in key locations around the city. On a smaller scale, this was repeated across the nation. Howard Jones led a rally in Bukavu during the CPC General Assembly meetings there in 1967 and brought powerful devotions daily.

The LECO building, home of Christ for All

Christ for All made the news on three continents.

"Rev. M. Makanzu made two tours of the eastern and northeastern sections of the country as part of this campaign. In both tours over 10,500 decisions were made, most of which were for receiving Christ as Savior and Lord. Government officials gave their support to these rallies, often requiring the attendance of prisoners and school children. The Word of God was blessed as it was preached with power. The spiritual healing of a nation was begun.

"The example set by Rev. Willys Braun and Rev. M. Makanzu was followed by several churches. In the western portion of Zaire the first church to appoint a full-time evangelism director was the Missionary Alliance (CEAZ). Soon afterwards the American Baptist-related church (CBZO) opened a full department of evangelism with a Zairian director and several sub-departments, each staffed by teams of a missionary and a Zairian.

"As we have indicated, the total impact of the campaign cannot be calculated, but what is known makes us realize that this was a providential leading by the Holy Spirit."

It was the Evangelical Library of Congo which sponsored the two-year movement. The director, Larry Rempel, was a genius in making the business profitable and had a generous heart for evangelism. Thelma and I had a fine workplace in the LECO building, a new Gestetner duplicator and a Congo typist paid for by LECO. In two years we wore out the Gestetner producing 17,000 newsletters monthly in six languages. Some days, paper printed on both sides was piled up five feet tall, collated, folded and inserted in envelopes, and the envelopes sealed, addressed and mailed.

God provided gifts from many unusual sources to pay for paper and ink. We were never in debt. We came to see immense changes in the spirit of the Church. We had long noticed the preoccupation of missionaries and pastors with the civil war being fought in the north, center and east of the nation and a corresponding indifference to ministry. But the whole month of prayer and the beginning of something forbidden by the Belgians, prayer cells, by the thousands, restored the eyes of believers to the King of kings. Three months of Bible studies on soul-winning, taught by lay pastors in villages and ordained pastors in cities, were followed by a month of every-home visitation and witness. By now, six months of nationwide focus on fellowship with God in new dimensions were having their impact on the people of God. Congo was turning back to Him.

We came to see that this nationwide movement was like a vast schoolroom in which we were introducing to 17,000 urban and rural pastors new ways to prepare, teach and involve their million believers in outreach to their neighbors one month at a time. Looking back 30 years, we see those monthly projects are still the basic building blocks of today's church growth. They were ministries introduced in 1966 and they have been maintained ever since.

For example, we introduced the exchange of pastors for weeks of evangelism, great outdoor rallies, the Three-Friends Campaign, Sunday school contests and massive Bible sales, along with many special monthly outreaches to youth, chiefs, women and children. Congo's churchmen enriched the life of the Church over 24 months of the Christ for All movement, and many of those elements of enrichment were never forgotten or discontinued.

Near the end of the first year, our great friend, Rev. Makanzu, was voted out of his booming church by pastors of his denomination, a matter of jealousy, not of discipline for sin. His freedom opened the door to our inviting him to join us as co-coordinator of Christ for All. His obvious gifts in preaching to his people easily defined his job description. The office work had kept us cooped up in Kinshasa. Here was an advocate who was free to travel anywhere. One happy day it came to us that Makanzu was inevitably to become the national

Dr. Makanzu, Congo's national evangelist

evangelist of Congo. He had been a brilliant pastor, but never an evangelist. But he liked the idea, so we arranged for him to hold a great outdoor rally for the city of Kikwit.

He gave his first sermon as an evangelist and began his first invitation. No one came forward and he lost his nerve. He came home a crushed man. "I can't do that!" he said in evident anguish. As we chatted further he observed that over a hundred people were waiting outside a pastor's house where he had visited on Monday. They were confessing sin and their need of a Savior. We had already arranged for him to preach for a week in our own mission area, so we encouraged him to be of good courage, to go try again.

He was an excited man when he returned from that trip. He slammed into the office exuding victory. At each message he gave an invitation and always there were serious seekers who responded. "I prayed with every one of them and could not go home until I dealt with every need," he assured us. From then on, Rev. Makanzu merited his title of National Evangelist and reveled in preaching the saving gospel to every group he could contact.

Large posters were printed with his picture and the words CHRIST FOR ALL CRUSADE, with dates and the name Rev. Makanzu, National Evangelist of Congo. Hundreds of these were sent out for statewide traveling crusades over a month or two. He preached to great crowds in every state and brought back reports rivaling the accounts of Finney, the great American evangelist.

We had made colorful banners for crusades in Kinshasa, and Evangelist Makanzu took some of those with him to be carried to the crusade site and erected over the platform. In one photograph of a march in a distant crusade we spotted a new banner. It read, "Prisoners for Christ." The warden felt his prisoners needed the Savior and had them march to the rally with their own banner. One could fill a volume with experiences of the evangelist. Never before and never since have the essential elements combined in Congo to produce another evangelist so given to indefatigable travel and preaching.

Christ for All did have other evangelists come to the Congo, from New Zealand, from China and from America. They played a tremendous role in lifting Protestants into full equality with Catholics in public life. In 1960, the year of Independence, Catholic missionaries and church members were said to outnumber Protestants 5 to 1. It is no longer the case. The 35 congregations of Protestants in Kinshasa in 1966 have now become nearly 1000, and many are crowded with thousands of believers.

There is a boldness and a confidence among Protestant churchmen which could never have been imagined when Christ for All began. Until Independence, the Catholic newspaper was the national leader, and it was filled daily with news only of Catholics. Belgians might pass a decade and never have the slightest notion that there were any people in Congo but pagans and Catholics.

It was the arrival of Drs. Howard Jones and Ralph Bell, our first foreign evangelists, both members of the Billy Graham team, that gave Protestants access to the stadium and to a first parade of two miles of marchers carrying dozens of street-wide banners and placards on sticks which said Christ for All. Never before had the capital seen such a sight as 30,000 Protestants boldly sang songs of praise while they marched proudly down the boulevard. It was the moment when Protestantism declared its presence in the nation's capital and its intent never to hide itself again.

On the platform of the stadium were all the pastors of the city. Great banners billowed over them. The stands and the field below were a solid mass of people. Impossible to miss in their white robes were Catholic priests, bewildered by all they were seeing. At each corner of the platform the government had stationed a soldier with a machine gun. By the pulpit were two government men with recorders, catching every word sung, prayed or preached. Never having seen Protestants together, the government wanted to be present as protector

Billy Graham Evangelistic Association sent Drs. Howard Jones and Ralph Bell to speak at Kinshasa's giant rallies.

and official observer. Having evaluated what went on, the government never again sent soldiers or recordists to our great rallies.

At that first rally a high official, a Catholic, congratulated all Protestants for their manifestation of their importance to the young nation as God-fearing citizens of the capital. He was most enthusiastic and won hearty applause from all.

Evangelist Howard Jones, a powerful African-American preacher, began his message with "It's good to be home again!" He was no novice in Africa, having lived in Liberia and preached on the radio there for years. The Congolese loved his identification with them, though at a banquet prepared in his honor by one of the churches, I recall that he said, "Willys, I can't eat this food." Clearly home cookin' for him originated in his Ohio kitchen, not in Congo churches. Congo cooking is delicious but can do strange things to American digestive systems.

His message was given with divine unction and many came forward at the invitation. When the people left, they knew that God had visited Kinshasa and changed the course of history in a most impressive way.

Other evangelists followed the Graham team. There was Evangelist Barry Reid of New Zealand, Evangelist Dzau of China and Rev. Richard Harvey of America. All had excellent rallies with much fruit and great joy.

Leighton Ford, President of the Lausanne Committee, wrote of one rally, *"Thank you so much for your letter of May 1 (1985). I was absolutely thrilled to hear about Bishop Bokeleale and have taken the liberty of sending a copy of your letter to Billy for his information..."*

It was Dr. Ford Philpot whose ministry climaxed the series of foreign evangelists in the second year of Christ for All. We had arranged with the Graham team and Dr. Philpot at the World Congress on Evangelism in Berlin to hold crusades in Kinshasa and other major cities. Ford sent two advance men to help prepare for the crusade. Together we reserved rooms for the 52 people he was bringing with him, sent ads to newspapers, radio and TV stations, and rented city buses to haul

Willys' drawing of Evangelist Ford Philpot

people from their churches to three gathering points from which they paraded to the giant, new stadium.

One bit of advertising we promoted was a huge banner to be towed back and forth overhead by a plane. I'll never cease to wonder that a professional banner harness was available to us in the capital. Nor will I soon forget the six-foot letters I painted on the banner on our lawn. The plane publicity caused a great deal of excitement and helped fill the 70,000 seats to overflowing for the great rally.

We had thousands of people nightly in various zones of the city, and Dr. Philpot traveled to major cities of the nation for giant

The Philpot crusade filled Kinshasa's new 70,000-seat stadium.

seems probable that those weeks saw the highest level of Protestant awareness since the gospel came to Congo.

And who was Dr. Philpot's translator? Who but Rev. Makanzu, the inimitable, now a seasoned national evangelist who communicated with his people as few could? In 1968, when Thelma and I ended our time with Christ for All, it was Rev. Makanzu who remained at its head. We helped him organize Congo's first National Congress on Evangelism, which was attended by churchmen of Congo and speakers and delegates of America, Latin America, Central African Republic, Cameroon, Malawi, Nigeria, Uganda, Rhodesia and South Africa. This congress spread the story and inspiration of Christ for All to many nations where leaders borrowed from Congo, as Congo had borrowed from Latin America.

Out of the National Office of Evangelism which we began in 1966 has come the National Department of Evangelism led by three Congolese with three earned doctorates. Incidentally, Rev. Makanzu received a doctorate from Asbury College in 1980. We had the joy of entertaining him in our home in Lexington, Kentucky, for three delightful days on that occasion. Later in that year Thelma and I returned to Kinshasa hoping to work with our beloved friend. Instead, we saw him on three occasions, twice on his deathbed, and then in his casket wearing his Asbury robes and mortarboard, evidences of the highest honor he had ever received on earth. He left a wife and large family, some thick volumes of an amazing depth of knowledge on which he had labored for years in early morning hours while the family slept. And, oh yes, he left tens of thousands of Congolese who had found Christ through his messages, and a nationwide Church much enlarged in every way because of his faithful proclamation of the Christ he loved.

Two diplomas were granted at our 1990 departure from Congo by Bishop Marini Bodho, new president of the Church of Christ of Congo, the umbrella organization serving 62 denominations. One diploma was for Thelma, one for me. They are identical except for the colored artwork and our names.

The Church of Christ of Zaire
DIPLOMA OF HONOR
We, the signatories, President and Legal Representative of the Church of Christ of Zaire, attest by the present that
Reverend Dr. Willys Braun
having worked as a missionary in Zaire since 1945, and in view of the record of his achievements and his engagement in the ministry of evangelism and of the formation of disciples,
deliver this Diploma of Honor as proof of our recognition of all that he accomplished in Zaire.
Done at Kinshasa the 8th of June, 1990
For the President of the Church of Christ of Zaire
Rev. Dr. Marini Bodho, Vice President
"How beautiful upon the mountains are the feet of those who preach peace, of those who bring good tidings" (Rom. 10:15).

Christ for All had an ending, yes, but its fruits are eternal. All that's done for Him outlasts the ravages of time. That's one of the joys of working for the eternal God.

21

OWED - OFFICE OF WORLDWIDE EVANGELISM-IN-DEPTH

A trip to Costa Rica in 1967 to a conference of the Latin America Mission on its Evangelism-in-Depth program introduced me to the exciting leaders of that very important mission movement. Their magazine, *The Latin American Evangelist*, had been mailed to us in Congo at some unknown friend's request. Its articles had thrilled me, for they showed Protestants who lived in strongly Catholic nations – like our Congo – marching down the boulevards of capital cities to huge stadiums for great public crusades of evangelism.

Wow! If they could do that, we probably could. The photos of those marchers didn't need one word of explanation. It was all written on their joyous Latin countenances. We must put such joy on our Congolese faces, I thought. And we have! Over and over and over. Evangelism-in-Depth was a landmark in global missions and it transferred easily to Africa by virtue of the magazine articles that communicated even the smallest details of what, why, who, how, when and where of the movement. It was on this magazine's splendid coverage of something going on in numerous countries of Latin America, an ocean away, that we built Christ for All.

In Costa Rica, delegates from Nigeria and Asia as well as Latin American nations met each other and heard the leaders of E.I.D. explain the philosophy and track record of this phenomenal, unique movement. On a free afternoon we were bussed to the grave of Dr. Kenneth Strachan, founder of E.I.D. who had drowned in a swimming accident. No mention was made of the fact that a foundation was to give a memorial grant to Latin America Mission in order to open two offices, one in Africa and one in Asia, to spread the message of E.I.D.

under the acronym OWED – the Office of Worldwide Evangelism-in-Depth.

We completed Christ for All and received an invitation to head the OWED in Africa. Our mission agreed to appoint Thelma and me to this project and we furnished a little cottage in which to live and work. For two years I traveled over Africa, north, east, south and northwest to 34 nations and to some repeatedly. It took one trip to help Rev. Wayne Beaver of Central African Republic (CAR) launch a powerful movement for his nation, which reported over 200,000 conversions, equal to all the members of CAR before he began the movement.

Cameroon required three trips before Rev. Bjorne Bue was appointed to lead a nationwide movement that over ten years saw a dramatic involvement in evangelism of the country's denominations. Eventually Rev. Bue returned to Norway for furlough, was ordained as bishop and rose to lead Norway into nationwide evangelism.

Ross Campbell and Peter Barker,
Ghana's men of vision

Evangelist Makanzu joined me in visiting Burundi to get that little nation started. Our Kinshasa office sent Rev. George Thomas copies of our mailings to inspire their leaders and they advanced very well until civil war stopped them.

Chad also launched out after my visit, and many thousands were converted before civil war struck that nation.

Liberia's Vice President, W.R. Tolbert, wrote to us on April 29, 1970 after visits during OWED years: "*Referring to your proposal for the organization of a national campaign of evangelism, I wish to indicate that I made a recommendation of same in my annual message to the 56th Session of the Liberia Baptist Missionary and Educational Convention. . . . I wish to assure you in the meantime, that I will endeavor to give all cooperation to Bishop Nagbe and Rev. Roland Payne in the formation and implementation of this program.*"

It was my visit to Ghana that inspired the most enduring national movement in Africa. Rev. Peter Barker was one of those rare foreign missionaries who worked closely with the denominational leaders and whose counsel was valued by them. In a special Ghana Ministerial Fellowship meeting called to hear my story about national movements, the Ghanaian chairman was thanking me and closing the meeting when Peter said, "Oh, brethren, we can't just walk away from this opportunity. Let's name a committee now to pursue this idea of a nationwide movement for Ghana." They did, and under the leadership of Rev. Ross Campbell it went on powerfully for 25 years. Ross then became the Africa worker for AD 2000 during the 1990s.

Trips were made to Angola, Botswana, Namibia, Zimbabwe, Zambia, South Africa, Malawi, Mozambique and Madagascar. Our influence in Zimbabwe, South Africa and Madagascar led to extra harvests on a short-term. I was received in South Africa by the Dutch Reformed Church's top leaders and spoke to their highest body of the great value of a national movement of evangelism. They changed their constitution, which forbade joining with other denominations in activities, opening the door to their participation in a national movement of all denominations. But my reception by leaders of other denominations was frosty. The churches were politicized to such an extent that to them the Dutch Reformed Church was the enemy.

*Willys traveled to 34 African nations
to introduce national movements
of evangelism.*

A few years later I met the head of the DRC churches in South Africa at the Worldwide Conference in Lausanne, Switzerland. I asked what came of my visit. "Oh, haven't you heard?", he asked. "It developed into a great youth movement in South Africa." I have no more detailed news than that, but from the excitement in this churchman's eyes I was convinced that God had been glorified there.

Some big denominations in Madagascar worked together in a nearly national movement for some time, but I never learned the results.

I doubt that our two years heading up the OWED work in Africa cost Latin America Mission over $10,000, but it was a high-water mark in evangelism on the continent. The common response of African churchmen in dozens of nations to my question, "What is your denomination doing with evangelism?" was, "Nothing. The early missionaries had to evangelize because there was no church. Now we have the church and don't need to evangelize." At the same time there were many large unreached tribes who were as pagan as had been the tribes now churched. It was and is common for some American denominations to proudly list the many unreached tribes in their nations where they have been ministering from 50 to 100 years. They called for prayer and gifts because of these unreached tribes. They should be ashamed to admit that they have ignored those tribes decade after decade, remembering them only for publicity purposes.

Evangelism was carried on until there was a church. After that, the focus changed to mothering that church. OWED was a voice calling these daughter churches to go out and win the forgotten, the ignored, and the lost. It fathered a resurgence of evangelism and of salvation around Africa. Liberals at the time had no use for evangelism. Their goal was to organize national committees of all denominations with strong liberal leaders dominating the agenda. In numerous nations the crass, faithless, Bible-less politics of these leaders led to a sharp division and separation of evangelicals from liberals.

The Association of Evangelicals of Africa and Madagascar came into being as a result of this harsh, angry division. It gave to evangelicals a base, a center that brought them together annually. It also hardened the liberal opposition. The long-term experience has been that the liberals' drive to organize and control all Protestants dried up.

Africans are not naturally unbelievers. As Dr. Makanzu said, "I will not give my life preaching what I do not believe. This book is God's book. I believe it, therefore I preach it." Evangelicals, through offering a plan of a nationwide movement of evangelism to every denomination, brought great growth and revival to vast areas. And because of that, evangelicals achieved what the liberals never could – unified action. They did not try to politically dominate. They showed them how to win the lost and to plant new churches far and wide.

OWED played a major role in this process. When Thelma and the boys and I returned to America in 1970 for furlough the OWED ministry ended. A sister ministry of great vigor, New Life for All, also ended. Africa had no one left proclaiming the need for and the glory of evangelism to reach great, lost tribes. Ten years were to pass in silence.

I cannot explain how the sponsoring bodies of OWED and NLFA could summarily chop off such strong evangelical movements in their prime. I suspect that men in America in high places so opposed the idea of all denominations evangelizing under a common banner that they shut off funding to stop it. Weird indeed, for evangelicals were convincing African denominations to preach the gospel to unreached tribes and to church them at last.

But to some American churchmen it was more important to divide the Church than to revive it and win the world. The great evangelical movement of nationwide evangelism of Africa was cut off at its funding source. For four years it prospered on the continent. In a few nations it carried on. But the greatest opportunity Protestants ever had to totally saturate Africa's non-Muslim nations with biblical faith and revival was killed in its prime. It did not die of itself.

22

ALLIANCE KEY '73

The Brauns spent a busy and happy year in California.

Over thirty years of missionary service we had only four furloughs, two fewer than normal, because we were too tied to ministries to quit on time. We were "happy campers" in Congo.

Our fourth furlough was spent in La Mirada, California and was an extremely happy one. La Mirada is the home of Biola College and my sister was chairman of its popular Christian Education department. She and Mother had a truly lovely home near campus and had found a rental nearby for us. For one year of our parental life we, and they, had close continuous fellowship in the fullest, most delightful sense.

Chris was in his senior year, majoring in Christian education. He had not yet found his true love Marcia, but would soon, as he continued in Talbot Seminary for three more years to earn his master's degree. Paul was busy in a flamboyant high school and came home wearing a $600 marching band uniform provided by the school. He later brought a football uniform – he was a punter. Phil was a grade schooler, totally fascinated by the pizzazz of California and of his two big brothers.

Thelma discovered that on furlough a C&MA missionary was permitted to earn money by working at a secular job. She signed up as a substitute high school teacher. Several times a week the phone would wake us at about five a.m. and an assignment would be given to her, generally in a school she had never seen, miles away in the tangle of highways of the greater Los Angeles area. Her Illinois teacher's license qualified her to teach in California if she took some night-school courses in a university. So she taught and studied and mothered two children – and me – and spoke in churches and held the fort in the four months when I was on missionary tours.

The year passed all too fast. When it was nearly time to return to Congo a letter came from Rev. L. L. Pippert, Home Secretary of The Christian and Missionary Alliance, asking us to head the new office of Alliance Key '73. We accepted eagerly, for this gave us an opportunity to learn whether what we had been doing in Congo's Christ for All and then the all-Africa Evangelism-in-Depth nationwide movements was applicable in Canada and the United States.

We graduated Chris and said farewell to him, to Mother and to Dorothy and began our drive to New York. It was a felicitous trip all the way except for one incident that had the potential to change all of our lives. At one motel Paul dove off the diving board into a too-small pool and cracked his head on the bottom. It was the kind of dive that has made all too many quadriplegics of high-spirited young fellows. By God's grace it did not do so for our son. A few days later it was just a scary memory. God had work for Paul to do.

When we arrived in New York the mission housed us in a large three-story, with basement, home in Nyack next to the Robert Cowles, the editor of the *Alliance Life* magazine, a wonderful family. The city of Nyack had not changed greatly since we attended school there 28 years earlier, though a new generation of teachers had come to Nyack College. Paul began his studies there and would meet Nancy. Phil finished grade school and grew up.

Billy Graham lent his name and fame to many great movements in the 1970s. His world travels and the Berlin, Lausanne and Amsterdam congresses on world evangelism, which he largely sponsored, gave enormous global incentives to evangelical missions. In America, besides his famous crusades, his presence on the planning committee of the Key '73 movement in 1970 gave this three-year program inter-denominational legitimacy.

In my lifetime I cannot recall any other movement which even approached Key '73 as an all-American crusade. Methodism provided a quarter-million dollar budget for Key '73 directed by Rev. Joe Hale, a young man who participated in Congo's first National Congress on Evangelism which we planned and administered in 1969.

Our office was in the old headquarters building in New York's Times Square area. All winter long we got up in the dark, drove to the city in the dark, drove home at night in the dark. Only on weekends did we see Nyack in daylight until spring and summer lighted our world. Snow abounded on the hillside overlooking the Hudson River. It was a considerable change from southern California and from our tropical Congo.

Our daily task was to write, design, publish and mail materials to 1400 C&MA pastors in Canada and the US for the next two and a half years. A splendid work committee of leaders of various departments had been assigned to write challenging articles to be published in a large three-ring notebook destined for all pastors. A national AK '73 congress on evangelism was held in Chicago, and was followed by district AK '73 conferences across Canada and the US.

Our work was overseen by Mr. Pippert. It was he who organized the national congress in Chicago and he did a truly great job. There had been a long discussion in the work committee about the usefulness of AK '73. Some dignitaries held that evangelism had no value until God sent revival. My experience led me to a strong conviction that doing evangelism was simple obedience to God, with or without revival, and that God revived an obedient Church. I called for wholehearted obedience in outreach with the expectation that God would reward our obedience with His gift of revival.

In launching AK '73 the C&MA officially obeyed God's requirement that its congregations focus on evangelism. It was not long before the Lord of the Church brought powerful revival to hundreds of C&MA churches in Canada and the US.

Revival is an awesome thing. It sweeps into congregations and brings cleansing and joy and love and salvation. It is carried like a holy virus by revived individuals and teams from group to group. It brings young and old together in complete harmony, heals long-term feuds, restores marriages and ends church divisions. It also increases giving to the Church, brings in new families and bathes a church in the warm presence of God. People of a revived congregation reported, "When we arrive on the sidewalk in front of our church the presence of God overpowers our spirit. We stop talking. We go in to a holy place where God is." That is different!

Revival was not a one-week event. Revival seemed to sit upon congregations for wondrous years. In the years of Alliance Key '73 the denomination recorded striking increases in conversions, baptisms and new members.

I recall an interesting experience with Rev. Pippert. He was preparing his annual report for the annual conference and was really frustrated. He had no good news for his report and regarded the past year as a poor one. I spent a few hours preparing a graph of membership growth of the past ten years. The graph showed a dramatic rise in the AK '73 years. One look at the graph put a big smile on the Home Secretary's face. His annual report was one of victory!

Evangelists of the C&MA were few and in little demand before AK '73. By the end of 1973, they were numerous and booked for years to come. We edited a monthly newsletter for Alliance pastors and in each issue reported on two more evangelists' ministries. We gave a paragraph to the evangelist's report of a certain crusade, a paragraph to the pastor's report of the same crusade, and a paragraph of an elder's report of the same. It became clear to every pastor that God was still mightily blessing His evangelists in Alliance churches.

A good friend of ours in the late 1960s was Rev. Wayne Beaver, who headed the National Movement of Evangelism in Bangui, capital of the Central African Republic. He was chosen by the Grace Brethren denomination to head Key '73 for them. He came to New York to see what we were doing and we gave him copies of everything to take back to his office. Many of those materials were used in their program which they called GROW '73. He saw great growth in Grace Brethren membership and later headed their seminary's mission and evangelism department.

Looking back, I see that evangelists were often regarded not as God's specially gifted heralds of salvation but as men who couldn't make it as pastors. Already evangelism was on its way out. It was no longer honored as a strong, permanent part of God's Church. The very fact that in 1971 anyone could convince denominations of America to launch a movement of evangelism was a miracle in itself. But the name Key '73 doesn't really include the word evangelism. Maybe we were the ones who so identified it.

In any case, God sent revival, a powerful moving of His Spirit to a reported 300 C&MA congregations. That is only 21% of the total, true, but those revived churches wonderfully impacted the whole Alliance and brought exceptional harvests of salvation.

In the C&MA magazine, *Alliance Life,* December 19, 1973, Thelma and I were encouraged by these kind words: "*On December 31 Willys K. Braun and his equally capable wife Thelma conclude their special assignment in the office of Operation Harvest.*

"*Those of us who have had opportunity to become well acquainted with this gifted, delightful couple thank God upon every remembrance of them.*

"*They have worked with an optimistic determination and a selfless dedication inspiring to see. Although necessarily absorbed in much detail work they have also been mindful of the broad perspectives. Only God knows the full extent of their contribution to the continent-wide Alliance evangelistic thrust of the past year and a quarter. Without discounting the gracious presence of God's Holy Spirit so manifest since the early days of Operation Harvest, we do not hesitate to say that Willys and Thelma Braun have been God's special gift to our Society for this hour.*

"*We admire them. We love them. We thank God for them. They have enriched our lives.*

"We wish them God's choicest blessing in all their future ministry for Him."

Other encouragement also came to us after the Key '73 movement: *"Thanks, Willys, for doing such a great job with Operation Harvest. I sincerely hope that this guidance from your office will continue because it puts a great tool in our hands, and the Operation Harvest news sheet helps to stimulate our people to do what others are doing"* - Rev. Anthony G. Bollback, Kapakulu Bible Church, Honolulu, Hawaii.

"Let me express my personal appreciation for your untiring and effective ministry in the Office of Evangelism during the last few years . . . much good has been done and many churches have experienced revival and the salvation of many souls because of your faithful leadership"- F. Paul Henry, Superintendent Western Pennsylvania District, The Christian and Missionary Alliance, December 19, 1973.

It was a marvelous experience for Thelma and me to work with the top officials of the Alliance for two exciting years and to have a part in this high point in the "old" Alliance, which ennobled evangelists and prayed for revival. In His infinite grace and mercy, Alliance Key '73 seemed to be His special effort to say to the C&MA leadership and to His Body, "This is how I bless the denomination that obeys me in active evangelism. I give floods of revival and salvation. Don't forget all of this as you strike off in a different path."

SECTION FOUR

27 E.R. YEARS

23

EVANGELISM RESOURCES

Apparently some Alliance churchmen thought Thelma and I had done something right, for as Alliance Key '73 came to an end we received thirteen job offers. The one we felt was God's call to us was an invitation from Dr. Ford Philpot to work with him in Lexington, Kentucky. He was ready to open an international office of evangelism in Africa and that was where we felt God wanted us to be. We moved with Philip and all our second-hand furniture to a rented house near a small stream in Lexington and got to work.

Work, for us, was to prepare crusades for Evangelist Philpot. In Congo we had pioneered mass crusades in the two stadiums and all over the huge city. In America, it was another story. The system was already well organized. Instead of being the inspirer and creative organizer of each crusade from start to finish we were largely following pre-set responsibilities. There was no lack of challenge. We traveled regularly to future crusade sites to meet with crusade committees and advance preparations.

Ford was a delight to work with. He had his own full-time printer to do his books, publicity and newsmagazine. We edited the magazine and did much of his publicity. He had a splendid quartet and various nationally known soloists. His TV programs were aired from coast to coast. His youth evangelist was also the pilot of his plane.

We enjoyed every part of our ministry with Ford, but our real calling was to Africa and the plan to go to Africa was nullified by a vote of the Philpot Board. A sharp recession in 1974 cut into income. Ford assumed that Thelma and I could raise money to pay for the move to Africa. We had no experience whatever as fund raisers in the Alliance and had no success whatever in the hard times of 1974.

Without money in hand, the Board did the only thing it could. It said no to Africa.

Dr. Philpot had had a heart problem for some time and after by-pass surgery his health was not what it had been. Income was inadequate and he needed to downsize. So with all good wishes on both sides we left the Philpot offices. After two and a half years with the Philpot Evangelistic Association we found ourselves unassigned for the first time in 32 years.

Then the Lord stepped in and required us to do something we did not want to do. He asked us to begin a new mission. If ever there was a mission born to fail, it was Evangelism Resources.

But the letterhead carried these globally-known names as the Board of Reference: Dr. Nathan Bailey, President, Christian and Missionary Alliance; Rev. Allen Finley, President, Christian Nationals Evangelism Commission; Rev. John Falkenberg, President, Bible Literature International; Dr. D. James Kennedy, Pastor, Coral Ridge Presbyterian Church; Bishop Kivengere, Evangelist, African

ER's Board - men and women of vision

Enterprise, Uganda: Dr. Donald McGavran, Dean Emeritus, World School of Missions; Dr. H. Wilbert Norton, Dean, Graduate Schol, Wheaton; Dr. R. Stanley Tam, President, United Plastics Corporation, and Dr. Alfred Whittaker, President, International Institute of Development, Inc.

Dr. Harold Spann, then Assistant to the President of Asbury College and later President of Wesley Biblical Seminary, brought a rare depth of spirituality and a breadth of practical experience in administration to the founding board of Evangelism Resources. Dr. Alexander Reid, distinguished Methodist missionary to Zaire, was Vice President, Thelma was Secretary, and Dr. Susan Schultz, (now Dr. Susan Schultz Rose), Director of the Library of Asbury Theological Seminary, was Treasurer. These were dedicated visionaries and they soon rounded up a group of equally distinguished members to add to the board.

But there were adverse circumstances that the Lord had to conquer. Our home denomination has a strong global missions program which greatly appeals to its members. It also is sternly protective of its congregations' expenditures. Over 24 years none of its congregations has supported ER ministries. Other denominations' congregations support ER, but none of our own. That is not to say that none of its members support ER. They do, but only as individuals. From the beginning we knew we could not expect its churches to help, not even our home church.

Our personal mailing list had about 400 families when we were with the C&MA. We cut that to about 75 for our first ER mailing, and only a few of those responded to our call for partners. Still our first fiscal year recorded gifts of about $50,000. If we had followed normal mission practices we would have rented attractive offices for about $12,000 a year, hired a secretary for $25,000 and given the chief executive officer a salary of at least $35,000. Let's see . . . $12,000 plus $25,000 and $35,000 comes to $72,000. Income was $50,000. We would have been $22,000 in debt with no overseas ministries whatever in our first year.

Instead we worked from our house, saving ER $276,000 rent plus all water, sewage, heat, light, air conditioning, garbage and grounds upkeep costs – over 23 years.

In that first half year ER purchased and shipped a $4000 gospel tent to Liberia. I made a four-month work trip to twelve nations in the first six months.

We edited, published and mailed *NEWS* every month to those on the mailing list, preached at missions conferences, kept up all correspondence, did accounting and banking and incorporated Evangelism Resources in the state of Kentucky.

For three years we followed this pattern, spending many months overseas and sending gospel tents to major cities. Then in mid-1980 Thelma and I moved to Kinshasa to build the International Center of Evangelism. ER had $15,000 in the bank, our total capital. We obtained rooms in a partially empty C&MA apartment. Specifically, we had a bedroom, bathroom and kitchen. The living room was almost full of C&MA freight. Gospel singers frequently used the empty part as their practice area. Mice and roaches shared the rooms with us on an equal footing, but we paid the rent.

We spent two months in Egypt, Nigeria and Cameroon in the fall of 1980 and expected to move to a rental house owned by an army paymaster, Colonel Pelo, when we returned. However, a month after our return the colonel had not freed that house of renters. He had instead bought land on a cool mountaintop and built a very large house with four bedrooms, an office, three baths and a living room as large as three normal living rooms. It was all his idea. He also installed decorative high-gloss tiles on all floors, including two porches.

The Kinshasa office building and Center staff

He showed us this marvelous place with no explanation until we completed the whole tour. Then he asked us if it was satisfactory. Only then did we guess that he expected us to rent this elegant villa. Shocked, we protested that we couldn't even dream of renting such a mansion. "Oh no," he assured us. "The rent is the same as for the house you originally agreed to take." He also provided expensive drapes for every room and built a seven-room office building free on the land.

When we moved in, we had no furniture. We bought mattresses and slept on the living room floor. The bedrooms were still being finished. We began furnishing the house, bit by bit, wondering how we could ever use all the space. No problem. Phil came to Kinshasa after graduation from Biola College. Steve Liversedge, single, lived with us for several years, as did Dale Garside. Many gatherings were held in the large living room, including conferences and some literature packaging on our 8' by 8' table. On the large front porch the Kinshasa Evangelism Committee met monthly for seven years, planning tent meetings, stadium rallies, full-year calendars of week-long outdoor gospel crusades in many zones, twelve-month programs for every congregation in the city and a five-year project of church planting.

Our family office had a double window, one that was screened shut to keep out mosquitoes. The other was hinged and could open to permit us to listen to visitors and to pass out money. We named it the "Window of Hope," because here every day dozens of people came with their personal agendas, were listened to and, in most cases, they departed with the funds they hoped to get.

There were poor beggars, of course. But there were also evangelists to the Bateke, the Pygmies and the Holos, Kinshasa church planters, tent evangelists, preachers wanting free literature, students of our three schools who had needs, sick workers or their families, unemployed people looking for jobs, builders needing money for nails, etc. The Window of Hope over ten years kept a great number of people in the Lord's work, and through them tens of thousands were trained in portable Bible schools, hundreds of Kinshasa congregations were planted and tens of thousands won to Christ in the capital city as well as hundreds of village churches.

It was at the window where we met the grass-roots people of Kinshasa and of all other states of Congo. We were available at the window six days a week. If a visitor had a project which needed discussion we would go out on the front porch and do business for the Lord, often with a cool drink to brighten the occasion. Our kitchen food store had four or five cases of colas or fruit flavors to meet the preference of each visitor.

If the visitor was an honored churchman we would invite him into our living room to have a good visit and discuss at length the project which brought him to our home. Over those ten years notables from all over Africa and other continents found their way to the International Center of Evangelism.

Our daily schedule was crowded. Thelma and I taught three class hours each day. Over seven years we designed and built six buildings with a total floor space of 27,400 square feet. We had ten adult missionaries, about 40 African workers and about 55 students. All of them needed money and I was the bookkeeper. Thelma was the salary payer and often in charge of feeding 70 people at lunch and 55 for breakfast and supper. It was a very busy life for us and for our 50 co-workers.

This should explain the Window of Hope. It made us available and helped us to settle each item quickly for dozens of daily visitors. If we had treated each visit as a social event we could never have done all that was required. Once seated as guests, Africans can happily pass hours with cool or hot drinks and a meal as part of the visit. There were not hours enough in a day for such relaxation. The Window of Hope worked two ways. The visitor hoped to get help. We hoped a decision could be made quickly so we could complete the day's duties.

Some missionaries locked themselves in their homes to assure that they could focus uninterrupted on their assignments. That worked for them. We chose an open window so more ministries could be encouraged. During the nine months of the year when we were at the Center, over 100 people were on our station daily. All came to the window, some to the porch and some into the living room from time to time. This way of life greased the wheels of a multi-ministry mission for a very rewarding decade.

Income in the 1980 to 1985 years stayed at about $50,000 a year. Over ER's first nine years it did not seem to matter whether we were two or three missionaries or whether we were in the USA or Africa. In 1979 Rev. Wesley Eisemann became a staff member and we traveled together in Africa. How we wished that income would increase so he could become a permanent worker!

A fourth and fifth house and the large two-story building for the International School of Christian Education, the International Institute of Christian Communication, the radio studios and a bookstore were built. This last building has a story of its own.

One of ER's Board members was Dr. J. C. McPheeters, president-emeritus of Asbury Theological Seminary. He was "retired" but was actually busy raising funds for the Seminary. One large grant that came to the Seminary in later years was because of Dr. McPheeters' friendship with a donor. It was my hope, of course, that our Board member would help ER. He did. He invited Thelma and me to the Redwoods Camp in northern California as speakers for two conferences. There we met several families and an excellent church became enduring friends of ER.

Dr. J.C. McPheeters
introduced us to Redwoods.

Rev. Edgar Nelson was then pastor of the First United Methodist Church of Yuba City, California, which for 21 years has faithfully supported ER ministries. Over fifteen years the Azim-Brooks Scholarship Fund has supported two students yearly, and more recently four, in the Kinshasa School of Evangelism and has ER alumni in many countries of Africa.

Winston and Joy Handwerker of Modesto, California enabled us to build the second large building on the campus. Each month a check came to our treasurer until the building was finished. Theirs was the largest project-gift ER has ever received. For years the building has been used by Sangu Malamu for its cassette-, radio-, and TV-program preparation as well as the International School of Christian Education and Dr. Zach Lumeya's four-year School of Missions.

In 1990, the year Thelma and I moved back to the States, we obtained a building next door to our large house. Dr. Gene Davis saw our need for more work space and provided a large part of the purchase price. The house had a very large rust-free roof and Steve built out beyond the original walls all around, creating a chapel for 300 with an outdoor seating area for 100 more. About ten other rooms were walled up, making what we then needed most, offices for our teachers and for various mission groups such as African Enterprise. I believe this building has about 5000 square feet of floor space.

The Center was given a bus by the Bluebird Bus Company, of Georgia. So far it has given ten years of excellent service to our students engaging in ministries. Other missions have funded the Richard Steiners, the John Mellors, the Philip Wileys and the Steve Nelsons for a total of 34 years of ministry, valued at $680,000. The Stanita Foundation's contribution largely went to train over 40,000 village lay preachers in portable Bible schools in eight nations of Africa and Asia.

A list of countable ministries of ER would include the following:

» Twenty-three gospel tents sent to the great cities of Africa.

» About 300 urban congregations planted in twelve denominations in a five-year project.

» The All for Christ nationwide movement of evangelism was supplied with annual shipments of monthly evangelism projects for 30,000 congregations for each of three years. These were published in French and five African languages.

» Maintained the largest Christian publication ministry in Zaire (now Congo) for years. Dozens of new titles by Africans and missionaries were printed. Tens of thousands of Bibles and Testaments and hundreds of thousands of Scripture booklets were received and distributed.

» A Kinshasa Committee of Evangelism met monthly over seven years at the Center and planned three mass meetings in the national stadium, with 70,000 in attendance. The KCE also planned dozens of weeks of evangelism in zones of Kinshasa and citywide, involving every church in years of growth.

» Operated the Kinshasa gospel tent ministry which won many Muslims to faith in Christ.

» Built and operated the International School of Evangelism to which outstanding churchmen came from 26 nations.

» Built and operated the International School of Christian Education and the International Institute of Christian Communication and provided numerous studios and offices for Sango Malamu cassette, radio and TV broadcasts nearly free of charge, as well as offices for Africa Enterprise and numerous other mission groups for twenty years.

» Supported gospel teams to the Bateke Plateau for over a decade and for Pygmy and Holo church planting.

» Provided scholarships for theological training for Bateke, Pygmy and Holo churchmen.

» Established a large Pygmy organization in 1991, MEPA, which has provided a church life for up to 400 Kinshasa Pygmies, some of whom were trained in portable Bible schools, in the International School of Evangelism and in three-year theology programs.

» Trained 30,000 village lay pastors in portable Bible schools.

» Operated Africa Network for five years. Literature was written in English and French for this office. Trips were made north and south of Kinshasa to about 13 nations. This brought students from many countries to the International School of Evangelism, influenced alumni to open schools of evangelism in Angola and Ivory Coast, and added to our international vision and ministries.

» Held an international conference on Pygmy outreach in 1994.

» Planned a Pygmy school of theology for Cameroon's south-eastern frontier, with a goal of training 100 Pygmies for ordination in central African nations. The Liversedges went to Cameroon in 1999 to set up this school.

· ·

The Wilmore office building

For twenty years, the Kinshasa Center was Evangelism Resources. At present Evangelism Resources is many things in many places. The Center had marvelous years of versatile ministries, but only the shadow of these and the high cost remain. Ceding the Center to colleagues better able to revive it is a win-win situation. The Center will live again and ER will be enabled to plant great, new ministries in Africa and Asia.

The story of ER must include the building in 1998 and 1999 of its offices in Wilmore. The building is modest in size. It has 3000 square feet of floor space but it has seven offices and a boardroom, printing room, kitchen, storage, three washrooms and a four-column porch in front, which makes it very attractive. It sits halfway up on a low hill, surrounded by green lawns and its parking lot. The new offices have permitted ER to add three extremely helpful workers to the ER staff, enabling ministries to jump ahead.

ER is not only ministries and buildings. It is people. Thirty-four adult missionaries have served God with ER in its 24 years. Besides these, we have supported 34 nationals in Africa and 140 nationals in Asia, with partial support for 40,000 students of portable Bible schools and thousands of students of Schools of Evangelism in Africa and Asia. Teaching churchmen and students learning to be leading churchmen are the compounding interest of investments made in ER.

Approximately $6,000,000 has been spent by ER over 24 years. It sounds like so much until one divides it by 24 and learns that on an average only $250,000 a year was received. That would pay for five missionary families' allowances, with nothing for the home office or for ministries. But ER has had as many as six families and two single missionaries and full plates of ministries going on in many nations at the same time.

Evangelism Resources can be described in various ways. My own focus is on ministries. This is where I spend my days and, often, my nights. So when I begin to write or speak of ER I delve into planting, watering and harvesting, both past and present. Eventually I get to the people who collaborated in those ministries overseas. In the 24 years of ER 34 missionaries did their parts, some for a year, some for five years. Rev. Wesley Eisemann has served God as ER treasurer for more than 18 years. These are the visible parts of ER, the reapers. But no harvesters and no harvest would be possible if there were not devoted Board members, faithful foundations and a body of compassionate, convinced and committed partners who pray, work, earn and give sacrificially to enable, enable, enable these ministries to go on.

In 1999 about 600 individual families kept ER ministries paid up. These families have their personal problems, burdens, illnesses, wants, needs, expenses and reasons to save for retirement, housing, future educational costs of children, future costs of parents, mortgages, health costs, etc. They give in spite of all these, and they give to God. The money is His, not ours, and in profound humility and godly fear we invest that money as wisely as we can.

Not only that. We too give of ourselves and our income. Wesley accepts no salary at all. Thelma and I do not work for two salaries, or for one. We work for less than a quarter of what we would earn working in normal mission administration.

It could be said that at our ages no one would hire us. But it should also be said that we are much more productive at this age than at any younger age. God has used the years since we were 65 to include all of the ministries of ER since 1983 when the Center was in its third year. God has not yet retired us, and every year ER leaps ahead. Praise His glorious name!

This chapter does not present all that can or should be said about ER. It is only a start. Under God's continued blessing, the best is yet to come.

ER's sterling Board members in 1996

24

ASIA

From age 16 to 53 I was fascinated with my world and with travel. Alliance missionaries of my generation flew to Belgium to study French. Thelma and I missed out on that. The war in Europe was on when our time to study French arrived, so we studied in America. It was a disappointment to us. But later we studied a year in Switzerland and traveled Europe's nations freely. Later the Lord took us to Hong Kong, Taiwan, Japan, the Philippines, India and Bangladesh.

The hunger to travel is gone now. Nights without rest, jet lag, sweltering heat, storms, hard beds and swarming mosquitoes, followed by more jet lag for a week, take the fun out of one more trip to here or there. I prefer TV programs on animals and birds and on distant cities. At 10 p.m. I can retire to my kind of bed and feel ready for a long, happy day's work in the morning.

But in 1991 Dr. Gene Davis and God called us to India. Interestingly, for four years I had felt that God wanted ER to minister in India. In the fall of 1988 Thelma and I were invited to London to speak at a DAWN conference. One of the speakers was Dr. Paul Gupta, director of Hindustan Bible Institute. He spoke with great power of the needs there. Later, back in Africa, I wrote to him of my interest but received no answer.

In the summer of 1989 Thelma and I attended the Lausanne II conference in Manila, capital of the Philippines. In preparation for the conference we printed 4000 brochures about portable Bible schools, some in English, some in French. These we distributed freely to delegates. The hotel where we stayed housed dozens of Indian delegates. We couldn't have been happier. Breakfasts were served at large round tables and Thelma and I chose to sit with a new group of Indians each morning. We enthusiastically told them about portable Bible schools and schools of evangelism but no one showed any

Dr. Gene and Vivian Davis.
They opened India to the Brauns.

interest in them at the conference. We returned to Zaire feeling that we were mistaken about God's wanting us to work in India.

The next year, 1990, we sponsored a national congress on evangelism. We had funded and organized the first in 1969 with Dr. Makanzu. Delegates from Uganda, Nigeria, Central African Republic, Cameroon, Malawi, Rhodesia, South Africa and America attended it as a result of my travels for Evangelism-in-Depth.

The 1990 congress was a smaller one but it attracted three visitors from Oregon, Dr. Gene Davis, whom we had met in London and in Manila and whose home we visited near Portland, and two Baptist missionary twin sisters, the Wisemans, whom we had known for years in Zaire. Gene stayed in our house, seeing all, hearing all, saying nothing.

The congress focused in part on the Pygmies. ER was just learning about the areas in which they lived in Zaire. We drew a large map and asked delegates to color in where Pygmies were. At that time we knew nothing of the big picture. A short time later, Marvin Bowers showed us a map of Zaire with the location of Pygmy camps in wonderful detail! He had bought it in Manila. We photocopied it and it has guided our teams ever since.

The other half of the story is that the map had been prepared and published by atheistic communists of the Russian block. (God, how You use the wrath of man to serve You!) He had His enemies do for us what none of His servants had done. Amazing.

Thelma and I left Africa in mid-1990 and reopened our USA office. Dr. Davis called us rather frequently and urged us to go to India. On one phone call I asked him why he went to Zaire. He said, "To check you out and see if you were for real." He obviously concluded that we were, for in half a year we were planning a seven-week trip to India, consisting of three two-week seminars on portable Bible schools and schools of evangelism, to begin in August 1991.

The first two weeks were spent at Dr. Gupta's HBI (Hindustan Bible Institute) in Madras. Before we left, arrangements had been made to open an ER School of Evangelism in HBI facilities in 1992.

Next we held a two-week seminar in southern Orissa and a plan developed to send ten Indian pastors to Lagos, Nigeria for a year of study in ER's School of Evangelism there. This was done, funded by Dr. Davis. Orissa delegates were also eager to learn what Orissa could do for a statewide movement of evangelism. I sent back a lengthy description of an Orissa Plan which over the next five years brought great growth to the denominations of the state.

Delhi was the third location for a seminar. A few pastors of neighboring states were included in the ten men sent to Lagos.

The Madras School of Evangelism was begun with two graduates of Lagos. Both returned to their home states, Rev. T. S. David to Rajasthan and Rev. Allen Mandal to Orissa. Rev. D. B. Hrudaya opened the second School of Evangelism in Balasore, Orissa. Its director was for seven years Rev. Mandal.

Rev. Hrudaya became the leader of the Orissa Plan and from 1993 to 1998 we carried on an almost weekly correspondence. He was enabled to open an ER-funded Teacher Training School of Evangelism and, on his own, a three-year school of theology. We became great friends. ER helped him with funds to train hundreds of men each year in portable Bible schools. Literally thousands of Orissans were trained by various groups funded by ER.

We funded the Reaching Every Village Survey program (REVS) in Orissa for two years with excellent results. It was headed

Rev. Hrudaya, ER's big investment in India

by Pastor Moses, who later served three years in Madhya Pradesh organizing portable Bible schools.

REVS was a two-phase outreach program. The first phase was a search for isolated families of believers in surrounding villages. The second phase appointed gospel teams to minister each week to target groups of isolated believers with the goal of planting a new church.

Rev. Hrudaya was ER's biggest investment in India for four years. The amount contributed in one year was over $30,000. Those were years of great growth for the whole state and the Hindus were the first to recognize that growth and react against it. It is no accident that murders, beatings, burnings and massive Hindu efforts to forcibly reconvert tribal Christians have focused on Orissa. And it was no accident that two mighty cyclones centered on Orissa, giving the terrorists much to think about beside tormenting Christ's people.

ER sponsored three large conferences attended by delegates from many states in 1994, 1996 and 1998. At these conferences Orissan churchmen who headed up portable Bible schools, REVS, schools of evangelism and the Orissa Plan presented reports on these ministries to the conference. Unquestionably the Orissa Plan, which was followed by the Maharashtra Plan, the Assam Plan and the Madhya Pradesh Plan, encouraged the formation of statewide Harvest Networks in states of North India.

ER was able to help Rev. Hrudaya in a very special way. His letters at times reported crises in income. His increasing schools required renting more and more buildings at great cost. Dr. Gene Davis had purchased land for a school building, but no one had money to build the school. After a particularly agonized plea I wrote a letter to a foundation proposing that a gift of $150,000 be granted to build an adequate school for Balasore. The foundation replied with an offer of $75,000 if ER could match it. We wrote to dozens of missions in India and to foundations over a period of months. Not one penny came in for the matching fund.

At last I wrote to the foundation reporting my total failure. Months later a phone call came to the office from another foundation and reported that it was interested in building a school in Orissa. I told about the $75,000 offer for a Balasore school and was told that

The Orissa 18,000 square foot,
rent-free building

they probably could match it. They did and they built the school. I had asked for funds for a two-story 12,000 square foot building. They actually built 18,000 square feet at a much higher cost than $150,000. So Rev. Hrudaya now has a large school building for his three schools, all rent-free.

In that period, Mike and Sharon Adams were ER missionaries in Hyderabad and Bangalore. Their new baby had acute asthma and they had to leave India. Happily, they interested Scott and Brenda Powell in portable Bible schools and they offered to work with us. They lived in Madras but they urged us to establish ER in Delhi in the north. Scott sent a pastor to northern states to meet leading churchmen and he returned with names and addresses of men who were to become directors of our schools of evangelism. Thanks to this information Thelma and I traveled to Calcutta, Bihar, Uttar Pradesh and Delhi, meeting leaders in many cities of the North.

We were looking for an ER office and considered Calcutta and Delhi. Delhi won. Gene Robinette was with us on the trip. He agreed to serve as an ER missionary and rented an apartment in Delhi. His first assignment was to visit our schools of evangelism and oversee portable Bible schools. ER was thus planted in India.

ER's entrance into India can only be considered a miracle from the amazing God we serve. How could aging missionaries, veterans of a long lifetime of service in Africa, be transplanted to Asia and find there an open welcoming door for the establishment of an extremely fruitful evangelism program and of tens of schools?

This is the work of God. Our amazing God.

25

DANI

The February 1998 trip through northern states peaked in a meeting of churchmen in Allahabad. The meeting itself was like others before. After the audience listened they responded with explanations why portable Bible schools, schools of evangelism and statewide movements would not work there. Actually, nothing we proposed was acted upon anywhere on that whole trip.

What made the trip valuable was that we met Bishop Stephens of the Church of North India and his head of evangelism, Rev. Stephen Rawate. Later we were to meet the Solomon Bodhans, who were to become the leaders of DANI, the Decade of Advance for North India. It was the Bishop's reprimand to his churchmen for their negative responses and his strong evangelical statement to them that imprinted itself upon my heart. In conversation with him later we learned that there was a second bishop in Agra. It was a long way to go but we drove there to see him, and he too spoke as a born-again proponent of church growth and evangelism. It was the very positive and zealous response of these two men, both of whom had a department of evangelism, which led to the concept of a special movement for the twelve states of North India.

ER had learned that great advances came from the inspiration of leaders of denominations to press forward in new outreach efforts rather than from conferences. These men brought exciting ways to grow to the forefront and this had value and needed to be shared.

Great cathedrals all over Europe are almost empty on Sundays. Why? I suspect it is boredom. Peasants were once drawn to these magnificent buildings and the colorful robes of priests and pastors. But when citizens worked in skyscrapers, lived in air-conditioned houses and had an education equal to the preacher's, the chilly cathedral didn't look good to them any more. And movies and TV made the old pastor's homilies sound quite dull. Modern people live in a culture vastly different from that which built the cathedral. But their denominations often insist on doing everything exactly as they did when Luther was alive.

In Africa, daughter churches imitated their foreign mother church – and in India it was the same. Handsome cathedrals in India are often nearly empty too. They were crowded when British government officials and army officers abounded. Indians who wanted well-paid jobs or powerful positions improved their chances by attending church in those days.

In these days, the only large group in attendance is made up of uniformed schoolgirls sitting together row after row. One or two dozen others straggle into the vast building. An ancient pump organ wheezes under the feet and fingers of a very, very old man. This could change if denominations could be brought together to share, pray and learn from one another.

The Bishops' Council in Allahabad January, 1999

June of 1998 saw planning for the Decade of Advance in North India and ten state Harvest Network conferences. At this time we began to see the value of bringing together key leaders with inspiration and vision. In 1999 DANI was launched at a Bishops' Council in Allahabad. It opened an office in Delhi and engaged Rev. Solomon Bodhan as executive director. He served one year. His successor is Rev. Stephen Rawate.

This letter is typical of many commenting upon the Allahabad meeting: "*First of all, let me congratulate you with much appreciation for the successful and blessed DANI inauguration conference at Allahabad. I, as a North Indian, am very thankful to God that the much-awaited move of the Lord has finally begun in North India. Praise the Lord! Hallelujah!"* - from a letter from Rev. W. A. Baria, Gujarat, India.

Dr. Luis Bush, International Director of AD 2000 and Beyond wrote this about the DANI movement: *"The decisions made and work-outreach items outlined for the Decade of Advance in North India seem well thought out, most do-able via God's provision and blessings, and compelling in total vision, purpose and inspiration. May God bless this movement mightily for His eternal purposes through His servants there in India – with prayers and support from those beyond."*

DANI drew upon the AD 2000 idea of "tracks" (departments). It drew also upon the Zaire movement, but instead of providing 24 Proposals for Progress for two years it will provide 480 proposals over ten years. Every three months a set of twelve proposals, one for each of the twelve departments, is sent directly to the headquarters offices of 900 heads of denominations.

In addition, DANI calls upon each of those 900 CEOs to launch a major campaign to advance in all directions in every congregation with these Proposals for Progress. Each is to name an Advance Team of twelve members, each representing one of the twelve departments. And each is to faithfully meet with his Advance Team each month and seriously evaluate every Proposal for Progress for its possible usefulness to his denomination. Those proposals approved by the CEO are assigned to the proper department representative to be developed.

There is more. Each CEO is encouraged to request each district superintendent to name a district Advance Team and then to ask every congregation, urban or rural, to name its Advance Team. The result is a network of teams ready and able to participate in every project the CEO sends to them.

The constant challenge of proposals received and the monthly strategy meetings of the CEO and his Advance Team are bound to inspire many, many dramatic advances throughout the year. Continued over ten years, advancing becomes a way of life. And life is the right word. Those empty cathedrals will fill up as new life flows through them to the populace.

Look at it this way. If all the Church does week after week is what mortal man can do, where is God included in the agenda? Much more gifted and interesting men are performing on TV and in movies. And for young people, boating and racing and fishing and driving and tennis and golf and shooting and visiting are more attractive than listening to a listless sermon. The world has changed enormously from the days of poor, weary, worried farmers to whom going to church was the bright spot of the week.

The willingness, then the eagerness of a CEO to add to the church calendar many new activities to reach out to seekers in new ways involves many more disciples, and each effort opens the door to the indwelling Holy Spirit in those disciples to do exploits in and through them. God moves into the congregation as the congregation stretches to serve Him in more ways, using more witnesses. DANI brings God into the action as the action spreads and covers the Body of whole districts and every congregation.

The reason why DANI was of major importance to India's Church was only partially clear to us when it began. We had seen 24 proposals sent to 17,000 pastors of Zaire bring enormous advances over 34 years. We knew that a simple office could inspire and challenge a whole nation. We knew India's Church was largely young and lacked widespread publications that kept new ministries reaching heads of denominations. Those were our foundational premises in 1998 and 1999, but in 2000 amazing news reached us – that in the past decade India had tripled her number of congregations.

This was an awesome advance worthy of endless praise. BUT the "blessing" faced denominations with a real crisis. Collectively they needed 200,000 more pastors and 20,000 more each year, not to mention 10,000 replacements a year for those retired and expired. These "green" or inexperienced pastors needed mentoring in their first years of ministry to encourage and guide them. Another 200,000 or 220,000 new churches, new bodies of elders, new Sunday schools, new everything was needed.

No nation has ever faced such an enormous need before. If India were wealthy it could, perhaps, have solved many of its problems by building more schools and more churches, printing more literature and hiring more district superintendents. But India is not rich and

Christians are its poorest people – the unscheduled castes, the tribals, the Dalits. Saved from their sin and social restraints they are moving upward, but are yet poor. Denominations cannot buy their way out of such tremendous needs as they face.

DANI cannot supply the vast funds needed, but it does supply essential information to this Church. When DANI began, the Hindu government was ratcheting up persecution of Christians in Orissa and Gujarat states because so many tribals were coming to Christ. For a year, heads of denominations tended to cancel out evangelism, to close down outreach, to batten down the hatches. DANI publications flowed into the offices of all North India's denominational leaders urging non-stop advances. No one talks about slowing down now, three years later.

The focus of DANI has shifted to a key need for every denomination to take inventory of its own growth crisis. Heads of small denominations probably know how many congregations they have and their needs. But a denomination that had 1000 churches in 1990 may have 3200, or 2600, or who knows how many? No one but God. DANI is urging every denomination to take a careful survey of every congregation to learn the needs of each and to learn the true total needs for more pastors, for church buildings, for mentors of inexperienced pastors, etc. Without such data, heads of denominations cannot plan adequate advances. DANI has sent to 900 denominations survey forms and survey gathering sheets which will provide the figures needed for comprehensive planning.

The major focus of the 1990s was on church planting. A graduate of one of our schools of evangelism can plant five new congregations in as many years, but he can pastor only one of them adequately. The other four exist in hostile communities and stand a good chance of failing. Those villages where a Christian congregation struggles and dies come to believe that Christianity is unfit for India. There will be fierce resistance to a second effort to plant a congregation.

Denominations must recognize that this is a new era in the Church, an era of crash consolidation of gains already made. This reality has not largely dawned upon leaders whose job description for decades has been to maintain traditions and be the decorative symbol of the denomination in major events. Missing in this job description was a concern for new, small congregations. Prior to the '90s there were not enough new churches to bother about. This is a new era. New churches now must become the major concern of churchmen. DANI is the spokesman to denominations of all India, calling them to give the leadership needed in today's crisis of struggling new churches.

DANI completed the first quarter of its ten-year publishing program in December of 2001. It has had a DANI council meeting each year and that Council voted to begin a DANEI Council in Northeast India, a DASI Council in South India and an AIDA High Council for All India.

Separate annual conferences are scheduled for DANI, DANEI and DASI and an annual conference for AIDA High Council.

Why? These regional conferences give opportunity for annual plans to be developed for some or all states in each region. By bringing leaders together each year on these levels, creative advances can be multiplied and expanded.

Our Lord pled for unity among His Apostles. He demanded it. Judas rebelled against this and ended up betraying Jesus and hanging himself. Peter publicly denied his relationship with Jesus to avoid embarrassment. It was a forgivable sin and Jesus' treatment of the sinner is carefully recorded in the "Peter, lovest thou me?" dialogue. Peter was back in the fold and still its leader.

After Jesus returned to the Father, it was Peter who kept the Apostles united. They named others to oversee the feeding of needy Christians. They met together to seek the mind of God and make decisions for the whole Church. When Paul brought up the question of the Gentile Christians, the Apostles met and listed a series of rules to be obeyed everywhere.

The Church grew as new house churches were added in Israel, Syria, Turkey, Greece and Italy. We read that believers of various house churches visited from house to house, creating the unity the Lord had required. More and more Christian evangelists, like Paul, joined the widespread Church, but the Apostles in Jerusalem maintained the togetherness of all, meeting often to respond to growing and changing needs.

The unity our Master wanted for His Church is growing strong in India. Denominations have not abandoned their "distinctives" in doctrine and practice, but they do not use them as a high wall. Rather, they accept the right of each denomination to cherish its uniqueness and its history. But they share a sense of togetherness in many, many ways. One of these is a profound appreciation for DANI's contribution to all denominations month by month.

The purpose here is not to create a great name, a great power base, a great movement. It is, rather, to bring together eager servants of the Master in a oneness of fellowship, a oneness of faith and expectation that God can work through. Titles, degrees, honors, politics and personal agendas should not figure largely in these conferences. It is a humble seeking of God's will which is wanted, with the confidence that He meant it when He told His servants, "Seek and you shall find." Such humility, such seeking, such purposing is bound to be rewarded by the Holy Spirit in ways beyond imagining. Seeking and finding under His initiative year after year for all denominations of all India is a noble enterprise, one fulfilling the prayer of Jesus for oneness of His people following New Testament patterns.

India is the world's second-largest nation, over a billion strong. Soon it will have more Christian churches than any other nation. Then I believe it will have more believers than any other nation. DANI has a major role to play in this miracle of the last days.

I cannot explain why, except to say that just as the Master laid the Pygmy race on my heart in 1989, He also laid India there. Why? Perhaps because I was listening for His voice. We had a great International Center of Evangelism which was impacting large areas of Africa. Who was better placed to church the Pygmies?

Similarly, having led the Christ for All national movement in Zaire and the Alliance Key '73 movement in the U.S. and Canada, and having inspired Central African Republic, Cameroon, Ghana and Burundi to begin national movements, who was more experienced and available for DANI?

The Lord from ages past asks the question, "Whom shall I send and who will go for us?" and ordinary no-bodies step forward and say, "Here am I, Lord, send me." God uses what is available. The pot is just clay. It is the indwelling Holy Spirit who does God's work, and the commoner the pot, the more visible the Spirit of the living God. Praise His Name!

· ·

Neighbor nations to the east and southeast of India have used the Indian proposals with adaptations since 2000, and Nepal to the north began in 2002. Pakistan to the west has churchmen interested in them. English-speaking nations of Africa, twenty of them, are expected to receive Africanized versions of India's proposals in 2003. French-speaking nations should follow. Arabic, Portuguese and Spanish mailings are being considered. The principles of the Decade of Advance are biblical and proven to be effective. Jesus' instructions to Peter tell us what was most on His resurrected heart: "Feed My sheep, feed My lambs, feed My sheep." Proposals for Progress are an almost endless supply of sheep food being made available over ten long, fattening, inspiring years.

That kind of food is needed in almost 200 nations of our world and it could be called a Peter Mission to the World!

26

AIDA

In February of 2002 a major advance was made, as the All-India Decade of Advance became a reality. The original DANI Council voted for the formation of an AIDA High Council to supercede it and for DANEI Council and DASI Council to be named to represent Northeast India and South India. These three regional councils met in November 2002, separately, to report state by state on what God is blessing in their state's denominations.

In order to broaden the scope of each state's report, each state delegate asked eleven other CEOs of denominations to answer a questionnaire about their denominations' experiences of God's blessing. This would bring to 336 CEOs the number reporting on their 28 states. Having participated in this way, CEOs would be curious to learn what the regional council did with their reports. These reports collectively became a national package, distilled, state by state, into a presentation read to the regional councils and then discussed and evaluated for inclusion among great ministries for 2003. The focus was, "What is God blessing greatly? Can it be replicated widely in 2003?" Twenty-nine greatly blessed ministries that are not already in wide usage were described for all in an 80-page *AIDA PACKAGE 2003*.

These were printed for all CEOs and were much discussed in ten state CEO Work Conferences in order to thoroughly acquaint all CEOs with the possibilities of each item. In essence, a national survey of all that can be learned by three regional councils was now presented in selective detail to all of India's heads of denominations so they could individually make up their own agenda for advance in 2003. The goal was to motivate maximum growth in Earth's second-largest nation.

After the ten-state CEO Work Conferences in January, AIDA met in March 2003. Its composition consisted of four members of each of the three regional councils. They reported on their council experience and their conferences, giving AIDA much to discuss, reflect on, evaluate and to act upon. AIDA is a national body with national as well as regional interests. It considers events, projects and ministries that might be attempted on a national, state or denominational scale.

In each state the state delegate invited his eleven CEOs to become a State Advance Team. Fifteen states now have Advance Teams. Each is a separate entity, free to draw upon all of the discussions of councils, conferences and AIDA and make their own State Advance Team plans for statewide events, seminars or projects which can help all denominations.

In one very bold stroke AIDA offers to India's other states what ER gave to Orissa in 1993. It has taken time to reach this point where a nation can be given a mighty boost, but the time has come and ER needs to act as God's ambassador – doubting nothing.

It should be noted that ER has diligently worked on its foundational organization, slowly building a network that is national. It has also worked very, very diligently on its content, or ministries. The untiring flow of *Proposals for Progress* has won the respect of India's churchmen and they are using them to their great gain.

216

Stephen and Shanti Rawate,
AIDA's able directors in India

There have been those who questioned the validity of sending out proposals. "Who uses them?" was the query. It was an inevitable question that had to be answered. Before beginning DANI it was seen that this could not change a nation overnight, or even in a year. Ten years was the realistic period chosen. Congo's Christ for All movement taught us how slowly denominations changed their agendas. But it taught us that they could and would change, not because of a proposal in the mail so much as because they saw their neighbor denomination doing something that was bringing it growth. We copy from each other much more quickly than we act on some printed proposals. But to get the copying going, printed proposals do show a few daring souls how to begin a new ministry.

We receive enthusiastic letters from such daring souls who launched out and harvested richly. Not many – yet. But the process has begun. We urge our School of Evangelism directors to teach and use *Proposals for Progress*. They are reporting that, yes, they are doing so. Far more revealing were the figures received from them in February 2002, in which I learned that 14 directors of our then 15 schools of evangelism are now CEOs of their own denominations, and that in an average of four years they planted 550 new congregations that last year baptized 4076 people. A director of one of ER's Schools of Evangelism baptized 1006 people in 2002 and over 700 by July of 2003.

What explains this phenomenal growth? The lessons of the 16 courses of the School of Evangelism curriculum are an important factor. Half of our directors did not head a denomination when they began our schools. Teaching the courses obviously led them to plant churches and begin a denomination. What else? The teachers are seriously teaching *Proposals for Progress*. Are they using these proposals? Oh, yes! This is the one group of churchmen in India that is really studying proposals with a purpose. And it is possibly the fastest growing fellowship of denominations in India.

It will take more time to get figures for the whole nation, but when they are in hand no one will question that AIDA was a watershed in church growth for this nation.

WHAT HAS AIDA ACHIEVED?

An Evangelism Resources Board member asked the question, "What has AIDA actually achieved?" Here are some achievements worth noting:

1. It has already created the largest body of very useable church growth plans available anywhere and will more than double that in five years ahead.

2. It has mailed to the headquarters of over 900 denominations a quarterly *ADVANCE* newsmagazine and a quarterly set of 12 *Proposals for Progress* over five years, with five to go, steadily challenging heads of denominations to give creative leadership to their congregations during a decade of their administration. The goal is to mentor a generation of eager, God-driven strategists.

3. AIDA has urged heads of denominations to name separate committees for women's ministries, men's ministries, youth ministries, children's ministries, etc., to plan annual calendars of events, conferences, camps and retreats for the whole denomination.

4. No one else is sponsoring every-state CEO Work Conferences where the men who administer the Church and who have authority and funds to make great new advances happen across the nation meet

and discuss the agenda given them in the new *AIDA PACKAGEs*. In fact, all of the items listed above are AIDA contributions to the Church of our Lord in India. And AIDA is Evangelism Resources' gift to God in India.

As India's denominational heads meet together and talk over the agenda items, they inevitably compare them to their own experiences. They hear from each other what kinds of ministry are bringing tribes to God, reaching youth, and involving men or women in new ways. They resolve to do what other admired leaders are doing. Here mere information evolves to challenges accepted. Bishops take ownership of proposals and put them to work when they return home. This is the long-term goal of ER and of AIDA. And here is where and when it happens.

Decade of Advance in Myanmar, DAM,
is an outgrowth of AIDA.

The AIDA National Council in April reports on what happened in the 27 State CEO Work Conferences and in State Advance Teams as a national report. It evaluates results. It plans for the future. It explores possible national events and it relates to top nationally active churchmen, seeking their notions of how AIDA can best serve the Church in its many parts. AIDA sees itself as a servant and not, in any sense, a master. It seeks to maximize its usefulness. It is wide open to suggestions. It gladly publishes articles by churchmen and advertises to everyone the good things offered by other agencies. It labors to make all useful ideas and materials known to all denominations so that new and old, small and large, are equally aware of options available to them.

State Advance Teams merit a description here. There were none in India in 1990. In 1991 we described the wonderful growth Congo experienced because of Christ for All, the national movement of evangelism, to the Orissa delegates at our two-week seminar there. Happily, Orissa State had a man who passionately longed for the Church in his state to grow. He learned of the basic principles of a national movement and began to spread the news to heads of denominations of Orissa. The results were phenomenal. Orissa had been losing ground for years. Missions and churches closed. Hope was gone. The Orissa Plan, which we prepared, was not immediately welcomed, but little by little leaders saw remarkable growth occurring where the plan was in use. Thousands of new workers were trained in portable Bible schools, hundreds in schools of evangelism. Hundreds of new churches were planted. Tribes were churched. In a statewide crisis, Protestants built a hundred homes for the homeless, took in orphans and supplied goats where poor families had lost theirs. Growth was excellent over a decade.

Other states copied Orissa to some extent. But only in 2002, ten years after Orissa began, were almost half the states of India manned with AIDA-inspired State Advance Teams. In 2003 AIDA published its first booklet for those teams. It is called *SAT-urate* and it provided an accurate report on the *SATs* and their early agendas and goals. Their reason for being is to constantly plan advances for the denominations of their states. They are the single organization in their states which serve all the denominations equally on a statewide basis.

They can develop marvelous ministries as they gain experience, vision and faith in the Almighty.

It should be remembered that these states, in many cases, have larger populations than great nations around the world. The fifteen states with teams have a combined population of 421,000,000, far bigger than the population of Canada, the USA and Mexico combined. We are not fiddling around in India.

FROM NOW ON

ER's unique ministry is its Decade of Advance in four Asian nations and in Africa's English-speaking nations. Our schools have great value, but other missions have schools and more will come along. If ER ceased to fund schools it would be a serious loss, but schools are popular and familiar and easily begun by whoever wants to begin them.

Not so the Decade of Advance. It stands alone in the world of missions, and the Spirit of God is still developing its scope and acceptance in India's original role model and in its imitators of Asia and Africa. As year four begins in India, the literature production carries on smoothly and on schedule, reflecting discoveries being made as the Church faces persecution, plants amazing numbers of new congregations and finds itself in a crisis of need for more pastors, church buildings, teaching of elders, deacons, Sunday school workers, prayer warriors, witnesses, etc. These needs are unexpected, unprepared for, even unknown by many heads of denominations who, in past decades, had such little church growth they paid no attention to the few new congregations.

This is a new day, with 20,000 new congregations being added yearly and a probable loss of over 6000 pastors to retirement and death. Training 26,000 men as new pastors each year is an incredible responsibility, but mentoring them, equipping them and providing needed literature for them as they begin their ministries is an administrative necessity for which there has been no past example. The 480 *Proposals for Progress* being mailed to heads of denominations over ten years is the sole ministry of its kind in the world.

Shaped to each continent's special needs, the Indian model brings to nations and their denominations resources that will enrich the Church steadily. Christian universities have maintained departments of Christian education for over half a century. Both my sister Dorothy and my eldest son Christian earned doctorates in this area of study. To me, the *Proposals for Progress* are the finest product of Christian education, for they focus on the heads of denominations where policy is conceived and carried out in the blossoming Third World countries. They are the apex of missions in that they provide a developing system of evaluating real needs of young denominations and of meeting those needs. No similar long-term research and response program has been made available to the young churches, and I believe it is God's provision for these days when so much of the Christian world has had only the example of western nominalism to follow.

Back home in Europe and America those role models are seeing their own populations abandon them for atheism or re-creations of ancient religions. It is as if the Spirit of God has wearied of us and our turning away from the Holy Word of God and from Jesus who set us free and made us rich and powerful and sophisticated in knowledge, but faithless in our hearts. In times of crisis we rush back to Him in shallow allegiance, but we are uncomfortable at His feet and drift away as soon as our fears abate, back to our God-lessness. We seem to have decided that we don't need God in the West.

Third World nations need God. They are emerging from paganism and poverty and live their whole lives as times of crisis. Wars, depression, early death, political violence and decadence, social injustice, ignorance and myth and hopelessness are the way of life. When Jesus is made high and lifted up, hope and peace enter society like a brilliant, sun-filled dawn after a crashing, hurricane-filled night. Hearts sense the forgiveness of their sins and the cleanness of their souls and of a world in which holiness and sweet obedience bring in a whole new kingdom of light and bright hope.

This is not just another god, this is the Creator, Savior of all mankind and the Host of the redeemed throughout eternity. No wonder students write of peace flooding their hearts when they come to the

Savior! In each case He commands the storm-driven waves of their private Galilee, "Peace, be still," and there is wondrous peace.

In this Third World, young believers in young churches face hostile societies of Hindu or tribal parents whose sons have been stolen from them by Christians. They despise these sons and drive them out. They hate the Christians and beat their leaders and burn their churches. They harass and threaten the "little flock" of the Good Shepherd and do all they can to destroy it. They want their sons and daughters back in the family, safely Hindu once more. The little flock faces big problems from the majority population in every one of the 200,000 congregations begun in the last ten years.

One hundred and twenty *Proposals for Progress*, with 360 to come, will make available the largest and most varied collection of practical options and resources ever assembled for the young churches of the world. These are especially valuable as a decade of continuous inspiration, in sets of twelve proposals, rather than as a ponderous volume of 600 pages, to be leafed through for fifteen minutes and forgotten. It is hard to forget 40 mailings spaced over ten years.

It is a fast-changing world. At this point it seems probable that this ER-sponsored movement will spread far and wide in developing nations. It is the one unique ER ministry and it is meeting real needs in Asia and soon in Africa, Latin America and the Islands. One day, China too can be greatly blessed by the treasure of proposals and annual conferences of council delegates who draw on the treasure to plan deeper and larger involvement in church planting and church strengthening for all denominations.

This is my prayer and purpose as long as the Master keeps us on the firing line of global missions.

SECTION FIVE

GIFTS FROM GOD

27

THREE BRAUN BOYS

CHRIS

An outstanding missionary doctor was in Kinshasa on February 26, 1949. We had entertained him for dinner the night before. He was Glen Tuttle, the personal physician of President Kasa Vubu and the builder of the large Kimpese Hospital. We awakened him to oversee the birth of Chris. His charge for services rendered was $15. We paid cash and gave him a watercolor painting by an English missionary who supported his mission with his beautiful, professional art.

Chris came two months ahead of time and weighed three pounds and four ounces. He lay in a basket lined with cotton baby blankets with two mason jars of hot water as an incubator. Mosquito netting protected him from flies, mosquitoes, roaches, mice, centipedes, etc. Catholic sisters were his caretakers. His chances of survival were so small that the hospital didn't bother to announce his birth to the newspaper, a normal courtesy. I had to do that myself.

Well, sir, Chris made it. I was awed by the number of items I was required to purchase at the pharmacy for that wee bit of humanity. While Mama was in the hospital with Chris I worked doubly hard every day, full of confidence that the Lord was in charge of my family. It was only as I drove out to the hospital each evening that my faith began to waver. Seeing them both in health restored my peace for another lonely night and long day. At last I was able to bring them home.

An incident I recall in that first year was the visit of our dear friends, the Osts. They had a husky two-year-old who learned to love tools from his architect father. One day he was standing over fragile, tiny Chris with a hammer in his hand. It was a frightening contrast.

Sonny was a sweetheart of a boy. But his strength and the hammer were a picture I never forgot.

Chris had amazing resistance to sickness. Kinshasa can get very cold at night in the dry season. Many a night I woke up to feed and change the wee babe and found his blankets off, his diaper wet and his limbs icy cold. Scared me silly every time. But it didn't seem to matter at all to Chris.

We took him to America on our first furlough and Chris was an immediate favorite with everyone. Full of smiles, happy to be held by anyone and everyone, he seemed born to please. He never lost that characteristic. And he was on the move. One winter day we couldn't find him in the house. There was an unheated second floor that we never used, but high up the stairs is where our mini-traveler was found. Months away from walking he was a veteran crawler.

We were assigned to Kinkonzi station for our second term. Dr. and Mrs. Dean Kroh were there with their twins, Davey and Danny. Cute as could be, they were built to play quarterback. Big and

Chris and Marcia

228

always double, they overarched wee Chris five to one. I thought they resembled a little fawn with two bull calves, solid, sure, curious about this li'l fellow. I guess growing up with such odds one learns to please.

Chris loved chickens, monkeys, puppies, kittens. He had plenty of them and feared none. One day our baboon broke his chain. This animal had jaws that could crack hard palm nuts with ease. When two Congolese saw the baboon come up the stairs they fled into the house, leaving Chris alone with the beast. He would not let me get near him because he never forgot that I had tied him up in the beginning. It was Mama who walked up to him, held on until I could get there and retie him. The baboon, nearly as large as Chris, could face down a large police dog and was Chris' buddy. They spent hours together before and after this event.

Chris loved sports and was catcher for his high school baseball team – as I had been for mine. He played the trumpet and edited the high school newspaper. In a school badly warped by children of aggressively liberal missionaries, kids who would refuse to enter the church and who scoffed at the Bible, Chris retained his faith in God and his divine call to missions. He served God in Zaire, Gabon and Ivory Coast and is now Rev. Christian Kenneth Braun, Ph.D., regional director for all Alliance fields in Africa.

But first there was Biola College where he met Marcia Mordhorst and married her. They had two great kids, Josh and Alicia. Her tiny fingers I taught to write A.L.I.C… , etc.

PAUL

The arrival of Paul was very different from that of Chris. We were at Kinkonzi Bible Institute and Dr. and Mrs. Dean Kroh, happily, lived there. Paul was born in our home, a full-term baby. The evening was more like a party than a birthing. We laughed through the whole time, Thelma as well. Once the pains subsided there was another joke and peals of laughter. In no time the baby was born and I took a pocket full of change, went outside with my shotgun and banged away until a crowd of African boys came out of the night to see what was happening. Amidst coins tossed all around I announced that Willys

Paul Braun was a member of the mission community and the next day the news spread everywhere.

With a big brother as a role model, Paul grew up rapidly and happily. On furlough we took our two boys to see Mother and Dorothy. I was present when Dorothy and Chris were together. Dorothy said to us, "Chris is so cute!" Whereupon Chris piped up, "Huh, if you think I'm cute, wait till you see my little brother Paul." Paul was a ball of fun. Before he could talk he was singing harmony. When it was his turn to pray he said, "Huh, huh, huh, huh; huh, huh, huh, huh; huh, huh, huh, huh, amen." The rhythm and ups and downs of his "huhs" sounded just like adult prayer.

Paul and Nancy

Paul had a boa constrictor at Nyack College. One summer, to earn money for tuition he sold Christian books in the south. The snake he kept in a cardboard box in a dresser drawer of his motel. While he was out selling, a black maid went in to change linens and noted a drawer was partly open in the dresser. She pushed it, but it wouldn't close. Something soft was keeping it open. Pulling the drawer out she reached in to remove the obstacle and, lo, her hand grabbed – a SNAKE. She was absent from work for several days.

The motel man investigated and insisted Paul take the snake out of the room forever. He put it in the same cardboard box in the trunk of his car. One day there was no snake. Weeks went by. No snake. Paul covered thousands of miles and came to our house in Lexington, Kentucky. The car had problems. We worked on it, took out seats and, yep, there was the snake wound around the springs. We took his tail and pulled mightily. He did not want to leave those springs. We were the stronger. When he finally released them and came loose he was fighting mad. We dropped him on the grass and let him cool down to his normal sweet disposition.

At Nyack, Paul married Nancy Van Kurin. They have three children, Michael, Matthew and Melinda. These are winners too. They get great grades, are musical, and Matt is a long-distance runner with a room full of trophies. They all love the Savior and are handsome, top-flight people in every way. I'll say no more.

PHILIP

Thelma's childbearing pattern was timed perfectly for our missionary work. We were married seven years before Chris joined us. Five years later Paul came along and five years more Phil joined us. If they had come closer together they could well have overwhelmed Thelma's professional ministries. Spaced far apart as they were, she hardly interrupted her daily schedule as a teacher, choir director of music, pianist, organist, author, etc.

Philip had two role models to grow up with. He was a very contented boy and quite convinced at ten that he was going on twenty. Even as a tyke he had answers. One day in Lukula he was feeding his

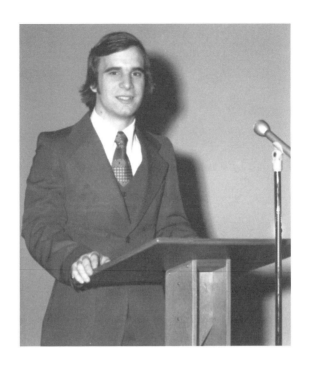

Phil Braun

puppy expensive peanuts. Thelma, hoping to stop the drain on her peanuts, stated officially, "Phil, dogs don't eat peanuts." Phil's huffy response, with finger pointing stiffly at his pooch, was, "Dogs is eating peanuts." Sure enough dogs was….

Several years later, in Kinshasa, Phil had two dogs. Chris and Paul loved to sing. Thelma would play songs they enjoyed and Mr. 17 and Mr. 12 would sing in fine harmony. Mr. 7 joined in, his neck straining for equal volume and both dogs howling to high heaven. What a quintet they were.

At seventeen Phil had a guitar and loud speaker system and sang in churches. He had the leading role in *No, No Nanette*, his high school's senior play, and discovered the excitement of a busy social life. His sport was soccer. He loved it.

At Asbury College he lived in a dorm room with three other freshmen. It was too much society. His grades plunged. He went to the University of Kentucky and lost interest in school.

It was in 1980 that Thelma and I went back to Africa with ER. Phil drove to California and entered Biola where his Aunt Dorothy and Grandmother lived. In four happy years he graduated and wrote to us indicating he would like to join us in Kinshasa. We were all alone and welcomed him with delight. He was a dedicated, loving partner and fulfilled our highest hopes for him day after day.

He knew a lot about electronics and installed a fine p.a. system in the International Church. We were building a small recording studio and he took that over very nicely. He went on a three-week evangelism trip with four African evangelists in the Plateau of the Bateke and came back thrilled with what God had done. Converted Bateke chiefs gave him a goat and a pig, which he brought home.

Phil brought home his gift.

Phil was supremely happy back in Kinshasa. He planned for a lady friend to visit him at Christmas and, if all went well, to ask her to marry him. He wanted to see how she responded to African life first.

Phil lighted up our lives. He was a very thoughtful and loving son and played an eager, active role in all the ministries we were developing. At the time, there were two other Biola grads in Kinshasa and a large number of young people from other schools. They had a busy social life, especially on weekends. On one of those weekends the young crowd drove down to Crocodile Beach. On the way, on a narrow jungle path they passed a small, isolated village. Phil talked to Christians there and they invited him to preach the next Sunday. He did.

The following Saturday the young folks went back. Crocodile Beach was a dramatic piece of scenery. The Zaire River rushed between twisting canyon walls into a wide, flat area. Floods had deposited sand on wide beaches and washed the soil away from enormous boulders on the shore, and the riverbed was crowded with these boulders which shot the water up twenty feet in the air and created broad, sluggish whirlpools on the surface.

Along these dramatic beaches, shifting river currents created quiet, shallow backwaters here and there which were ideal for swimming. They were, however, invaded from time to time by rushing water, which could sweep swimmers out into the riotous mainstream. A missionary's daughter was relaxing in such a backwater when a massive invasion of current swept her out from shore. Several boys were on the bank and saw this happen. Phil shouted, "Come on, fellows, let's help Cindy." He jumped in. The others did not. For about two miles the young people followed the two along the water's edge. At one point the current swept Cindy into another quiet backwater on the Zaire side and she was safe. Phil was caught by another current and washed across the vast river toward the Congo side and disappeared, never to be seen again.

A helicopter, plane and ground search parties covered the area to no avail. A month later, a memorial service was held with Phil's brothers present. The Comforter did his divine work in our hearts.

Hundreds gathered for the memorial service.

Phil was with his Lord. We did not know it then, but we had decades of mission work to do before we could join him. We thank our God on every remembrance of him for the years he lighted our lives.

. . . .

For several happy years the Chris Braun family was our neighbor at the International Center of Evangelism. Wonderful people. The second large school building was built because of Chris' eagerness to begin an International School of Christian Education. That school is in its twelfth year now, I believe. The evacuation of 1992 and destruction and violence in the city that caused it resulted in a deadly dismantling of those institutions which had made family life livable in Kinshasa. Chris could not bring himself to take his family back to Kinshasa. Understandably, many families left Zaire forever at that time and the exodus of missions became almost total. The years the Chris Brauns were there left strong, beneficial fruit at the Center and in the lives of the family and added new dimensions to their future ministries.

In 1999 Paul became president of Evangelism Resources. In that year the staff left our house and moved into its new office. Timing was right. The glut of new responsibilities in Asia has filled my time, my thoughts and my energy. I have none left over for administration. A new broom sweeps clean is an old adage which applies nicely in this case. Paul is on the move at age 46, sweeping very clean. ER ministries are covering more and more of Africa and Asia, demanding more income, more visits, more decisions, more attention and work.

We have feelers out to China, Malaysia, Indonesia, Ghana, Ivory Coast and Angola at present. In which of these the Lord will ask us to work we do not yet know. Time will tell!

As this chapter ends I am very aware that I have not given their due to Marcia and Nancy, both beautiful Christian wives and mothers who have kept their husbands' love, their children excelling and following the Lord. Both are professional women admired by all. I leave the finer details to their proud husbands to record for posterity. And of course, there is so much that God has poured into their very fulfilling lives that I have not even begun to relate. They will write their own books when the time comes.

The Braun Family in 1995
Front Row: Marcia, Alicia, Willys, Thelma, Mindy
Back Row: Chris, Josh, Paul, Mike, Matt, Nancy

28

THE HOUSE

Rev. Donald Shepson and his wife Dorothy were beautiful people. We met them in 1943 at a young people's rally where Don was the speaker. What a dynamic preacher he was! I was 26 at the time, attending Nyack Missionary Training Institute as required by the C&MA for applicants for overseas service. Thelma and I also pastored Nyack's Old Stone Church and we had taken some of our young people to the rally up near Hyde Park on the Hudson River.

Don was about my age but he seemed older to me. He pastored a fast-growing congregation across the river from Nyack and was already on the Board of Managers of The Christian and Missionary Alliance denomination.

Looking back I can see the way God moved. It was our pastoral duty to take the young people to the rally. There we met the Shepsons and admired them at once. On that first meeting we asked Don to preach a week at our church.

Don and Dottie Shepson

We became fast friends in that short time.

Thelma's playing and singing impressed Don. The next summer he rented an empty building in downtown White Plains for special Saturday-night evangelistic services. Thelma was asked to play and sing each Saturday for the series and I did a chalk-talk. Outstanding speakers were invited to preach in those services. I recall Dr. V. Raymond Edman, president of Wheaton College, and Dr. William Ward Ayers, distinguished pastor of Calvary Baptist Church in New York City. His Sunday morning radio broadcasts came on as our wee Old Stone Church congregation was going home. Sunday after Sunday I had listened to this master preacher's powerful messages just after I had preached my own. This Saturday evening I shared the pulpit with him for a brief moment in time.

One of the speakers was a one-of-a-kind Alliance district superintendent, Rev. H. E. Nelson. Since he lived in Nyack as we did, he invited us to ride with him and his wife. I did my best to make small talk to brighten up the half-hour trip, but there was no response from Mrs. Nelson in the back seat and only discouraging grunts from the driver. After a few minutes I became a silent passenger wondering how this discourteous, tiresome old man ever became a district superintendent.

I found out in the service. After being introduced, he greeted the audience solemnly, read from the Gospel of John, chapter three, of Nicodemus' secret conversation with Jesus in the dead of night. At that point the audience may well have felt they were in for a rather dead evening. But Howard Nelson turned out to be a very entertaining man. For half an hour he kept everyone in that service alive with laughter. Then for ten minutes he preached the most soul-wrenching salvation message I have ever heard and gave an invitation to repentant sinners to come forward and beg God for His pardon and salvation. More people responded that night than any before or after.

On the way home the preacher chatted incessantly. So occupied was he with his conversation that he missed the turn to Nyack and we found ourselves back in White Plains where we had started. The ride home was hilarious. Even Mrs. Nelson chuckled quietly in the back seat.

My classes on homiletics never got close to the preaching style of Rev. Nelson. Our professor was a classical orator and focused mainly on outlines and content. The Nelson sermon would have horrified him but many listeners came to Jesus that night, just as Nicodemus had.

The Shepsons were called to pastor the large and popular Toronto Avenue Road Alliance Church and we went to Belgian Congo for our first term. On furlough we received an invitation from the Shepsons to preach in their church one long weekend. On that visit we spent a day at a summer camp where Don was chaplain on week days. Don loved the lake and arranged for a swim, but our bodies had been tropicalized and the icy water was too much for the Brauns. We found a ride in a motor boat much more to our liking. We were to boat with the Shepsons in California, Florida, Switzerland and Belgian Congo in later years.

The meetings in Toronto were challenging and thrilling for us. Thelma and I divided the time, a practice we have followed for fifty years. We returned to our rented furlough house at the Alliance's Beulah Beach grounds near Toledo, Ohio and, at the end of furlough, took ship to Matadi, Congo's port city, and began term two as director of the Kinkonzi Bible Institute.

Same size in dresses was a help!

Each furlough the Shepsons invited us to their church to renew fellowship and to have a series of missionary messages. They were still in Toronto during our second furlough and we had a great time with them. Dottie Shepson and Thelma wore the same size dresses and Dottie decided she was weary of much of her wardrobe while we were with them. The Toronto church had many wealthy families and Dottie dressed as fashionably as any of the church women. In one week, Thelma was outfitted for a spectacular decade!

Back on the field, I proposed that Rev. Shepson be invited to come to Congo as the annual conference speaker. We set up the gospel tent in a distant market center and Don preached every night. It was a joy to translate for him and the Congolese responded wonderfully. One of our Bible Institute students, the bass in the school's popular quartet, was married by Don in the tent - a memorable experience.

There was never a more generous visitor from America than Don. He gave the missionary children's school money for a small swimming pool which was enormously popular. A missionary family on our station received four new tires for their car. Money to buy a pump to supply water for the six houses on our station, and pipe and bathroom equipment moved us all out of the outhouse era. Don changed so much for so many people.

Back in Toronto, Don gathered a few of his well-to-do friends together and told them that he and Dorothy had been saddened over the fact that as missionaries, the Brauns could never save enough money to buy a house when they retired. They, as a family, had decided to open a savings account for our retirement, into which they would put $200 a year. He asked his wealthy friends if they would like to do the same.

We knew nothing of this for twenty years. After a nine-year term on the field without a furlough we took our boys home in 1970. In 1971 we were asked to head the Alliance Key '73 program which was so blessed of God. The program ended the last day of 1973 and we loaded up our furniture and family in a rented truck and moved to Lexington, Kentucky to work with Dr. Ford Philpot, the illustrious Methodist evangelist.

Thelma and I flew to the Lausanne World Congress on Evangelism that year, as did the Shepsons. In fact, Don raised the money to pay for Thelma's ticket. One evening Don took us to dinner in a lakeside restaurant. At Don's request Dottie and Thelma wore formal gowns. Obviously this was a very special evening, but Thelma and I had no idea why. After a delicious meal, our table was closed off from the rest and the four of us were alone in a small but handsome room. Clearly nervous, Don stood up and began a recital which greatly changed our lives. He was a skilled preacher and radio evangelist and he was at his dramatic best as he told of our visits to the Toronto Church so long ago.

"You two have been in America five years now and will not be going back to Africa, so the time has come for us to tell you what happened after your visits." He described the agreement with his friends. He told us their names one by one. As he spoke of each, he laid a check on the table. Last of all, he laid the Shepson check down and totaled them. He added that two more were coming. All together they were enough to pay for two-thirds of a house!

What a stunning gift! What amazing people! At the end of our time in Switzerland we returned to Lexington and began looking for a house to buy. It was a lengthy process. After many visits to available houses we arrived at a house near the Cardinal Valley Alliance Church which we attended. I have no idea how many cats the owner had, but from the moment the front door was opened to us we breathed the strong stench of an overflowing litter box. When we finally exited that house Thelma was discouraged and burst into tears.

We did not know that a block away a string of new houses was being built, one of which would soon be ours. It was on a hill overlooking a park and horse farm where colts raced on the horizon. It had a large living room and a basement which we paneled and decorated over the years. Best of all, it was very close to the church.

One of the many proposals we had sent to the 1400 congregations of Canada and the USA Alliance was called "Pack Every Pew." I had first tried it in a church in Connecticut and it worked wonderfully well. Now in Lexington I pasted a number on each pew of the church and gave every faithful member a numbered pew to fill two nights of the week. The pews seated eight people. The rule was that anyone could ask anyone to sit in his or her pew on assigned nights, but that two of the eight had to be unsaved.

It is obvious that these rules created a lot of "horse trading." Husband asked wife to sit in his pew two nights and wife agreed if he would be in her pew two nights. Parents lined up their children to attend and aunts and uncles were invited, etc.

Sunday attendance at best was generally about 125. On Monday the church filled up with excited people. The evangelist had expected a handful of weary saints and had prepared a "pep talk" for them. When the pastor indicated that there were many unconverted visitors he made a quick shift in plans. "The Spirit of God has led me to change my message tonight," he said with a big smile. He preached a rousing salvation message and people responded to the invitation to pray at the altar.

Seems he couldn't believe there would be a full house on Tuesday, so once more he informed the people that the Holy Spirit had again led him to change his sermon plan. For the whole week he preached salvation and repentance and many were saved, so many, in fact, that the congregation grew and grew and had to build a large church which ultimately recorded 700 in Sunday worship.

A Chinese family attended the church and Dr. and Mrs. George Chin received two pews each to fill. To the amazement of us all, they packed two pews with Chinese friends every night. This was a marvel to me and I asked Dr. Chin if his friends might like to continue meeting on Sundays for a Chinese Sunday school class. He thought they would. There was no room free in the church so they used our nearby house every Sunday until the larger church was built. They moved into a chapel in the church and grew in number and in God's grace over 21

ER's Lexington home and headquarters

years, at which time they built their own church building where they now worship.

The house made the Chinese church possible. But it also made Evangelism Resources possible. A year and a half after we bought the house it was recorded on incorporation papers as the official address of Evangelism Resources. From mid-1976 until late 1980 it was home and headquarters.

Paul and Nancy were now in Lexington increasing our ER home staff from two to three full-time workers. Ministries were begun in Nigeria, Moscow and India. The little house was too small for all the new activity. Paul and Nancy moved to Wilmore and arranged to have my retired sister, Dr. Dorothy Braun in California, to move to Wilmore too. We began looking for a house in Wilmore and found one with a large work area on the first floor, right next door to ER's treasurer, Rev. Wesley Eisemann, and his delightful wife, June. It could not have been a better choice. Over the next eight years Wesley was to take us into the computer age and be a perfect neighbor.

But consider this, from 1976 to 1980 and from 1990 to 1999 when the new office was built, ER paid no rent, no taxes, no insurance, no heat, no electric, no water, no garbage and no grounds upkeep. On that lovely, sparkling night the Shepsons made possible thirteen years of growth in the house of God's provision for what none of us could have anticipated.

Great is the Lord and greatly to be praised!

Don became an enthusiastic ER board member until his death and his son Don succeeded him. Son Don was a busy international pilot and unable to attend board meetings year after year. He dropped off the board but continues to be interested in ER's progress. Dottie Shepson outlived her husband over a decade and we visited her frequently until she moved to Shell Point, Florida.

A happy time related to our Lexington house stands out in memory. Thelma and I had dragged tons of limestone rocks from excavations by builders of houses near ours to our back yard where I built two retainer walls to hold the soil for a garden. The earth was rich and I planted cherry tomatoes which ripened at a time when the Shepsons paid us a very happy visit. I showed them the back yard's newly planted bushes and flowers but it was the tomatoes Dottie liked best. She stood among the bushes popping them into her mouth until I thought she would burst. She was a very happy lady and when Dottie was happy - which was almost always, - everybody was happy.

The Wilmore house is now "all ours." We have replaced the air conditioner, the roof and the hot-water heater, and planted bushes and trees and vines with all the American flowers we could not have in 40 years in Africa. The Shepsons are with the Lord but the Eisemanns are still our wonderful neighbors.

That is the story of 523 Talbott Drive - until now – and of one more of the Lord's miraculous provisions for the work He called ER to do.

Our home at 523 Talbott in Wilmore, Kentucky
The house next door belongs to our dear friends, the Eisemanns.

29

PROTECTION

Looking back over eight decades, I cannot miss seeing the hand of God protecting a toddler, a child, a man living an oft-endangered existence.

On an early spring day after our afternoon Sunday school, I found myself with other youngsters at a flood-filled quarry by the Mississippi River. There were discarded railroad ties and old, rotted boards lying around, and one of the kids began nailing together a raft. Together we finished it and pushed off from shore, each a ship's captain braving the seven seas. Suddenly the raft came apart and we found ourselves in cold, deep water, none of us swimmers. By the grace of God, all escaped what could have been a tragic experience.

Water has always attracted me. A quarry with vertical sides near Leslie, Missouri, was full of water. On a hot summer day my older cousin, John, and I decided to cool off in it. Suddenly a leg cramp yanked my calf painfully against my upper leg and I slipped away from the shore and was sinking into the depths when my cousin reached for me. Neither of us could swim, but he was able to cling to the brush and to me and get me out of that perilous place. It was a brief experience together, but both of us knew we had faced death.

Johnny was an active hunter. One day he was cleaning a pistol. I walked over to watch. Pistols were exciting things. I was itching to get my little hands on it. "It's broke," he said, but he let me hold it. I knew what to do. I pulled the trigger and the broken gun worked fine. It shot a 22 bullet right through Johnny's hand. There was a bucket on the log cabin floor for food scraps for the hogs. Johnny's hand bled on and on into that bucket. At last it stopped and his hand eventually healed 100%. God was at work again, but this time it was Johnny He saved.

Back to my youth in St. Louis. My friend and I had hiked all day, had supper and put down our sleeping bags in a beautiful stand of pine trees. We had chosen poorly. The ground sloped so much that we kept rolling down hill. In disgust we walked up to a paved road and went to sleep. A shout awakened us. A horse pulling a milkman's wagon stood almost over us. The milkman was in a frenzy. We moved off the road and let him continue his route, glad it was not a truck with poor lights.

As a boy I rode my bike far and wide in St. Louis. This bike had no brake. It had only a single chain and one sped up by pumping and slowed down by pushing against the momentum of the pedals. One day I found myself going down a hill so steep I could not slow the bike down. I went careening out of control into Broadway, a very busy street. Seeing no car coming on my left I turned into that lane, but my speed carried me into the other lane, my bike slithering on its side. The front wheel stopped as a car shrieked to a stop on top of the wheel. A shaken driver backed off the bike so I could get up. I carried the ruined bike home. My age – perhaps 15.

A group of students arranged to drive a new car and trailer from Wheaton College to San Francisco on vacation. We made good time across the plains and were driving in Wyoming at night. I was in the trailer asleep with Tom Parks, president of the freshman class. Suddenly we were flung from our beds. The fridge and stove were crashing from side to side. The trailer whip-lashed violently then rolled over and crashed to a stop. To our amazement we were all alive and unhurt, but the car and trailer were in terrible shape. Age – 22.

On a college vacation up in British Columbia a Wheaton College friend invited me to climb to the top of a snow-capped mountain. We rode horses up to the upper edge of the trees, but had to traverse deadfalls and loose shale on foot for hours. Each of us wanted to give up at various times but always the other prevailed in going on.

There was a vertical rock face we had to traverse at one point and I was moving slowly with no foothold, simply holding by fingers to a small ledge above. I looked straight down what seemed like hundreds of feet with my fingers giving out. Just in time my foot found a place to take my weight and I moved on to safety. I have often testified to God's mercy to me on that day.

We made it to the top, took off our shirts and undershirts and threw snowballs at each other. We had a glorious view over western Canada's range of mountains. It was the handiwork of the Creator, the One who saves college students who risk all for adventure.

We were in our first term on the jungled mountain at Vungu – age – 24. Meat for the table had to be shot in the jungle. I thought it would be a good experience for Thelma to hunt antelope with African dogs and game drivers. I placed her in a good spot and cut some plants behind which she could hide. "When you see movement, don't expect to see the whole antelope," I told her as I left her to await the drive. "If you see part of it, shoot." I went on and found a place to wait. The drivers began coming toward us to frighten hiding animals toward us. Nothing stirred. There were no shots. The drive was over. I moved over toward Thelma. She had her gun on me. Dear Lord! I wasn't very smart.

The motorcycle with sidecar traveled to many villages.

One night years later I was riding toward our mission home on our motorcycle. It stopped running near a village called Kinzau Mvwete, so I left it with the local preacher and began the walk home. The first part of the walk was on the automobile road, flat and wide.

I had a flashlight but its batteries were weak, and I thought it wise to save them for the narrow, rough jungle trail up the mountain.

As I walked through the blackness an urge to turn on the flashlight came and I pushed down the button. The dull light revealed a Gabon viper lying one step ahead. These sluggish killers make no effort to move away. They bite with savage speed, however, whatever comes near to them. I backed away from death, found a heavy stick, returned, clubbed him lifeless and threw his body in the tall grass. To me, God made me push the button on the flashlight and once more saved my life.

On five occasions seven-foot long black cobras have had occasion to strike me. One dropped out of a tall tree at my feet, then turned away. Another chased me, his hood extended, for about forty feet, then turned and left. One had me trapped in a chicken house and decided to leave. One stared in my eyes, two feet away, from his hiding place in a pile of kindling. And one, after I tried to mash him with a boulder as he lay in a ditch and after I fell to earth from the effort, rose up above me, hooded with anger, stared long at his enemy, then withdrew into the jungle.

We were away from home for an annual conference in Congo. Returning by car in the early morning hours, we opened the door and walked in to be greeted by our gentle pup, now snarling and snapping at one and all. He was rabid. We didn't know that so I put him outside so we could get some sleep. Early next morning I woke up to see him barking and snapping at African workers peddling their bikes. By now I had guessed the problem and had to catch him without getting bitten. I did and chained him up. He died two days later of rabies. Age – about 48.

The rain poured deafeningly on the metal roof of our house at Lukula. Phil was asleep in his room. Thelma and I slept in another. A thief pried the screen apart on a window and walked in while we slept. He took the keys from my trousers and opened a closet in which we had money to build a mission house. When we woke up in the morning the sun was shining. We were confused to find the locked closet open, the money gone, our keys gone, our typewriter gone. In the mud I tracked the thief up to a nearby railroad track. There I could not see tracks. Back home I found a rock about the size of a softball on a table. If Phil or we had awakened, the thief would have broken our skulls. Age – 44.

I was in a taxi with about seven passengers. We were en route together, all strangers, I the only white, from Lagos to Benin's capital. Afternoon turned to night. From time to time the driver stopped and he and the other passengers got bottles of beer. After awhile the alcohol began its work. There were sinister whispers in the back seats. Things were getting ugly. Not a soul on earth knew I was in a taxi between Lagos and Cotonou. Only God knew and cared. It would have been so easy to kill the white man, roll his body in a river and divide his money and clothes. So easy.

In Nigeria and Zaire, crazed soldiers have sighted their army rifles on me, eager to pull the trigger. Two planes in which I flew hit severe downdrafts and almost crashed in Africa and India. Strong ocean currents have carried me away from shore. We drove an icy highway along which we saw hundreds of snow-trapped vehicles as we drove 400 miles in a blizzard, non-stop. Over and over and over, my life and Thelma's have been "in the valley of the shadow of death" and God has kept us alive and well.

And there were more of these kinds of experiences, riding the rails in Canada, hunting buffalo and red-river hogs in Congo, other thieves in other houses, near accidents with our motorcycle in the '40s and cars in the '50s. God's angels, unseen, have been kept on high alert to preserve us to this hour.

Behold, what manner of love the Father hath bestowed upon us.... What a great God we serve!

30

HUNTER AND HUNTED

My uncle judged me big enough to own a gun. He sold his to me for $7.00. It was a nearly new single-barrel, single-shot 12-gauge shotgun. And I was a wee bit taller than my gun. It would be my major meat-provider for 34 years. Squirrels, rabbits, doves, chicken hawks and snakes were its victims the first 19 years, mostly on my uncle's farm. The closest butcher shop was 13 miles east of the farm and in those depression years there was no money to buy meat. On the farm there was chicken when company came, rabbit, squirrel and 'possum in winter, dove or pork preserved in lard. Guns provided much-appreciated small game in hunting season and they also provided sport in a work-filled life style and protection against chicken thieves, hawks, wild cats and bad dogs.

My cousin John had a double-barrel shotgun and he was a crack shot. One day we were walking through a woods and a squirrel jumped from one tree to another high above us. It never reached its objective. Johnnie's gun roared over my head and killed the squirrel half way across the open space. On another occasion we had hunted rabbits with no success and daylight had turned to dark shadow as we returned home. Suddenly a rabbit rushed away from our path and was visible for only a second. It was enough. Johnnie nailed it.

I was a young city boy. The way to hunt squirrels was to sit by a large, hollow tree for a half-hour, absolutely unmoving. Mosquitoes, flies, eye gnats and unhappy muscles were sheer torture for me. Worse, my imagination saw squirrels where there were none. I have shot leaves, sure they were fat, juicy squirrels. I have shot knotholes in trees because I saw a squirrel looking out. Then I climbed large oaks to fish the dead squirrels out. I never got a squirrel that way.

There was a huge sycamore tree at the edge of a limestone cliff below which a shallow creek flowed. A squirrel was in the top branches. I had no gun that day so I climbed to the top branch of the tree to catch the squirrel. Looking down at the stream below I seemed to be a mile high. The squirrel easily ran down the branch on the backside and I descended a wee bit wiser. Hunting was in my blood. Cousin Johnnie had a 22 rifle that he carried wherever he went. Rabbits like to hide in the brown grass of autumn and winter, and my cousin often spotted them sitting along his path. A 22 shot killed without tearing the animal to shreds. This old 22's shell ejector was worn out, so Johnnie kept a heavy wire ramrod in it to poke out the cartridge casing after each shot.

On one occasion I had just arrived from the city and we were walking on a dirt road. Johnnie had his 22 and saw my bright eyes looking at it. "Want to carry it?," he asked and handed it to me. My young fingers were fiddling around with the hammer and trigger imagining animals hopping up everywhere. Suddenly there was a loud "Crack" and the ramrod buried itself into the hard ground very close to my cousin's foot. Lesson learned: "Don't play with the hammer of a rifle."

One day I was walking to the mailbox four fields from the log cabin farmhouse. I had my gun. As I came to an abandoned farm's pond I spotted a blue-racer snake. Not wanting to waste a shell, I used the stock of my 12-gauge as a club in an effort to kill the snake. I don't recall whether I killed the speedy snake. I do remember that the stock broke off and I had to carve a replacement.

In my teens, on a summer vacation my uncle offered to buy me a 12-gauge automatic if I would cut down young oak trees in a pasture area. It was a wonderful offer but those oak trees were hard to cut. They were about six inches through and there were hundreds of them. I spent a whole morning cutting down a few. Hot and weary I calculated that I'd be too old to lift the automatic by the time I cleared the pasture. Anyway, I was satisfied with my single shot 12-gauge gun. It was an old friend by then.

· ·

The old gun went with us to Congo in 1945. The Africans loved hunting and my gun looked great to them. Their guns were all homemade muzzleloaders. The barrels were three-quarter inch pipe. Out of chunks of iron they fashioned a hammer, trigger, spring and small tube that carried a match-head flame to the powder in the gun barrel, exploding the shot out of the open end. My gun could change shells to fit the game to be shot. Bird shot, monkey shot, antelope shot and buffalo shot were different. For changing the kind of shot and for reloading for a second shot, I had every advantage over their muzzleloaders. So the Africans were eager to have me (my gun) in each hunting party.

Only a few weeks after arrival on our jungle station of Vungu I was invited to go on a first hunt. We started out at 4 o'clock, "the time of the first chicken" (rooster crowing). By early dawn we were in a dew-soaked prairie grass area and the "president of the war," the head of the hunters, stopped frozen in time. He then led us out swiftly into a herd of red-river hogs. I spotted one circling and blasted away. It fell dead. The president shot too but his animal kept moving, dripping blood.

It was decided to follow the wounded animal, which we did through jungle thickets on hands and knees. Every time more blood was seen the president whooped, "Menga mama!" - here is blood - and we were hyped up for one more mile of tracking. We never found his pig so we hunted for some hours and then returned to "my" pig. Some men trussed it on a stout pole and we started toward home. I felt good – proud, happy. It was hard work carrying the game so many miles home. I decided to be very generous with my pig. These were good men.

When we got home I discovered that it was not my pig. It was their pig and they had an exact system for dividing the meat. I got a hind leg. The rest went to my companions. But after all, they found it, they took me to it and they carried it. All I did was shoot it. Any dullard with a good gun can do that. But even if I shot it, if they had waltzed off into the jungle I'd never have gotten "my" pig home. Those pigs were in a grass wilderness as distant and unknown to me as the dark side of the moon.

Well, the ham was in time for Thanksgiving and Thelma, Grumpy, our tiny pointer pup, and I enjoyed it to the full. To me, this mission field was a hunter's paradise. I thought I would shoot countless pigs in days ahead. The country was full of them. Little could I have imagined that in the 14 years I was to have a gun I would never see another red-river hog in the wild. But I would kill more pigs!

We had walked endlessly from our Vungu station to get to Kai Vungu on a Saturday. There were services all Sunday and an interesting incident occurred that day. The old pastor was to my young eyes quite ancient. His hair was a crown of white wool. One of his sons was my age. He taught school on our station and I had taught him to skin out birds for the American Museum of Natural History in New York.

Thelma and I woke up in our borrowed hut on Sunday morning. I dressed and went outside. There was Rev. Isaki Malonda cuddling a tiny baby. I oohed and ahhed over this bit of the future and asked who its parents were, assuming this was a grandchild or a great

Grumpy was ready to hunt.

254

grandchild. This sweet and kindly pastor stared at me with cold, hurt eyes. I had insulted his manhood. He was the father! White people could be so – so stupid.

Monday morning we ate our last crumbs and started the long walk home. There was no food at all for Grumpy. The path led up a heavily jungled mountain and I asked the carriers to lag behind me as I hunted the jungle for a bird or monkey for Grumpy. Well ahead of the others, I heard a heavy body rushing toward the path and brought up my gun. The red head of a hog showed itself and I fired. Down it went! My second pig in my first couple of weeks in Africa.

The carriers came up, took one look at the pig and gazed in horror at me. I had shot a red village pig out foraging for food in the jungle. The village was an eighth of a mile further up the hill. When we reached it, a deacon in our party told village men about the shooting and before I knew what was happening I found myself in a village tribunal where I couldn't understand a word.

I did understand the shouting, angry emotion. These men could see the pot of gold that had just dropped into their laps. Children who broke another family's clay jar had been made slaves for life in such tribunals. The owner of the dead pig loved and adored that beautiful animal more than his wife and children. How much would it cost us to assuage his grief? There was no sum large enough. As they shouted over my fate I looked at them wondering at all the fuss. Finally it ended. A month of our salary was to be paid the smitten, suddenly rich owner. We left the village to eat its pig, which I had bought a dozen times.

Two weeks later a man showed up from the village. Seems that a black pig in the bushes had received part of the shot. No one had seen it but it was found dead – a female with six unborn piglets. I had to pay for all of them. Of course the village ate the meat – the most expensive pork I ever bought. By then I was no longer an over-eager hunter of pigs. Antelope were more easily distinguished from village sheep and goats.

They were, however, neither plentiful nor easy to see in the jungle ground foliage. My first experience with the small red antelope came in a dense jungle area. I had learned how to imitate the call of the antelope and did so on this occasion. It was a plaintive, high, nasal "Ny aaap, ny aaap, naap, naap." I was new at it. I heard running sounds, saw a red body flash partly into view and shot. Away went the antelope. I couldn't believe I missed. Examining the spot where he had been I found the buckshot embedded in a slender sapling I had not even seen. It had collected the whole load.

Not long before that an African had called antelope, seen part of a moving body, shot and had his scalp ripped off by the wounded leopard. The man lived.

On an open grasslands years later, at night with a full moon, I went out with an African hunter to call antelope. A larger antelope rushed up. I could see his shadowy shape and I shot. He ran away. The hunter was closer than I to the antelope but he didn't shoot, counting on my superior 12-gauge to bring the animal down. We walked home empty handed.

This was not the usual pattern. I often went out in nearby jungle areas with my gun, compass and sharp bush knife. In the sundown period each day, hornbills and blue tree pheasants called out loudly to get their flocks together for roosting. Guided by their calls I would consult my compass, then cut my way toward the big birds. They were not easy to see in the high foliage, but they supplied many meals with good meat.

Monkey meat is delicious and though there were few near our station, they were numerous two hours walk away. Some of the most exciting moments were those in which a troop of monkeys followed each other through a set "path" in the treetops. On one occasion my gun barrel got hot from repeated shots at monkeys that, one by one, stopped at a certain point. I shot six times at monkeys that stopped at that point and each one dropped. When the last monkey was shot I worked my way to where I expected to find six dead monkeys. There were none. No blood, no hair, nothing to indicate that even one animal had been touched. My conclusion was that they were too high, too far for my ammunition to reach. It was exciting while it was happening. The game drivers must have thought two armies were at war for a few minutes.

One day I brought a dominant male monkey down, the defender of his troop. Buckshot had paralyzed his back legs but his arms were long and powerful and he was as ferocious as a leopard.

Large canine teeth were bared and snapped at me as he roared with fury. I shot him quickly to end his pain but his rage and courage facing me remains indelibly imprinted in memory.

My gun was the cheapest, simplest hunting piece I ever saw in Congo. Other missionaries had high-caliber rifles. I dreamed of having one. As our first term drew toward an end, Thelma and I were in the capital city in charge of LECO, the large press and bookstore. We had a week of vacation coming and decided to visit our great friends, the Osts, who were building a very large church at Boma. A store in Leopoldville had Winchester repeater 35-caliber rifles for sale for $125. I wanted one of those beautiful guns with all my heart for the vacation. Thelma said, "Get it," and I did.

We took the train to Matadi and the riverboat to Boma. Nate fixed the sights for about 200 feet and we went hunting. On that trip I shot a horse-antelope that was so far away it appeared smaller than the front beadsight. I aimed the gun about six feet over its back and

A feast for the Bible School men

fired. The antelope fell down. When we got to it, we saw the bullet had gone through its body and was pushing the skin out on the far side. What a gun!

When we returned to the capital I sold the gun for the price I had paid. It cost us nothing but provided the greatest hunt of my life. It was not the only fine gun I had. On furlough I told hunting stories to Sunday School children and a widow woman came to me after a service and said her husband had died and left an automatic 12-gauge shotgun, which she wanted to give to me. It was new, in mint condition, a magnificent gun. I loved it. But back on the field I was faced with so many financial needs that I became miserably uncomfortable having so valuable a gun. By that time we lived near a city with a butcher shop and I rarely had time for hunting. I sold the gun and used the money in ministry.

The Osts were assigned to build a small vacation house by the ocean. There were vast sand flats about a mile from the ocean where one could drive for many smooth miles. Nate Ost had a used Jeep. At dawn we would drive up to the flats and look for small antelope. Nate would drive at one and it would rush from side to side. I had my old gun and shot at the jumping, twisting animal from a bouncing, swerving vehicle. It took awhile to learn how to time a shot. One morning we got four and salted them down for preacher-students at our Bible school.

There were bustards on the flats. They were like miniature ostriches in appearance. One species had the body weight of a goose, another species had the weight of a chicken. The smaller bustards were not disturbed by a car driving up to them. My gun was just right for them. But the larger ones flew away if a car approached. Nate would drive toward them until he saw they were getting nervous. Then with his rifle, he would shoot one. They were delicious birds.

One day I wanted Thelma to experience a Jeep hunt. At dawn we drove up on the flatlands and spotted some big bustards. Nate said, "Willys, get out behind that bush and I will herd the birds to you so you can shoot one." I did. Off went Nate with my wife and disappeared over the horizon in a cloud of dust. Gone, nowhere near the birds. I sat, bewildered, behind my bush.

After awhile I heard the motor and the Jeep came over the horizon chasing an antelope toward me. The antelope was dead tired and Nate was trying to herd him within range of my gun – when the motor died. I took a long shot, hoping to kill the antelope but it was too far away. The shell wouldn't eject from the gun. Nate and I ran after the animal. It would lie down exhausted and we would run up to it only to have it jump up before we could grab it. Since I couldn't get the old shell out, I used the gun as a club, trying to stun the beast, and the stock broke.

We were wearing out when I finally got the shell out and a new one in and shot the antelope. Now we had a dead antelope a long way from the stalled Jeep with Thelma in it, miles from home on a searing hot morning. It could have become serious for there were no roads or towns nearby. Fortunately, the motor started easily, we loaded up our antelope and drove home for a cool swim in the ocean.

We ate well. We lived well on vacation. It was a memorable time for us all. The Osts lived in a grass hut under a baobab tree – near the ocean, almost like Robinson Crusoe. They preached to an unreached tribe and saw fruit. Life was beautiful. Married for years and childless, the Osts had a son there. He was Sonny, a strong, big boy, their first. It was the golden age for Congo and for missions, a time of great openness for the gospel. Nate and Helen, Thelma and I had our annual vacations and guns played a role in them. But our years, our lives were given to ministry and God gave the increase.

Guns were not only essential to put meat on the table. They were useful for celebrations. When Paul and Phil were born on Kinkonzi station I filled my pockets with 12-gauge shotgun shells and big mimpata, coins worth about five cents. Shot after shot rang out bringing children of Bible Institute teachers and students running. When the shells were all shot, surrounded by kids, I began emptying my pockets of mimpata, tossing them everywhere among the scrambling youngsters. They were a happy bunch and wished us dozens more babies….

One day a mad dog raced up to our Kinkonzi house, looking for someone to bite. The Africans screamed warnings. I nailed him with the old gun. On two other occasions in Kinshasa, rabid dogs bit a neighbor's child and our dog. I had had to surrender my gun before

Independence in 1960. In Kinshasa, I had no gun. Rabid dogs could be chased away with rocks or sticks – chased away to bite and infect others over and over.

In the violent, pre-Independence period I had come to the conclusion that I would not shoot an African who threatened us. We had come to Africa to bring salvation, not death to these people for whom Jesus died. At that point to own a gun was to risk using it on evil men, or having them use it on us. An old friend, a regional judge, asked to buy it and I handed it over.

I have not owned a gun since. The grocery store supplies our meat. There are no jungles in Wilmore. I love living animals and have no desire to kill them. Life has changed American society enormously in the 1900s and my jungle now is a computer-dominated office. My gun is a lowly ballpoint pen, which communicates continuously with churchmen overseas and with American partners of ER in high-harvest efforts to win peoples in Asia and Africa to Christ.

From gun to pen

31

GOD'S MIGHTY MEN

No man is an island. No man stands alone. My life has been shaped – and blessed -, by a host of men and women, most unknown to you who read this but some world-famous. I write of them as part of who I turned out to be. Some stopped by my side for a very short time. Some never knew I existed. But some became lasting friends. Come to think of it, they are almost all with Jesus now, but in the times of which I write they were lively servants of the Almighty.

Alfred Gibbs was a superb preacher and an admirable tennis player who sailed from South Africa to minister in summer conferences and camps at a Brethren campground in Cedar Lake, Indiana. He had heavy three-inch slides of Pilgrim's Progress which he projected in the boys' camp I attended at ages 15, 16 and 17. I loved those ten days (cost $10) each summer. We slept in rough cabins, ate in a wide open dining hall, played ball, had crafts and swimming and boating and services, and I met my Lord as personal Savior there. Thirty-four years later I sat at the Lord's Table in the South African assembly that sent Alf Gibbs to America – a holy moment.

Dr. John McMillan was a spiritual giant along the way for us. He was editor of the *Alliance Weekly*, which is now *Alliance Life*. He was also one of Nyack's professors and our very dear friend. For long years he served as chairman of the C&MA mission in the Philippines. It was a nation in which demons held sway over many of the population, and John McMillan's faith and boldness cleansed many tormented persons and led them to Jesus. From impenetrable hardness the people turned to openness and revival as their tormentors were driven out of them by this quiet, authoritative servant of God whom we knew intimately and loved.

Because of transportation difficulties in 1944 due to the war, the Annual Council of the C&MA was held in Nyack. We had sold our cork belts and had extra money on hand. My salvation in a boys' camp, three years as a camper and three years as a leader, left an indelible impression on my heart that the Church needed more boys' camps. As pastor of the Nyack Old Stone Church I led a boys' camp in an abandoned army camp. Every camper went home testifying to his salvation. Now, about to graduate and with money to spend, we bought some used army tents, new folding cots, mattresses, cooking utensils, tableware, etc., enough for a camp of 30 boys and their leaders. Dr. McMillan arranged for me to introduce this portable boy's camp to the delegates of the Annual Council, which gave the idea a rousing ovation. I can't picture that happening in an Annual Council in these days.

Dr. V. Raymond Edman, president of Wheaton College, was a strong role model in my early twenties. He was a consummate story-teller and became a personal friend who, to my astonishment, walked down a street in Omaha, Nebraska about twenty years later, saw Thelma and me and, with his winsome smile, greeted us by name.

I made a bas-relief clay plaque of him and the Wheaton College seal when he was named president. By covering the clay with liquid rubber I made a mold of it from which I extracted plaster-of-Paris copies. These were stained brown, waxed and sold in the College Stupe – its snack shop - for a dollar. My last copy lies forgotten in some attic, stored there when we went to Congo.

When Dr. Edman assumed the role of president, he turned over his Sunday evening preaching services to, of all things, a student named Billy Graham. He could be pardoned in later years if he quietly patted himself on the back for having made an exceptionally good choice.

Recently the Bill Gaither Choir honored Billy Graham on its regular Saturday night TV extravaganza. Ruth Graham was there and enjoyed the marvelous memories and music of the rallies in America and Europe. Cliff Barrows and Beverly Shea took part in the program. The greatness of this man could not be missed as the hour passed with views of masses of people, of thrilling songs, of presidents and, best of all, of thousands of people coming down out of the stands on an eternal trek to meet King Jesus.

Billy's greatness was reflected in a brief period in America's history when he was the spokesman for the Savior to our nation, and

262

movie stars and famous men came forward "just as they were and waiting not." It was the high tide of biblical faith in our country, and year after year he was the first on the list of "Most Honored Men." Our family furloughed in California in 1954 and watched Billy and Ruth on TV, Grand Marshals of the Rose Bowl Parade.

He was THE Christian of that era. Presidents, kings and queens sought his visits. Any Christian author or leader of a movement who had a Billy Graham testimony of approval was accepted everywhere as theologically true. Thelma and I attended a Youth for Christ conference as C&MA representatives at Winona Lake. Billy was the speaker one evening. The Billy Sunday Tabernacle had never been filled since its construction and Mrs. Sunday had a longstanding offer of a brand new station wagon for anyone who could fill it. The crowd that came to hear Billy Graham overflowed the Tabernacle by the thousands. Bob Pierce was a speaker of the week as well, and Billy gave the station wagon to him. Unforgettable days, those!

But Billy had a less well-known global influence that may well have launched a hundred nations into crusades of evangelism that brought more millions to Jesus than his great rallies did. His world congresses on evangelism brought isolated churchmen into a glorious international and inter-denominational fellowship that changed forever the often-angry relationships of churchmen of many nations. National conferences grew out of Berlin, Lausanne, Amsterdam I and Amsterdam II, and the Church became warmly one at last in prayer and purpose in dozens of nations. Explosive church growth resulted and, in spite of the secularism in Europe and America, Christianity became the largest and fastest-growing religion in world history.

One day Thelma and I sat in the Lausanne World Conference in Switzerland, awaiting the start of a closing communion service. To our delight we found that Ruth Graham was sitting behind us. We had a nice chat. At the end of the service I boxed all the used communion cups for use in churches in Zaire – just as I shipped all the styrofoam letters used in the Berlin World Conference back to Congo for Tous Pour Christ use in campaigns. "Go to the ant, thou sluggard" has spurred me on lifelong. The Great Depression made scavengers of us all in the beginning, and the Bible encouraged economy and conservation for decades after.

Classmates of Thelma whose names were nationally known for a lifetime were Robert Evans of Greater European Mission and Abe Van Der Puy of HCJB radio of Latin America. Peter Stam III, another of that well-known family, rose to head Africa Inland Mission and Carl Henry pioneered the Fuller Seminary in Pasadena, California and *Christianity Today*.

Carl visited Congo in the '60s and invited American missionaries of the capital to a lunch downtown. Most of the local missions then were strongly liberal and, after eating, the men began a loud attack on their guest's Bible-based faith. This was not unexpected. Liberals were on the warpath in Africa – all over, and had been for decades before.

As for Carl Henry, a big, robust, eloquent, powerful protector of the faith, he rose from his chair like a great grizzly bear among yapping jackals and roared fearsomely – for God. His answers, his declarations, his quotations and passion held the others spellbound. They had eaten at the table of a world-class theologian that day.

Of Wheaton's "brave sons and daughters true", one became my great friend and best man at my wedding. Paul Freed, son of C&MA missionaries to the Arab lands, pastored a church, earned his Ph.D., ministered with Youth for Christ, then founded Trans-World Radio, one of two global radio missions. I wrote of our joint venture making what we called a collapsible boat. It was well named. Floating was what it did well until someone got into it. Collapse is what it did best. Then it earned its name. But Paul was a worldwide servant of God lifelong.

He had an attractive sister, Ruth, who wed another student, Ben Armstrong, son of a C&MA district superintendent. Ben began the National Radio Association, which regularly had U.S. presidents speak at its annual meetings.

It occurs to me that Wheaton graduates of that period were exceptional visionaries who dared to begin global or continental organizations, many of which are now famous and very large. Missionaries who served their missions tended to do their assignments until retirement with no opportunity to begin a new agency and no desire to do so. It was free-lancers who saw needs and met them who launched Campus Crusade, the Billy Graham Evangelistic Association, Trans-World Radio, etc., etc. It took Thelma and me 31 missionary years to reach the point where God could open our hearts to begin Evangelism Resources.

Makanzu, the Billy Graham of Congo

In Africa, there were great Congolese men of God who shaped our goals and activities. Most outstanding of these was Dr. Makanzu, the Billy Graham of Congo and a superb author and pastor. When we met him he was pastor of the Dendale Baptist Church, which was the largest in the capital. He was a genius in involving believers in ministry. We wrote a booklet about his 25 action committees that kept over 150 of his members in church life activities. It was easy to get 5000 people to his church compound for an outdoor meeting with a guest evangelist. We had great times in his church.

One Sunday morning young Chris and Paul played a trumpet duet in Dr. Makanzu's church to a packed house when a naked man strolled down the central aisle waving his arms like a bandleader. Everyone knew this man. His name was Cinquante-Cinq, which means 55. He roamed the streets, normally clothed, telling folks that they would soon have independence in 1955 - this was in 1965 when Congo had already had five years of independence. To my amazement, the boys kept playing as Cinquante Cinq planted himself firmly in front of them leading the rhythm. Happily, Christian men quietly surrounded him and, with a giggling audience all around them, soberly assisted their guest back up the aisle to the doors. All in a day's worship.

Dr. Makanzu was unceremoniously voted out of the church by jealous fellow pastors one evening and he found himself unemployed. A matchless preacher, he had no options but to get a job teaching Bible classes in the public schools – until we invited him to join us as traveling evangelist in the Christ for All national movement of evangelism. We printed large posters advertising his meetings and arranged tours for him all over Zaire. He kept a diary of his meetings and took slides of them with huge crowds in outdoor meetings holding banners we made. The people had never seen anything like this and he often had crowds of 5000, 10,000, even 30,000 hearers. His journals are not unlike those of American revivalists and we estimated that well over 50,000 people testified to their salvation in Jesus in his great meetings.

We spent exciting hours together. I recall driving with him one day in Kinshasa, talking about future campaigns. He turned to me and said with much sincerity, "Tata Braun, you teach us everything you know and then we will do it better than you!" This one sentence defined our relationship. I was the teacher from a long-experienced foreign church and I was to tell him every ministry, every way God was working and blessing in my church. Then he, knowing his people and his times, would shape those ministries to fit his people and bring God's blessings to his nation.

Thelma and I worked in a publishing office in the capital for years in what could have been a dull, secular activity, but we chose to teach the evangelist new, lively ways to bring salvation to his people everywhere and to teach 17,000 other preachers of Zaire how they too could reach out farther and more effectively to their towns and villages.

Rev. Makanzu was awarded a Doctor of Divinity degree by Asbury College in 1980, due to our enthusiastic writings about him. He stayed with us in our home in Lexington for several days. We had no indication that he was ill, but cancer was destroying this amazing man of God. Months later we moved back to Kinshasa and saw him twice in the hospital. He soon died and was buried in his doctoral robes – an enormous loss to his nation.

A missionary to Congo must be included among those who shaped our lives. Dr. Alexander Reid was an extraordinary missionary. If he had been in the armed services his chest would have been heavy with medals and bright ribbons. He was a hard-working strategist driven by an urgent vision to fill heaven with Africans.

This is not typical of missionaries. Many of those I have known did their daily assignments and spent their off-time "hanging out" over Chinese checkers and soft drinks. Alex was full-time planning and doing soul saving and church planting lifelong. He led a revival in the Methodist area in which tens of thousands of Congolese gathered under thousands of square feet of arbor-type shade provided by palm branch roofs. These prolonged revivals touched the lives of two men who would lead all or some of the nation.

Moise Tshombe was prime minister of Congo and a splendid Christian and politician who was out-maneuvered by the army's Col. Mobutu in a bloodless coup. He died a prisoner in Algeria as arranged by Mobutu.

The other man baptized by Dr. Reid was Lumumba, who turned from his Lord and became a violent monster shrieking his rage over the radio day after day. Violence was his agenda as Prime Minister. He held the nation in nervous shock until arrested by soldiers sent by Kasa Vubu, the president. He died in a prison break in the southeast of Congo, the Katanga.

It was Alex who counseled Dr. Shaumba to ask us to design a national movement of evangelism in the paralyzing days of civil war. He took me to Matadi where the Congo Protestant Council was in session and gave me time to present a 24-month plan for Christ for All. It was Alex who introduced me to Dr. Ford Philpot, who gave the churches of the capital their first mighty crusades of evangelism. And Dr. Reid arranged for me to visit Asbury College and Seminary in Wilmore, Kentucky and then became a founding member of Evangelism Resources' Board and its vice president.

So many Americans have inspired and enabled us to develop E.R. through the years that I don't dare start listing them lest I forget

Dr. Harold Spann.
He believed in the dream.

many who deserve to be mentioned. But standing tall among them is Harold Spann who had the courage to believe in our dream when we first talked to him about a new faith mission, Evangelism Resources. We had met him in the Collingswood, New Jersey UM church pastored by Phil Worth, described in the Wheaton chapter. Harold came from his post at Asbury College to address the large missions conference. He was the key speaker, we were the visiting missionaries. We could understand the almost instant bonding of spirit when we learned that he had once longed to go to India as a missionary, but defective eyesight made that an impossibility.

Years later, after we had settled in Kentucky we recognized that the call to Africa could not be stilled. ER came into being under the skillful and diplomatic leadership of Harold Spann. His counsel led us to contact outstanding leaders for the ER Charter Board and he opened numerous churches to our testimony and appeals. His faith in God and loyalty to us his friends qualify him eminently to a stellar position in this chapter of mighty men.

In recent years seemingly out of nowhere came a Spirit-guided veterinarian of Portland, Oregon, Dr. Gene Davis, whom we met in a DAWN conference in London and who visited us in Kinshasa to see our work close up. He must have approved of what he saw because he took us to India and, with his wife Vivian, hosted Thelma and me for seven long weeks in three areas of India. He paid to have ten pastors go to our School of Evangelism in Lagos, Nigeria to learn the courses. As a result, ER is in four Asian nations and has 22 schools of evangelism. There is much truth in the saying, "It isn't what you know, but whom you know."

Now the president of Foreign Mission Foundation, Gene has a burning passion for India. A recent letter to us states,"*God has used you...to bless the world. I am in Gujarat with a couple hundred pastors... We are going to see the knowledge of the glory of God cover the earth as the water covers the sea.*"

In India, two men have been strong colleagues. They are Rev. D.B. Hrudaya, who led India's first statewide movement of evangelism, and Rev. Stephen Rawate, who now leads DANI. We have interacted closely over wonderful years of harvest.

Knowing Jesus the Savior and Lord, and God, His magnificent Father, and the resident Holy Spirit, guide and empowerer, underlies every good thing that my life has known, beginning with a pious mother and going the distance with a God-filled wife. God's mighty men often get their valor and victories from His mighty women.

Rev. Stephen Rawate

Rev. D.B. Hrudaya

32

PERSONAL INTERESTS

PUBLICATIONS

High school for me was an unwelcome interruption of my sports life and farm vacations. I just didn't get the point of it. Dorothy actually enjoyed school and made excellent grades. I wanted to quit and get a job in the zoo, but Mother insisted that I finish high school. I did, but not proudly. My grades were poor in all but art and mechanical drawing. I felt challenges to excel in these manual arts, but grammar, history, mathematics or a foreign language were an infringement on my human rights, from my point of view.

When I bowed to the Lord He opened my mind. In my senior year in high school I suddenly wanted to learn everything. A little old lady near retirement age taught English Literature and she caught my attention not only by dramatizing poets and playwrights as no one had before, but with situation-problems which required much thought in seeking a solution. These solutions with supporting reasons had to be written out in compositions. She gave me excellent grades on these thought-essays and I began to hope that in my skull resided a brain that could do adult learning.

This teacher fascinated me. In those days, people traveled by streetcar. I liked to see new places in the city and, unseen by her, I boarded the streetcar she went home on and, at a distance, followed her to an attractive apartment in a very nice neighborhood. My curiosity satisfied, I returned home never to see that neighborhood again. I honored her as the teacher who readied me for college study. Her name I have forgotten but her voice is easy to recall as, with an English accent, she recited with high drama, "That's…my last duchess hanging on the wall… Looking as if she were alive." In my mind I saw the beautiful face of the "last" duchess and as the story went on, a tiny birthmark unnoticed before appeared on her cheek – so small.

But the arrogant duke described his dissatisfaction with this blemish that soon was all he could see when he looked at her! There she was "looking as if she were alive."

Words can stir the imagination, the emotion, the soul! I had read hundreds of Indian and cowboy novels and learned so much of the old West. Now I began to discover another world of artists and philosophers, poets and historians and I began the process of learning acceptable English and of expressing my thoughts on paper. It was a sea change for this teenager which came to fill my working days in mature years.

· ·

Useful writings began with a monthly news leaflet which I called *Today and Tomorrow*. News bits about the five Assemblies of St. Louis and items of interest to the generation of "Today" were added to devotionals encouraging them to move confidently into "Tomorrow" with their Lord. When I left St. Louis for study at Wheaton, other young men kept *Today and Tomorrow* going for years. It had a part in keeping Brethren youth together and hopeful until they were integrated into the leadership of the Assemblies.

Seven years of study followed and writing essays, reports and examinations kept my pen busy. But it was in Africa that writing became a ministry. Thelma and I took out a mimeograph in 1945, an offset printing press in 1950 and a heavy letter press, with lead type, in 1956. There were a half dozen thin Kikongo books on sale when we arrived in Congo in 1945 and I bought them up in quantity and sent out colporteurs throughout the villages selling them. Africans were hungry to learn all about God and the larger world.

We published more new books than any other mission in the Kikongo region and sold many books to neighboring missions. In 1964 LECO, the large press in the capital built with funds from many missions, called us back to work with the editor of a Christian Kikongo monthly magazine called *Moyo (Life)*. I did the artwork and layout, and oversaw printing and distribution. We published tons of these magazines and distributed them over all Lower Congo for years.

An idea came to me one day to organize all the churches to distribute a packet of special literature free to every family in the capital city. Eventually we obtained a million pieces for 200,000 packets. It took a staff of five three months to get it all packed for trucking to 35 congregations. Each Sunday for a month, 50,000 packets were given out to 50,000 homes by 1000 Christians. The immediate impact of that month was to give Protestants a new sense of unity and of ownership of their city, for they had been a hidden minority and had never worked together on any project before. No doubt my monthly visits to the 35 churches of the city with bundles of magazines gave me both a needed confidence and familiarity with the pastors to undertake such an effort. Soon after that the tent ministry and Christ for All were launched. All of what followed did so because of the one-million distribution project.

Thelma and I were asked by Dr. Shaumba to edit *Congo Mission News*, a quarterly magazine for missionaries. We wrote, photographed, secured articles, did layout and oversaw printing, mailing and accounts in a period of civil war. One issue carried 40 pictures of Protestant martyrs killed by Simba gangs. The article accompanying the picture was titled "Tears in God's Bottle." The front cover showed a stone monument with the 40 names and a stone angel weeping at the side. I had seen a monument in Switzerland with a weeping angel and the memory set my fingers to work with pastels simulating the stone monument and angel. The names were printed on the drawing. I still have the original in the year 2000. It is a moving sight to me.

By the way, one day one of the 40 martyrs walked into our office. She had been carried off by one of the officers and was in the jungle for months. Her mission reported her death to us and to the English government. We heard she had quite a time getting herself reinstated among the living.

A bound volume of *Congo Mission News* contains 534 pages and is in our library.

In 1966 we started the Christ for All nationwide movement of evangelism and for two years its literature needs filled our lives. We completely wore out a new mimeograph running over three million pages through its rollers. Over two years 17,000 preachers were sent monthly mailings, and each mailing introduced to them a new way to win their populations to faith in Christ.

In 1970 we returned to America, ten years after our last return home in 1960. A year later we were called to New York to head Alliance Key '73. For two and a half years we wrote, wrote, wrote to 1400 pastors of the C&MA in Canada and the USA. A big red notebook 1½ inches thick holds part of what was published then. There were separate publications, tracts and posters that would not fit in the notebook. The C&MA had over 300 congregations report revival in that period.

Thelma began *Jottings* for *Congo Mission News*. She continued it in Ford Philpot's *Storyteller* magazine, which we edited for two years, our second magazine. When we began Evangelism Resources we began our third magazine, *NEWS from the Fields*. There are now three bound volumes of this and the beginning of a fourth. They measure four inches thick and are the teaching, sharing and challenging "voice" of ER headquarters to an ever-growing number of supporters and non-supporters. Income for ministries has grown over 23 years because families have shared our vision concerning overseas ministries and written checks to enable these ministries to go on.

A fiscal policy of our leadership has been to enter every open door and believe God would pay the bills. For 22 years He paid the increasing costs as they grew from $50,000 a year to $750,000. In 1999 I agreed to open many new schools in Asia. That was the year ER entered its new office and had extra costs from it and additional costs in Africa. We went month after month with too little money to keep Asian schools paid. I cut off three schools in South India for the next year's support, but took on four new schools. Income had increased in 1999 but not enough to meet the much larger need. Cutting back was a sad episode.

Back to literature. In ten years building of our Kinshasa campus, teaching led to producing two textbooks in English and French. One was *Pastoral Evangelism in Africa* and the second was *Evaluating and Escalating Church Growth*. In these ten years we were the largest publisher of Christian books in Zaire. Dozens and dozens of titles were written and printed.

To enlarge the number of African writers, publishers and booksellers we opened a third school, the International Institute of

Christian Communications. The school was excellent, but the timing was not. Zaire's economy was in a free fall and literature was a money-losing ministry because $100 worth of books lost value daily. If you got 100 books for $100 by the time you sold them your money would buy only 60 books this round and 35 books the next. Keep up the business and your $100 would be lost altogether. A zaire, once valued at $2, fell so low it took a million to buy a banana. We had to close the school.

But we continued to publish and give books away. We were given thousands of Bibles and hundreds of thousands of tracts. We gave them all away and paid transportation costs. The International Center of Evangelism earned its name and was a strong center of learning, literature and tribal evangelism.

Rev. James Falkenberg, President of Bible Literature International, wrote, "*It's from a grateful heart that this letter comes to you – gratefulness for all that both of you mean to me, personally, and to BLI's ministry-at-large. You have helped us forge some pretty important goals and directions over the years, and we thank our God for you.*"

In ER's library are three three-ring notebooks, five inches thick, with single copies of our publications in many, many languages and many dozens of titles – a record of a day now past, for the Center no longer has the needed staff nor income to maintain such literature productivity.

In 1990 Thelma and I moved to America and managed the home office in Lexington for a year, then moved to Wilmore. Writing has filled these ten years. Our ministries grew to include Nigeria, Russia, India, Bangladesh, Myanmar and Nepal. Instead of two schools we now have 30. Instead of 30 overseas workers we now have 135. Correspondence has increased greatly. Overseas trips have increased. Fund-raising activities also increased. The scope of ER overseas ministries has expanded, especially with the beginning of Decade of Advance programs in North India, Bangladesh and Myanmar.

The concept of DANI developed as a result of Thelma's and my trip to six cities of North India and meeting two bishops of Uttar Pradesh. These bishops both had departments of evangelism, something I had not seen earlier in India. And both were keen advocates of evangelism. In North India we sensed a strong self-consciousness in north India's churchmen. Christianity's strength is in the south and northeast. Its weakest area is the twelve states called North India. There was a pervasive resentment of being viewed by the south as a mission field. The north longed to be seen as equal. A movement in the north that bound them together would be very welcome.

The Decade of Advance in North India was such a movement and, indeed, it was welcome. But unlike other "movements" it required something more than attendance at a conference of denominations. In fact, it called for a lot of creative energy. That is why it was a veritable movement. Too, unlike other movements that the mission world has seen, it offered a non-stop series of *Proposals for Progress* to all denominations, giving 480 fresh ideas of how twelve departments of the life of the Church can move forward month after month.

You can see where writing was a major part of DANI. We had to describe every facet of DANI for the January 1999 conference and more and more thereafter for the first full year of proposals, *ADVANCE*, departmental questionnaires, addresses of 400 CEOs, of 144 state coordinators, 22 DANI Council members, 12 Central Coordinators, etc. Letters to Gene Robinette, letters to Scott Powell and letters to the Bodhans numbered over 100.

And there were Bangladesh and Myanmar with their DAB and DAM programs. They too required writing, as did Malaysia, Angola and Ghana.

The little English literature teacher in Central High School, 66 years ago, would never know what she had started. But she was God's servant, unknowingly, for the moment and I am forever grateful to Him and to her.

PUBLICATIONS BY THE BRAUNS

Advance of the Church in Africa (120 pages); *Pastoral Evangelism in Africa* (92 pages); *Evaluating and Escalating Church Growth* (100 pages); *Roots and Possible Fruits of AD2000* (160 pages); *Evangelism Resources* (143 pages); *Collateral Readings*(124 pages); *The Status of Pygmies* (40 pages); *The Timothy Project (India, Russia,* 48 pages); *Winning Zaire (*54 pages); *Partners in Conquest (*36 pages); *Called to Shepherd God's People (*112 pages, published in over 25 languages); *Congo Mission News* (504 pages, five years);*Story Teller* (240 pages, 2½ years); *NEWS from the Fields* (1000 pages, 22 years); *Christian Education the Other Side of Evangelism; AD 2000 To Help Double the World Church; Empower the Church in Your Nation; Multiple Planning Teams; Saved* (6 languages); *52 Bible Themes* (5 languages); *What is Going on in Zaire?;Proposals for Denominational CEOs; Where in the World Is This Happening?; Elements of a Movement of Evangelism; Open a Door Wide to God; A New Thing in Africa; Pastor, You Can Make a Big Difference; The Orissa Plan; ADVANCE; REVS Project Materials; AD 2000 Calendar 1993; Orissa Teams of Ten; A Decade of Advance in N. India (DANI); He Married a Princess; Jottings* (36 Years)

These are available in the archives of Evangelism Resources for in-house review or photocopying.

THE ARTS

My father was a commercial artist in St. Louis. After he left us and was divorced, he married an accomplished artist who had worked for him. He was one of several Plymouth Brethren artists in St. Louis. Two of these had been partners with my father. Both made excellent livings. Both were close family friends whom I called Uncle. Uncle Carl Walters had a beautiful suburban home and two sons, one of whom was a Board member of ER until he died. His name was Donald. Uncle Charles Hendrick also had two sons, one of whom was Donald. Both sons supported their families as artists in St. Louis.

I am forced to conclude that my father could have prospered as an artist there too, had he persevered. An ink- and water-color drawing of his shows excellent mastery of the drawing pen. The oil paintings which I saw in his West Hollywood home were of exceptional quality but they had been done by his wife and son. Interestingly, his son Bill had made a wood carving, a bust of his father which was well done. I suspect that while I was wood carving in Belgian Congo, he was doing the same in California. Genes?

In this chapter I simply want to record my own artistic activities. They were surprisingly varied, but my era was one of global curiosity. American presidents enjoyed big game hunting in Africa. Rich men built grandiose museums with enormous bull elephants fighting furiously. It was a time of awakening to a reachable, knowable world, and my life was shaped by this American renaissance in which the greatness of our land was being explored and publicized in newspapers, magazines and books.

By the time I reached 80, television and movies had made every nation a familiar neighbor. There were few animals, birds and insects which were unfamiliar to the kids roaming malls in search of something new and exciting. The world has changed. Exploration now lies in the bottom of an ocean or on planets in the skies. Microscopic medicine and electronic horizons beckon today's youth. Mine was an earlier time, and it defined my interests.

I list those interests and activities largely in the order of their occurrence, though some continued for decades.

Childhood was largely limited to pencil drawings and crayon coloring, none of which remain. In high school years I fell in love with animals and birds and bought a course on taxidermy. A crow, a fish, a mole, a squirrel, an owl's head, a black bear's paw inkwell and the skeleton of a squirrel set in wax for extra credit at Wheaton followed.

My biggest dream-project was to mount a whole lion shot on a Mississippi island by a "big game hunter." I read about this cheap shenanigan in the paper. An old circus lion had been bought by the hunter and his cage was boated out to a small sand island. With reporters safely protected, the cage was opened and the lion strolled out to "freedom." He hardly had time to smell the breeze before he was shot down. I didn't approve of the way this was done, but the vision of mounting a whole lion was exciting. Few people had cars then, but street cars covered the city. I hopped on one, then another and another to reach the address of the hunter. My time ran out before I reached the man's area and I had to return home - lionless.

In my junior year at Wheaton I was asked to do the artwork for the yearbook. I had seen some very interesting paste-ups of cloth, leather and ceramic faces and decided that this was more interesting than the usual pen drawings. I think the French call this "montage." It was a new idea then. Looking through the yearbook I see nine of these, all with Ivory soap heads and hands, with pinheads as pupils. Some are amateurish, but others are of professional level and all are fun. There were two wax sculptures with plaster of Paris powder mixed in to give a marble look. One shower room "cartoon" was composed of a singing trio of two carved sponges and a bar of soap.

There were three two-page displays of a block of Ivory soap specially ordered. These measured about 18" x 12" x 2". The surfaces were carved in bas-relief motifs of the fall, winter, and spring season's sports. Using plasticene clay on wire armatures I modeled figures about 10" high. The first showed a young winter slaying an old summer, standing on a large dead leaf. The second showed the Wheaton Tower building, about 16" long, with King Winter behind it. The third had an aged winter being driven away by a young woman spring, both standing on an 18" flower. These clay sculptures were

Wheaton yearbook's clay sculpture shows
Spring chasing away Winter.

painted black to give a better contrast with the white soap and some highlights.

I didn't know that yearbooks were graded by an organization until I was told that the artwork for the 1942 yearbook received the highest mark possible. Looking back, I imagine I could have made a living as an artist. But my first three years at Wheaton were very seriously dedicated to a career in sociology. The Lord of life wiped both of these goals out of my heart. He called me to missions. Four years later, Thelma and I were in Belgian Congo, opening up all kinds of new opportunities to be "me."

For two years we studied at the Nyack Missionary Training Institute. To make ends meet, Thelma taught English in the college and I pastored the Old Stone Church. It was an abandoned Methodist Church so small that 125 people crowded it out. Average attendance was 60 in Sunday School and 25 in morning worship. Our average weekly income was $13, giving a total of $676 a year. The old church has a window over the front door. Salmon's head of Christ was very popular at the time. I made a 5' by 3' oil-paint picture of the Lord on glass so it resembled a stained glass window with light streaming through. As far as I know, it is still in place.

The trip to Congo was complicated by World War II. German submarines were sinking ships in the Atlantic, so our freighter kept close to the mainland as it plowed southward. As it reached the bulge of South America it angled over to Capetown, where we disembarked. Our trip north through South Africa by train gave us a few days at the Livingston Falls where there was a large, free trade in lion and leopard skins. We couldn't afford such luxuries, but I picked up some scraps of leopard and later made a hat and purse. That was in 1945. We still have the hat but I think it was never worn. Women's hats went out of style about then.

Our train to Congo terminated in Port Franqui, where we took a river steamer to Leopoldville, the capital of Congo. One of the passengers was an ornithologist who was collecting bird skins for a museum in Brussels, Belgium. He was a fascinating conversationalist and advised me to write to Dr. James Chapin of the American Museum of Natural History. The greatest collection of Congo birds in the world was Dr. Chapin's, I was told.

This conversation led to my collecting over 100 birds of the Bas-Congo area and to being mentioned in books written by Dr. Chapin. When I visited him he gave me a brass tube machined to fit into my twelve-gauge shotgun and hold 410-gauge shells with fine bird shot so as to avoid damage to specimens. Termites riddled several thick volumes of Chapin books and none remain.

For seven years, birds were a delightful focus for me. I still have about fifteen watercolors of birds of Congo. Most I painted with the live bird on my left hand while I sketched and painted with my right hand. All of these were painted at the Vungu Mission, on top of a mountain clad in virgin jungle, a place abounding in birds.

One incident stands out in my memory of those years at Vungu. I often relaxed in the evenings by walking the high jungle paths with my gun, hoping to get meat for our table. One day, and only once, I heard a whirring of wings and a loud chatter of birds slowly coming my way. Suddenly hundreds of birds of many kinds, large and small, whirred into the place where I stood and then swept onward. A migration? No. It was a multi-species drive in search of insects, lizards, snakes and whatever a jungle could yield to hungry birds.

It resembled the jungle drives of Pygmies with their nets and spears and distant criers and bell-carrying, voiceless dogs. It was like a driver ant crusade which often covered half an acre of jungle. But these different species were "lone rangers" which privately sought out their dietary preferences. What memory in their genes rallied them to join in a common, united, purposeful front to rouse and gobble down insects in large jungle areas at one time? For me it was a unique experience and thought-provoking. Was there a Napoleon among them to call them all to war? Or was there a seasonal clock which once in a decade brought them excitedly together as a single flock?

Africans learned that I would buy the skins of game animals and they brought quite a variety to me. It was my way of learning what animals lived in the jungles of the area. One man brought a raw leopard skin which he had dried on the wall of his hut. The skin was longer than the wall so he angled part of it to make it fit. Our Vungu house had a fireplace and I put the skin up on the wall over the fireplace. Thelma said the crooked skin made her sit crooked in the chair facing the skin.

Before the skin was put up, there had been an oil painting, a portrait I made in America of Thelma. Every meal time I sat across from her and the portrait was right behind her. I couldn't avoid seeing the need for improvement in the painting. One day I got out my tubes of paint and began to "improve" the likeness. The trouble was that I could never get the original flesh colors. The palette was simply incompatible. In the end, I could no longer abide my botched job. If it wasn't Thelma 100% it wasn't acceptable. Somewhere along the line the portrait was sadly destroyed. I never tried again. However, I became a patron of a young Congolese artist who did a very nice pastel portrait of Thelma, and it appears now over our piano in Wilmore.

During the Vungu years I gave considerable effort to manufacturing levels, masons' trowels, hacksaws and drills and purchasing bolts of white duck cloth. This was a subsidized activity to help make tools available for pennies and white suits for preachers for a couple of dollars. Tools which could be used to build a brick house were sold to anyone who wanted to build a house. Many people moved from huts of branches into houses of bricks as a result. And many poor village lay pastors looked very handsome in gleaming white suits.

On our first furlough I painted a second window. This one was for a round area above the pulpit of the C&MA Church in Mansfield, Ohio. Thelma and I were the first couple married in that new edifice. The window was 6' in diameter and I bought two 6' x 3' panes of pebble glass and painted two hemispheres with a flaming torch. A round frame was built to surround the glass. Eventually the congregation outgrew that building and a new and larger church was built. The window was built into the new structure and remains there today.

Our second and third terms were spent at Kinkonzi station where I was station manager and director of the Bible Institute. They were wonderful years of church growth. Here I designed and built dozens of dormitory and kitchen buildings, a large two-story Bible Institute and a large extension and tower on the church. We made clay bricks and burned them in kilns. In the summer dry season over 100 brick makers, masons, carpenters and earth movers were employed.

Here I painted my third faux-stained glass window, 6' x 12' in size. It took three pieces of pebble plate glass for this picture of the Lord Jesus seated amid flowers. The church platform was part of a recessed sitting area which jutted out of the back wall. We cut out bricks in this wall for the window. A large choir platform was built in front of the pulpit and fluted cement columns were added to the two corners of the platform area.

In this period a cathedral-sized church was built at Ndingi and I bought four large panes of pebble glass and on each painted designs. One represented God the Father, one God the Son, one God the Holy Spirit and the fourth the Word. Never had I such freedom of expression and of the use of color. To me, these were glorious. Unfortunately, I ran out of linseed oil and experimented with kerosene as a thinner. In order to secure translucence, I thinned the paint considerably. It dried hard and I took the windows to Ndingi feeling very good about the business. Business? It was a gift to the church, of course. To my total chagrin, people of Ndingi told me that the heavy rains had washed most of the paint off the glass. The kerosene had ruined the binder in the paint. I was never able to repair the damage.

At Kinkonzi I had two or more carpenters all the time. I designed furniture and pulpits and doors and brick molds, garages, houses, cages for jungle animals, churches of the district, etc. It was a very creative time and situation. There I carved a bas-relief of Peter shocked as he heard the cock crow and remembered that Jesus had told him of his coming denial. The wood was butter yellow with a close grain. Today it is on our wall at the head of the steps in our living room, a warm tan in color.

A second carving in the display of 15 sections is a humorous hornbill head and neck with the background cut away. The bird was colored in its natural colors and varnished.

On a two-week trip home by freighter I carved a fetish piece, copied from a postage stamp, in bas relief and gave it to Rev. Phil Worth, a Wheaton College housemate, pastor of the very large United Methodist Church in Collingswood, New Jersey and ER Board member who visited us in Kinshasa. We had great times with the Worths and shared his pulpit with many of America's great preachers.

Our fourth term was mostly spent in Kinshasa, first with the Evangelical Press of Congo and, later, as head of the African Office of Worldwide Evangelism in Depth. This was a term that lasted nine years. There just was no time to stop what we were doing.

Regarding art, I bought a small ebony log in Kinshasa and had it sawed into thin boards. One section of this, about 7" x 9", I carved in bas relief to depict the bowed, thorn-crowned head of Christ on the cross. An ebony frame brought its size to 13" x 15". It shone like black marble and the wood was almost as heavy and dense as marble. I loved this piece above all others. Sadly, I presented it as a gift to Kasa Vubu, the first president of independent Congo, when he visited New York to speak to the United Nations. Kasa Vubu had studied for the priesthood in Catholic seminaries and he could appreciate the carving of the Lord. After his death I visited his home in hopes of regaining the ebony, but no one was home.

On furlough in Nyack, New York I worked on a clay and armature head and shoulders bust of Kasa Vubu. When it was finished Thelma and I drove with it to the city to have a ceramic copy made of it. It was finished to look like aged bronze. When flicked with a finger nail the sound was a high, clear ringing one. I made a thick rubber mold of the bust and blocked it with plaster of Paris. Removing the original, I poured a plaster of Paris copy. The original was sent to the president in a steel drum. The copy was later cut back in size to fit a container and it is currently in the garage, painted bronze. It is a nice piece of work, but who cares now about Zaire's first president?

I went to visit President Kasa Vubu after his forced retirement. The purpose was to obtain a paragraph expressing appreciation for Dr. Glen Tuttle who had been his personal physician and who built the large Kimpese Hospital - and delivered Chris! We were editing *Congo Mission News* during five years of that term and I frequently illustrated articles with pencil portraits. Dr. Tuttle's retirement had a two-page drawing of the doctor and of his hospital as well as our article, Kasa Vubu's testimonial, and another by the national head of the Department of Health.

We had fun in those days. Leafing through five years of *Congo Mission News* I found my pencil portraits of Dr. Pierre Shaumba, President of the Congo Protestant Council, and of Mr. Marthinson, pioneer of the Congo Bible Society, both great and enduring friends. And Thelma began *Jottings* in that magazine.

Someone sent to me three thick volumes of a Famous Artists course in that term. I sent back to their school several pencil renderings and a black, gray and white watercolor of a farm. The watercolor is presently on a wall downstairs in our home in Wilmore. It is a study in lights and shadows and is not a copy of anything. It reflects my very happy vacation months, and I can almost feel once again the itchy hay on my back as I look at it being unloaded into the barn. The attic of the log cabin captured us for frigid winter nights because of heat which leaked up through the ceiling. But with warm weather, the barn gave us freedom to laugh and talk as long as we wanted before sleeping.

Stone provided only one bit of art for me. It was a very meaningful ear about life size, carved in white soapstone. Thelma gave the stone to me for a depression-time Christmas gift. It measured 1 1/2" x 6" x 1/2". It suggested to me the pierced ear of the love slave in the Old Testament. I wanted to be the love slave of my God. With

*Willys' drawing of Thelma to
accompany her "Jottings"*

the aid of two mirrors I sketched the shape of my own ear on paper, then began to carve. The wee stone was longer than my ear so I cut off the extra and, later, glued the ear upright on the left-over as a base. The piece was polished and glowed like white marble but it was not finished. I crafted a tiny drill out of a paper clip and drilled the hole through the tab of the ear. The stone became my flesh, for me. I was, I am the love slave of my God. Somewhere the ear was lost. I have a larger stone, another gift from Thelma, which for a quarter century I have wanted to carve into an ear but always there have been other priorities.

In the 24 years with Evangelism Resources I have made two more windows. One is in the stairwell of our Kinshasa media building. It shows the cross over the African continent with African lips speaking, an ear hearing and a hand writing. To protect it against the rain and the damage Ndingi's window suffered, we put the painted side inside. African fingers just couldn't leave it alone. A scratch here, a scratch there and, after a few years, it had to be touched up. When we saw it last, it was bright with colored light.

The last window of the series can be seen in the ER office building. It has the ER logo of the cross over the world. The glass is 6' x 6' plate glass and the painting was done in our garage over a winter. There was less light there than in the wall where it was placed. I blame the low light for the rough brush strokes. I simply was not seeing them clearly. But it is a good addition to the building. The paint is on the outside to protect it from fingers, and slanted sheets of quarter inch plastic protect it from rain but permit air to circulate freely.

Collections were made in the 1940s of butterflies and other insects. Living creatures were kept, three kinds of monkeys, a baboon, three kinds of antelopes, a long-tailed genet, tame goats and parrots. These made up our Braun zoo while the boys were growing up. Stamp collections and coins from 50 nations were collected for the boys.

Thousands of slides and photographs make up ER's collections today.

Oil paintings were collected. Currently, 45 oils decorate the new office - all collected and framed by us over 25 years. Copper work, Gabon soapstone carvings, ancient leg and arm bracelets of brass, fetishes and wood carvings, including full figures and heads of ebony and other fine woods, plus some brass figures from Nigeria and a host of souvenirs from around the world are displayed in our living room. Asia, Africa, the Island World, the Near East - all have contributed to the collector spirit which has always been ours.

The life of a career missionary and of missionary children is rich and varied. It calls for creativity and provides freedom and inspiration to be all that the human spirit and the Holy Spirit within invited one to be. I have never regretted spending my life as a missionary - so far 56 years in this 2000th year of our Lord.

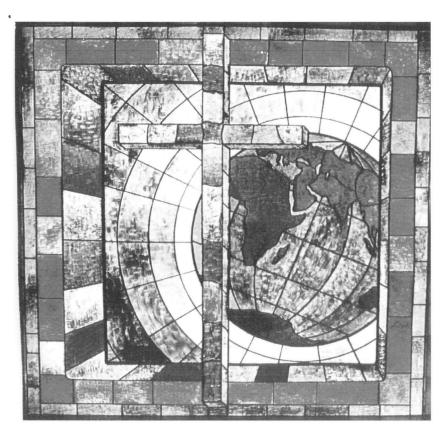

The ER stained glass window

33

MINISTRIES

CROWDS

Thelma in her teens had preached in many thriving churches crowded with people who wanted to see and hear the girl evangelist. Curiosity was replaced by surprise or awe at the mature Bible messages they heard and the blessing received.

When she married me she had to start from scratch. Our first church was the Old Stone Church in Nyack, New York. Our average Sunday morning attendance was only 25 but we built up the Sunday school to 60. At age 26 I felt socially closer to kids than to their parents.

In our first term in Congo we were isolated on a mountaintop, many miles from villages other than the two tiny ones on the mountain. A good crowd was about 30.

In our second term we lived on Kinkonzi station with about 400 grade schoolers who left for their villages on weekends. Bible Institute students increased from 17 to 93 over ten years. Hospital patients were attended by relatives who fed them and cared for their needs. Thirteen villages were within an hour's walk. With all of that potential, the weekly Sunday school averaged 168 people in attendance. We accepted this as normal for years.

You read earlier that in 1954 the Sunday School contest at Kinkonzi increased the six-week average attendance from 168 to 1300. Those Sundays passed with growing excitement and explosively increasing crowds, with over 2000 attending one Sunday. The next year we expanded the contest to 300 congregations and they reported that overall growth was three times the attendance of the year before.

From that experience I learned that drifting along at 168 was not the will of God. We learned how to bring 1000 people out regularly.

Kinkonzi Sunday School crowd

We organized joint-district open-air rallies with 3000 in attendance for three services. We brought 1000 to 10,000 people together for tent rallies out in rural Congo.

In Kinshasa we brought people together in dozens of outdoor evangelism rallies by thousands and by 10,000. They marched in giant parades 30,000 strong to the smaller stadium and five times to the national stadium where 70,000 people gathered, and several times some 15,000 responded to the invitation to come forward for counseling and prayer.

The Center led in beginning a Kinshasa Committee of Evangelism, which met monthly over eight years to plan citywide zone-by-zone crusades as well as stadium crusades. We provided the loudspeakers, platform and pulpit for each zone week after week.

Evangelists were invited from China, New Zealand and the USA. For each there were mass rallies all over the city. At one in Ndjili a fence of palm fronds surrounded a crowd of over 10,000, including the embassy personnel of free China, to hear Dr. Timothy Dzao of Hong Kong.

Rev. Makanzu, the leading pastor of Kinshasa, found himself without a church in 1967 and we invited him to co-chair Christ for All with us. Zaire had never had a national evangelist but needed one, so we asked him to accept the role. He was equipped with numerous banners, large posters and travel money for two years of crusades in every province of the country. He preached to great crowds up to 30,000 in these tours of evangelism. No Christian had preached to so many Zairians nor seen so many come to Christ. In Kinshasa he was the voice of the Church in crusades, universities and churches and in the offices of President Mobutu.

Crowds gathered for Jesus were never before, nor since, so frequent or so large in Zaire-Congo. They were a gift from God in the 1966-1970 and in 1980-1990.

There were converts by the tens of thousands. The Alliance field's first tent saw over 40,000 come forward to accept Christ. Kinshasa's first tent recorded over 50,000. Over 75,000 came forward in five rallies in stadiums of Kinshasa. Thousands more were saved in every-zone week-long outdoor crusades. Dr. Makanzu recorded untotaled thousands who responded over 13 years. The twenty-seven tents we provided for the capital cities of Africa reaped vast harvests.

There were other gains, especially for the Church in Zaire. Protestants were a minority and oppressed by Belgian priests who believed the nation was theirs. As a result Protestants saw themselves as threatened, endangered, second-class citizens. But when they marched 70,000 strong through the city and into the national stadium they discovered their mass, their right and their power, and they never went back into their holes to hide again. In a day they became unstoppable citizens, which explains the explosive increase of Protestants and of their churches, some seating 3000, 5000 and 10,000.

Another by-product of the steady emphasis on evangelism was the emergence of evangelistic preaching all over the city and of great leaders of evangelism such as Dr. Mengi and Dr. Diafwila, heads of the national department of evangelism, which I began and which Dr. Makanzu led after me. One can appreciate the enormity of the spiritual change in the capital only by knowing that Kinshasa knew little about evangelists or evangelism until we introduced the gospel tent with an Alliance tent evangelist to Kinshasa's 35 pastors and churches in 1966, and that later over 1000 Kinshasa congregations all know and do evangelism.

One more fruit of evangelism in the '60s and '80s was the explosive growth of bands and choirs in the city. When we began in 1966 the only band in a Protestant denomination was that of the Salvation Army, which led every march and every major crusade rally. A few years later there were numerous bands in large churches.

Choirs played a major role in tent, street and stadium gospel meetings and eventually every congregation had one, two, three, four or more choirs. There were men's choirs, women's choirs, children's choirs and mixed choirs. Congo's people love to sing. At one time President Mobutu demanded that all youth groups be stopped in the churches. The pastors obeyed. They simply turned youth groups into choirs – of all ages. The president couldn't stop his people from singing. He didn't even dare try.

And those choirs turned to writing and singing hundreds of new songs. The church loves those songs that are learned from their choirs. And every choir records its own songs, and "spies" record all possible songs by other groups. They all wear distinctive uniforms and travel widely to other churches to sing. When you start something new in God's Church in Kinshasa you never know how far it will go.

In Asia, Christian crowds were not a logical goal. They threatened Hindu radicals and led to terrorist reprisals. In India, the best way to grow was to plant a multitude of small churches and train a multitude of lay pastors, ordainable pastors and tribal missionaries. Keeping a low profile was important for safety. Multiplying explosively the number of congregations and helping them grow and branch off in new congregations was the way to expand in all directions. Training tens of thousands of preachers to shepherd these new congregations was crucial to the growth process in Asia.

That is what we focused on in our first nine years in India. About eleven thousand men were trained in ER-funded portable Bible schools in that period and 1936 were graduated from our 20 schools of evangelism. In 2000, we graduated over 600 students from our 23 Asian schools of evangelism. In 2001 the expected number is over 700.

CONFERENCES

From 1945 to 1953 Thelma and I only attended conferences planned and led by others. In 1954 we set up tent rallies in most centers of our Alliance field with attendances of 500 to 10,000.

Before Independence riots began we held a crossroads evangelism rally at Mayunda, another at Yema and a third at Ndingi, with a total of 11,000 present and many conversions. The church was at its most popular point in those years. On our Kinkonzi station we had many weeks of evangelism and could bring 1000 people together regularly.

Three new movements challenged the church at that time. A Makukusa cult sprang up which introduced "holy dancing" in all-night orgies. The Kimbangu Church swept through the land, totally suppressing mission congregations in large areas and building palm frond roofs for huge outdoor meetings. Their message was healing, independence, and an African Holy Spirit. The third was the frenzy of pre-Independence, with an eventual mass forsaking of the laws of God in a nationwide spree of looting, killing, burning and kidnapping. Missions were equated with colonial rule. In 1960 and for years after, major flights of missionaries culminated in 1993, when most missions pulled out forever.

We left Zaire in 1960 for furlough and a year of French study and returned in 1962. We got tent evangelism going again on a steady basis and held one conference for about 100 deacons at Lukula. In 1963 we were assigned to Kinshasa where over a million people lived. We provided evangelism tents from 1966 to 1986. An estimated one and half million people attended and well over 50,000 claimed to have received Christ.

In 1966 Christ for All was voted in by the Zaire Protestant Council. We held a four-day national planning conference for two delegates from each province. These men laid out a two-year plan for all denominations, named me as the director, and called for six Provincial Conferences and about 40 Denominational Conferences to launch the movement.

In the two years of Christ for All, besides calling 17,000 preachers to conduct 24 monthly outreach ministries and supplying them with reports and detailed descriptions each month of the outreach of the month, we invited a series of evangelists from overseas and from Zaire to hold evangelistic crusades, as follows:

» 1967 – First stadium rally with Howard Jones and Ralph Bell of the Billy Graham Team. 30,000 marched to the stadium with large banners and placards.

» Evangelist Timothy Dzao came from Hong Kong and preached to tens of thousands in six places.

» Evangelist Barry Reid came from New Zealand. He preached in the second stadium rally and in eight other places.

» Dr. Richard Harvey came from the C&MA in America and preached in eight places in Kinshasa and other places outside of Kinshasa.

» 1968 – Dr. Ford Philpot, TV evangelist, was the first to preach in the national stadium to 70,000 people as well as in five other Kinshasa rallies and in three other cities.

» Dr. Mavumilusa Makanzu, Zaire's national evangelist, preached in the smaller stadium one Easter after a citywide week of evangelism. He preached all over Zaire for 13 years, frequently to 5,000 people and up to 30,000 outside of Kinshasa.

» 1969 – Zaire's first National Congress on Evangelism with about 200 delegates from nine nations.

» 1968-1970 – The Alliance appointed us to the Africa branch of OWED, Office of Worldwide Evangelism-in-Depth. In this period 34 nations of Africa were visited. Denominational heads met in those nations to hear what God was doing in Zaire. As a result, Central African Republic, Cameroon, Burundi and Ghana launched national movements of evangelism like Zaire's, winning great numbers to Christ and giving those nations a strong majority.

It is this band of Christian states that stretches three-fourths of the way across the waist of Africa and meets Uganda, Kenya, Tanzania and Rwanda to complete the last quarter. God sent revival through those nations, due to the preaching of Dr. Joseph Church, joined by Evangelist Festo Kivengere. It is this impenetrable belt of Christian nations which stopped Islam's thrust southward for a hundred years.

Of these many activities, only teaching in the schools was our assigned missionary task. All of the other ministries were over and above what the Alliance expected of our family in the 1944-1973 period in which we were its missionaries. I can only believe that it was God's Holy Spirit who kept urging us to both see and meet new needs and new options to bring Africans to salvation and to life-long service. I do not hesitate to believe that millions came to Jesus as a result of ministries listed above. But I profoundly regret that no one did them before or after us, except within the limits of their own denominations.

» 1980 – Back in Kinshasa for Evangelism Resources we organized and funded church-planting teams for 11 denominations. We met with the teams each month and held one large church planting conference. Hundreds of new congregations were begun.

» 1983 – Dr. Philpot again preached in the National Stadium with our leadership.

» 1985 – Dr. Marini, Vice President of the umbrella service organization to 62 denominations, spoke in the national stadium.

» 1987 – Dr. Bokeleale, president of the above organization, spoke in the national stadium.

» 1990 – The Third National Congress on Evangelism was held, with special emphasis on the Pygmies.

» 1995 – An International Congress on Pygmy evangelism was planned and funded by ER, a unique experience.

In addition, between 1983 and 1996 30,000 laymen studied in portable Bible schools in Africa. They used the *Called to Shepherd God's People*, written by Thelma, in eight languages. These were not conferences, but they changed the lives of over a million people scattered over the continent.

From 1985-2000 our ER Kinshasa schools trained hundreds of able leaders from 26 nations. Again, these were not conferences, but tens of thousands of lives were transformed through the ministries of alumni.

God urged us to go to India and to offer to its Church what ER supplied so generously to Zaire and all Africa. I take up once more a listing of our activities – this time in India and spilling over into four other nations: Bangladesh, Myanmar, Nepal and Pakistan.

From 1991 through 2003, 73 ER conferences were held in India. It is easy to picture the two types of schools ER has in India. It is less apparent what we do on our trips to India. Thirty-seven of those 73 conferences were funded and planned by ER but led 100% by Indian colleagues. Thirty-seven were planned and funded by ER and we participated in them.

It is our mailings of *ADVANCE* magazine and over 200 *Proposals for Progress*, along with these 73 conferences, that make the All-India Decade of Advance a major encourager, informer and challenger of 700 heads of denominations, and a major factor in deepening faith and daring and causing victories nationwide in this enormous sub-continent. Our goal is to rouse up the Church in every possible way to think bigger, pray more, do better and fulfill the whole purpose of God for His Church in India. Two thousand years of near-hibernation is being replaced by a massive grassroots march to Christ Jesus, led by newly-inspired denominational heads. To accelerate nationwide, this process of winning India is Evangelism Resources' assignment from the living God. We are eager to complete the assignment.

My brief summary of some of our activities could be, should be seen as acts of God in a window of time when the Church was ready for Him. In those seven years Zaire and North America were open to nationwide evangelism. Today, 30 years later, such a concept is unthinkable, not because God has changed, and not because He no longer blesses evangelism and revival. Rather, His Church in America no longer invites evangelists, and Zaire's chaos prohibits a nationwide movement. God opens windows of opportunity, of salvation and lasting revival. And man shuts them.

It seems unquestionable that what we experienced in Africa was needed in India. God gave the burden. God took us there. God gave us co-workers. Then God gave the vision for an India-wide movement of evangelism.

The word evangelism as used here covers much more than the ministry of evangelists. It includes church planting, church growth, and church nurturing. It includes church cleansing, revival and holiness. It includes Bible reading, verse memorization and teaching the Word. It includes total surrender, commitment, obedience and service of many kinds. The goal is nothing less than the fulfillment of the whole purpose of God by His Church.

TRAVELS

Old passports inform us that we have been in about 72 nations. In the Americas, we have been in every state of the continental 48 plus Alaska, but not Hawaii. We were in Canada's states from Quebec to British Columbia. We entered Mexico at several US border crossings and the capital. In Central America we touched down in every banana republic on our way to Costa Rica. We have not traveled South America. We did visit Haiti.

In Africa, of the 50 nations, we have not been in Guinea, Mauritania, Upper Volta, Niger or Libya. We have been to the other 45.

In Europe, we have been in all but Scotland, Ireland, Finland, Poland and Czechoslovakia. In the Near East, we were never in Free China, Iraq, Afghanistan or Pakistan. In Asia we were in India, Bangladesh, Nepal, Myanmar, Thailand and the Philippines. We go where we think God wants us to establish ministries.

Since 1968 we have never traveled like tourists when in new countries. Our goal was to meet the heads of denominations in each capital city, for we had reports of God's moving to relate, and proposals for churchmen to evaluate and to act on, if they chose to. In 34 nations of Africa these visits led to bishops and presidents of denominations sending some of their best men to our schools at the International Center of Evangelism. Actually, students from 26 nations flew to Kinshasa to study in this unique school.

Now it is Asia's turn. Travel takes less of our time. Since 1990 we are overseas about three months out of twelve. We have established ministries with Asian leaders who keep them going. We can fulfill a very vital role from our Kentucky desks through post, fax and e-mail 75% of the time and go overseas for numerous conferences and fine-tuning in the remaining 25% of the year.

SECTION SIX

OBSERVATIONS

34

DOUBLE PORTIONS

When I went to Wheaton I was 21 – a man. Out of the roughly 600 girl students in the school I wanted one who would love me. She had to be a Christian and mine. Those were about the only limiting characteristics in mind. Blond, brunette, black-haired or red would not have mattered.

God was much more careful. He picked out a real star and said to her, "Love this poor, lonesome creature," and for the next 61 years she did.

· ·

I gave a lot of thought to selecting a major field in college. As an ardent Christian in a world of economic depression I determined that I could best serve my Lord helping people. So I worked hard to master sociology. I planned to go west to earn a Master's degree and a Doctorate in sociology in Portland, Oregon.

God got me headed east to Belgian Congo. In 1944 Thelma and I became missionaries of The Christian and Missionary Alliance. Why the C&MA? That was Thelma's church and it had a strong missionary vision and passion. There were 13 C&MA missionaries overseas from this one church in this little city of Mansfield. The four Assemblies of the major city of St. Louis, where I grew up, had none. I had no concern whatever for the unreached peoples of our world, but God gave me a wife with a passion for that lost world, and He gave me a call to go where they live and win them to Christ.

· ·

In Congo I was content to sleep in a palm frond hut for a week with hogs grunting and scratching their tough hides against it and malarial mosquitoes whining outside and inside our nets all night in order to win a few village believers to faith in Jesus. That was being a real missionary in my thinking then.

But God showed Thelma and me a way to attract 50,000 Africans and Indians to study in portable Bible schools. They were already in those 50,000 villages, not for a week but for a lifetime. The goal was not just to win them to faith in Christ but to disciple them lifelong and to win the next generation. God did it! We simply followed His guidance.

· ·

Assigned to be principal of the Kinkonzi Bible Institute, we were happy teaching Bible to 17 students. What else?

God sent us a student body of 93 after awhile and the Bible Institute added so many new forms of witness that it became the outreach center for the whole mission. It sponsored the first four-part harmony traveling choir. It began tent campaigns across the field. It sent out gospel teams far and wide. It operated a printing plant, a bookstore, provided employment for students. It terraced the dormitory hillside, built dozens of dorm family units, planted hundreds of fruit trees and dammed a stream to produce fish. It had a radio studio that prepared half-hour programs five days a week. It organized mass rallies where thousands gathered for evangelistic preachers and held fieldwide Sunday school contests for 300 churches. God used what the school introduced to the Congo field for many years to come.

· ·

In Kinshasa, Congo's capital, I was content to cooperate with an African editor in publishing a monthly magazine called *MOYO*. That means LIFE in Kikongo, our African language.

But God had a much bigger idea. He led an African churchman to assign me to head a nationwide movement of evangelism called Christ for All which provided monthly challenges to 17,000 preachers in six language areas. Numerous new ministries were introduced to all of Congo through this movement. Thirty-two years later, those "new" ministries are still the backbone of church growth in the churches. God guided us into launching that nationwide movement and to the 24 monthly challenges sent out during it.

Our fourth term, instead of being the usual four years, lasted nine. When we left Congo we had three boys and wanted only a quiet year at home.

But God had other plans. When our year was about to end, headquarters in New York called us to lead a program they were participating in called Key '73. We moved to Nyack, NY to a fine old house owned by the denomination and drove into New York City every weekday. Fourteen hundred congregations in Canada and the United States were taking part in this movement which was to go on two and a half years. It did. We produced a two-inch thick notebook of ways to make a congregation grow, and grow those 1400 congregations did. The numbers of converts, baptisms and new members rose wonderfully. Giving was far ahead of budget and revivals, some lasting for years, were reported in over 300 congregations. God brings revival. God guides His laborers. God blessed the whole C&MA in those years, and its evangelists were booked up for meetings for years to come.

. . . .

In moving to Kentucky, for once I had a BIG goal. Dr. Ford Philpot was a very creative Methodist evangelist who had citywide crusades and a TV program on numerous stations. When we were leading Christ for All, we had invited Dr. Philpot to preach in Kinshasa stadium. He had a wonderful crusade and we became close friends. My BIG goal in joining his association was to establish an international Center of Evangelism in Kinshasa. He liked the idea and we went to Lexington as an interim place to live until the Center was built.

God had another idea. In 1974 America suffered a serious recession. We could never raise a nickel to buy or build a Center. The project was refused by the Philpot board. After two years, our time with Ford ended. What now? Little by little we came to feel God wanted us to depend on Him and build the Center as a new mission. This is how Evangelism Resources came into being.

. . . .

By then we had been in America for six years. We had begun to buy a house and expected to direct the mission from Kentucky.

The question we had not answered - in fact, had not asked, was, "Direct what mission?" This was a mission without any overseas missionaries, without any stations, without any ministries. By 1980, after many trips to Africa, Europe and the Near East, the Lord sent us back to Kinshasa. My BIG idea there was to rent a house and begin a little school of evangelism.

Again, God had a much, much bigger idea. He gave us a house three times as large as any we would have designed for ourselves. In it we were able to house Phil, our third son, Steve Liversedge and Dale Garside over five years. We held conferences in the very large living room. We had two offices in it and six office rooms in a separate building. Later we were able to build four missionary houses and a campus of three school buildings with 27,000 square feet of floor space. Clearly God had a bigger idea.

By 1990 we had completed ten more years in Africa. There were ten missionaries, well trained for the ministries, and we were

The International Center of Evangelism in Kinshasa

able to return to America and open a home office. The International Center of Evangelism had three exceptional schools with students from 26 nations. It had planted hundreds of new congregations. The century-long resistance of the Bateke had been broken and hundreds of villages had believers and lay pastors. Portable Bible Schools had trained 20,000 men across the nation. A national program of evangelism had been in operation for three years. Pygmy evangelism and churching had begun and almost every denomination had a department of evangelism trained in our International School of Evangelism. Oh! God's idea was much bigger than any we had!

· ·

So in the last half of 1990 we returned to our house in Lexington, Kentucky. What were our reasons for this? We thought we might be able to serve the workers and the ministries better from America. We expected to preach in more churches and have more ER dinners leading to a gradual increase of funds for the field.

Again God's idea was so much larger than ours. A few months after we returned to the USA an amazing opening to Nigeria took us back to Africa to set up an International School of Evangelism there. A year later Thelma and I spent seven weeks in India, from which came ER's entry into Asia. Thirteen years later, there are 30 Schools of Evangelism in nine countries. 45,000 lay pastors have been trained in seven nations and the Decade of Advance in North India is four years old with clones in Bangladesh, Myanmar, Nepal and twenty African nations..

The concept and elements of the Decade of Advance can be a tremendous blessing in many nations of the world. It has global potential. It brings together the continuous challenging of heads of denominations with hundreds of *Proposals for Progress* – new ways to reach out on twelve denominational fronts – with a network of denominational district and congregational teams which can develop new ministries at the grass roots level in 700 denominations across all India.

The Lord God has, as you can see, consistently taken my little goals and built upon them at every stage of life. When I think small, He thinks big. When I think BIG, He thinks BIGGER. When, in my old age, I begin thinking bigger, He drowns my highest hopes in a flood of His BIGGEST achievements.

Life long, He has doubled - and doubled again - His portions. And I feel in my bones that I have recognized only a fraction of the ALL that He has showered on Thelma and me. What a God of grace and mercy and power He is!

35

LOOKING AHEAD

The time of our Lord's return cannot be known by anyone on earth. Numerous books have been written in the last ten years on the subject. As I look back over the history of the Church, I note the miraculous rise of Christianity through the centuries as a small band of fishermen grew to a vast body composed of the citizenry of the Roman Empire. It swept through the Near East and Europe, wiping out ancient religions, not through jihads, terrorists and armies, but through the missionary travels of other fishermen, farmers and tradesmen. The irresistible Christ changed hearts, emptied pagan temples, won emperors and civilized primitive cultures. It is a story of spiritual conquest and of redemption and of transformation, which was to cover the earth in time.

How much time? Two thousand years seems like a very, very, very long time indeed. But at age 86, I see that only 23 periods of 86 years add up to 1,978 years, and that is just 22 years short of 2000. One could say that there have been only 23 generations of 86 years since the Cross. We can get a handle on 23, can't we?

Something of enormous significance occurred in the seventh of those 23 "generations." A man named Mohammed wrote a book called the Koran. The book declared that sons of Abraham through Sarah's housemaid were to regard as infidels all who did not accept the new book and slaughter them all. His followers were quick to obey. They poured out of Arabia and took the Near East, North Africa, Eastern Europe and Spain. For hundreds of years they ruled Spain and moved against France but failed. Europe at last organized against them and over 1000 years drove them out of its nations apart from Albania and Bosnia. Europe even ruled in the Near East and North Africa for a time, but it never routed out Islam as a religion in those nations and eventually abandoned them.

In the twenty-third "generation," enriched by oil and emboldened by terrorists, the Islamic offspring of Abraham are once more on the offensive. They are obeying the Koran's injunctions to slaughter the infidels. Explosives are their new swords. Airlines fly them worldwide. They are a huge majority in dozens of nations and are in total control. Their radicals have come to dominate once peaceful nations. Arab riches flow to them to buy weapons and bombs. Boldly, they threaten the whole world. Sixteen percent of the world's population is shouting its battle cry at 84% of the world, and the 84% tremble.

Christians wonder why the Creator put billions of dollars worth of oil under Islamic lands. We wonder why God, in Abraham's time, promised Hagar that her offspring would be as the sand of the sea. Why did He permit Mohammed's terrorists to capture forever nations which were Christian? Why, why, why?

We shall have to wait for heaven to learn the divine wisdom which arranged all of this. One thing is clear, power has been enjoyed by Greece, Italy, Russia, Spain, France, Sweden, Germany, Portugal, Egypt, England, America, Brazil, China, Japan and on and on. It seems the Almighty raises up people after people and that in the judgment day, no nation will be able to say it never had a chance. Arabs were desperately poor until oil was found in their lands. When oil no longer enriches them, their deserts, mountains and rock-strewn lands offer them only poverty. But in this generation they dream of conquering and slaughtering, as the Koran requires of them.

In past centuries European armies were able to subdue their nations and Muslims lived in relative peace. In this "generation" western armies can bomb them and drive out their rulers. But it is not clear that they can be subdued to live quietly in the world. The openness of Western democracies and the ease of travel have made it almost impossible to protect our citizens from the rage of the Koran.

Russia was a mighty power worldwide until it invaded Afghanistan. Its empire fell apart after that. Is it possible that the USA will exhaust its wealth and military might in Muslim lands? It is logical to take up arms against terrorists wherever they are. In so doing we take our fight to them and show Muslim rulers that the cost of harboring terrorists is very high. Yet the cost to the USA is also enormous.

Islam maintains fanatical control of its many nations and even when one is defeated in war its populace remains loyal to its religion. No Christian nation has so strong a bond, so uniting a force to keep it through adversity. The Koran has achieved what the Bible is losing in Europe and America, its once strong core. Fortunately, great numbers of new Christians in Asia and Africa still hold the truth of God as the size of Muslim families is making Islam an ever-growing menace. All of this is true.

But it is also true that in the past 86 years the Church of the Lord Jesus Christ has grown faster than Islam. And it has done so by word of mouth, not by the machine gun. It is no surprise that a billion Muslims can conquer weak nations by invasion and terrorism. But that Christians have brought even more people to faith in Jesus peacefully by simply talking is astonishing. In truth it is God's miracle. His divine power is clearly the only explanation for such growth.

The Bible gave the world the ability to live together in peace and prosperity. It gave us concepts of human rights and of equal justice, of democratic unity where a billion people can speak the same language and live under the same flag. It opened men's minds so we could discover the laws the Creator built into earth's atmosphere, its land and its seas. We click a mouse, we set a thermostat, we answer the phone, we learn from radio and TV and universities and endless books. We explore the galaxies; we walk on the moon. We swim among whales and wolves and "invent" new ways to penetrate the mysteries of our brains and our cells. We mine the earth for energy and new building materials for factories and laboratories. We collect and analyze each plant for substances which heal our sickness or add to our sight, our hair, our strength, our years. All of this and more are gifts of God through His Word, His Son and His Spirit.

The Koran's gifts to mankind are few. Its peoples have been suppressed. Oil, found and extracted by Christian people, has given them unearned wealth with which to buy the means of waging war and conquering weak nations in our day. Oil buys the parts for bombs which blow their carriers to smithereens – along with any nearby Jews, Christians or fellow Muslims. But it is the Koran's declaration to its readers that they must kill all infidels and conquer all peoples which drives the "faithful" to deeds of terror. The book's teachings have created a political power structure in which mullahs not only rule but also are the voice of God, heard and obeyed by the people.

We find incredible the masses of Muslims who come together for Muslim holy days. We find the suicide bombers impossible to understand. We cannot comprehend the resistance of Muslims in Iraq to our efforts to free them from tyranny and poverty. It makes no sense – to us.

The whole world has become a shooting gallery for Muslims, the targets being a market place or two proud skyscrapers. These Muslims rarely field an army to be destroyed. They train in secret specialists to bomb civilians at work. Their suicide bombers self-destruct and leave no guilty persons for reprisals. It is world war with no front and no victories, no peace.

Two factors, beside oil, favor Islam. One is the census factor. Muslim wives, whatever their modest dress, produce more babies than Christian wives, whatever their sexy dress. Muslims increase at alarming speed because they have larger families. Secondly, the social glue is far stronger among Muslims than among Christians. While they are prostrating themselves five times a day to Allah, our schools are forbidding prayer or any mention of God for Christian youth, and our laboratories are inventing ever more effective birth preventatives. The Koran is adored, protected, obeyed – a book of jihad and endless terrorism. The Bible is rejected, its God dethroned in the nations to which it gave liberty, wealth, long life and power. Humanly speaking, the odds are all in favor of the Koran's people. They will outnumber, outvote, out-terrorize and outshout post-Christian peoples.

Christianity was born a struggling minority. Its strength was the indwelling Holy Spirit who transformed individuals, families, tribes and nations. Islam had every advantage in Africa for a thousand years. It was established on the east coast, on the north coast and across the vast northern half of Africa. But it was Christian missionaries who explored and inhabited the land until Christian nations began colonial governments in the nations. And it was missions which won strong majorities of populations of Congo, Rwanda,

Burundi, Kenya, Uganda and Tanzania, creating a bulwark against the Muslim tide.

Secular society mourns every death of its soldiers in Afghanistan and Iraq. TV, radio, newspapers and magazines make headline news of each death. But the endless parade of missionary deaths received no notices whatever. Yet it was the missionaries who won nations to Christ, the net result of which is the fact that no American soldiers will be needed in them. There are museums for football players, basketball players, baseball players, movie stars, race horses, artists, war heroes, scientists, animals, birds, insects, gems and collectors' items. Almost the only recognition society has come up with for its overseas missionaries is the Billy Graham Center at Wheaton College, and almost nobody knows it is there.

The greatest force for peace and friendship for Christian nations is its international army of gospel preachers, but few citizens consider that. In fact, the liberal media is prone to criticize missionaries for disturbing primitive societies in their paradise, ignoring the fact that those people are endangered species as civilization takes their land and brings starvation and new killing diseases. As the population increases there is less and less room for pandas, tigers and isolated tribes. People either come to terms with the new realities or perish.

THE LORD'S RETURN

Only a few generations back, there were untraveled seas and continents and peoples. No longer. The two billion-plus nations, China and India, are traveled freely, studied comprehensively, and both have burgeoning bodies of Christians. The number of unchurched tribes grows smaller year by year. Seven years from now India can have a preacher for every one of its 600,000 villages and far more churches than the USA, the current leader.

TV, radio, and the press carry the gospel message to the remotest valley. The requirement that this gospel of the Kingdom shall be preached in all the world for a witness to all nations, and then shall the end come, was an impossible dream fifty years ago. It is a reachable goal today. And "the end's" coming awaits its achievement.

Armageddon, the horrendous war to be fought over Israel, was unimaginable fifty years ago. No longer. As Islamic jihad expands and as Europe sits on the sidelines, awaiting the collapse of America's economy, the showdown against the hated Jews can burst upon the world with appalling speed.

God's purpose is to bring the people of every tribe and nation to salvation and to His heaven. The event that triggers His return in absolute power is the great battle. A billion Muslims hate the Jews and are becoming bolder and bolder in their war against Jews and Christians.

In my day science has changed so much of man's experience as it learns more of the mysteries that God built into His Earth. It seems that the Spirit of God is taking humanity on a guided tour of electronics, weather phenomena, planetary knowledge, biochemistry, oceanography, medicine, genetics, geography, history, zoology, botany and more. Why? Is it because He wants men and women to be awed by His omniscience, His omnipotence and His omnipresence as the time nears for His coming?

And when He comes, who will be the most surprised? Muslims! No more jihad! No more Koran! They will not go to the Jews for an explanation of His ways, His laws, and His power. Nor will they go to our scientists. A new day for missions will dawn as believers become the new mullahs, leading them to shout "Jesus, Akbar!" and have it right this time.

This is as I see it as I complete this wee book in my "generation." Even so come, Lord Jesus.

36

WHO WILL GO?

A question which every Christian should ask himself as life moves from decade to decade is, "Has my life made things better for other lives?" Is it possible to be a Christian and live a good life, but only good for one's self?

A radio interviewer in Ohio once charged all missions, and me in particular, with disrupting the idyllic life of primitive societies to their hurt. I quoted the figures of school children being trained in Congo at that time and spoke briefly of slavery, the poison cup, tribal wars, poverty and the high cost of low morality. I might have mentioned that after thousands of years of "idyllic life" there were only 13,000,000 people in the nation, whereas in only 100 years after that the population jumped to 45,000,000, due to the intrusion of whites upon their populations.

A further result of this "invasion" was national peace, national unity, the national language, the concept of a nation with a Congolese president, cabinet, parliament, department of justice, army, police, postal system, a network of roads and bridges and river boats, trains and planes, with prosperity for all.

Thelma and I gave forty years to this development. Our area of service was evangelism, Christian publications, both secular and Bible training of children and adults, and church planting/church mentoring on denominational, national and international levels. That does not limit its significance in the political arena. The fundamental contribution made by missions was the moral revolution in the hearts of unreached Africans, who for about fifty years did their best to obey God's laws. In so doing, they made possible all the good things that came to them in that period. The words that apply accurately to that "blip" in the ages of their paganism are "God's blessings." They tasted the blessedness of walking with God for a season.

We were very active partners in that season and can rightly say, "Our forty years there made a difference in the lives of 500 pastors and 30,000 lay pastors we trained, and thousands of school children whose schools we built and directed, and millions of new believers who found eternal salvation in great crusades we organized, in tents we provided in many nations, and in the national movements of evangelism."

And in Asia? God led us to enable a corps of about 28 men to be directors of schools of evangelism, organizers of portable Bible schools, heads of denominations and state representatives of the AIDA, All-India Decade of Advance (and of Decades of Advance in Bangladesh, Myanmar, and Nepal), which, in India, is involving several hundred heads of denominations in statewide planning of new ministries, events and projects. Schools of Evangelism are training thousands of men for passionate lifelong evangelism, missions, church planting and pastoring.

Since Thelma and I first went to India in 1991, portable Bible schools have trained over 15,000 laymen to pastor villages and new congregations. Our 25 Schools of Evangelism in Asia train about 675 students annually and seven clone schools train about 175 more. Five ER-funded schools in Africa add 125, bringing the total to near 1000 graduates per year in 2003.

Enough. The purpose of this chapter is to simply say, "God used our lives, insignificant as they are, to make life better for other people." But that is only part of what we wish to say. The other part is that this was true only because we responded to God's Great Commission by obeying. Our sons did the same. It is a response possible to our grandchildren and to all young believers. The call still rings out, "Whom shall I send? Who will go for us?"

This generation is smarter, richer, healthier, better equipped in every way than Thelma's and mine. Travel is faster, safer, and familiar to all. Populations are shown on TV, their languages are known, their cities and roads, even their animal life is documented. Anyone can get "there." Any young person who says, "Here am I, send me," and chooses to fulfill training requirements can be sent. Or, as so many hundreds have done before, a man can begin his own mission ministry and see God raise up needed support.

Our national constitution has it right. All are born free in America. In Christ, with a few exceptions due to age or physical problems, all are both free and equal to heed the call. God did not show the Brauns favors that are not available to others. Those favors are still there awaiting simple obedience. For those who go and go and go and go, the harvests grow and grow and grow and grow. Nothing mystical about that. Nothing at all. The most amazing harvests are the result of sweat and weariness involved in planting ever-larger fields.

Every young Christian who reads this book can accurately say about all that is recorded, "I could do that. I can do that." In Africa or Russia or Asia – anywhere, you could do what God enabled us to do. You can do far more than we ever did in this age of planes and cars and e-mail. There is a world to "Go ye into." It still needs eager volunteers who see the glory of the Almighty God whose call rings out through the approaching night, "Whom shall I send? Who will go for us?"

EPILOGUE

by Thelma Braun

A WORD TO THE READER

After a full and normal day of work at the Wilmore office September 29, 2003 Willys spent a pleasant evening gathering up garden cuttings and putting items into the suitcase for his trip to India the following Sunday. Little more than an hour after his usual sleeping time he awakened and was quickly called into his heavenly home. His life on earth was abruptly ended, but his work for the Lord he loved continues and is flourishing in many nations around the world.

Words poured easily from Willys' pen. A creative thinker driven by his life's goal of reaching the world for Christ, each of his dreams had to be transcribed, the details carefully analyzed, the means of reaching the goal clearly drawn. Little surprise then, that the events of his life flowed from his ready pen. Willys thought deeply, he cared passionately, and he wrote with painstaking accuracy.

For the preparation of the manuscript I am greatly indebted to Letha Jones, who transferred Willys' handwriting from his ever-present legal pads to the computer. The Lord then sent Rhonda Dragomir to employ her superb technical skills to format and bring the pages into printable form. Both of these ladies worked lovingly with complete dedication and devotion, obviously believing in the work Willys lived for, the extension of Christ's Kingdom into all the world. They are wholehearted devotees to the Great Commission mandate.

Perhaps I should mention that family played a large role in Willys' heart, and some of his writing was primarily intended for his sons and their offspring. But since origins play so vital a role in the formation of a person's character and personality, I decided to retain family history so you will know him better.

Arranging the book for publication has been for me a mixed emotional task of sorrow and of joy, joy at the recounting of shared blissful experiences, pangs of loneliness and sorrow at the loss of our beautifully shared life.

Willys penned the last words of the story of that life in mid-2003, and we have not tried to update the figures he used – the number of schools and students, and the total picture of finances and progress were accurate then. For current information on the exciting recent developments in the ministries of Evangelism Resources you may contact us at the address in the front pages of this book.

For friends who were not acquainted with ER in past years, let me revert to parts of the letter I sent to friends in Spring 2004. Written on floral stationery, it was labeled the Rose Letter.

This year was starkly different from any before – let me highlight its months for you.

The beginning was wonderful. Alicia had been with us for nearly a month in the summer before, weeks of sheer delight, and she came back from Wheaton College for Christmas vacation, and that idyllic time ended with the wedding of Mike and Meredith. Then came New Year's Day when I recorded in my journal: "No new resolutions – just want to live closer to the Lord than ever before." The recurrent theme in the diary held these words: "These are such happy days!" When I had a bit of a cold Willys said, "Maybe you should stay home. First sick day you've taken in 65 years." That was a bit of an exaggeration, but almost true.

February had a terrible ice storm. Willys had noted its coming before Valentine's Day with his typical upbeat attitude, "It's going to rain tomorrow. Let's celebrate today!" and celebrate we did! There were some heartaches in that month and I noted that Isaiah 26:3 was a superb refuge: "Thou wilt keep him in perfect peace whose mind is stayed on Thee," and His peace we had, even in the dark hours.

We left for India in March, John Musick making the trip all the happier and exciting. The best part of India? – meeting with those sterling AIDA leaders in the Delhi conference, then the new top-notch evangelism school down at Lucknow – and oh, I mustn't forget the outdoor meetings at Jaipur, the Rajasthan city with so many elephants and camels roaming around. Every time we go to India I wish we were decades younger so we could emigrate there. But having a part in training and equipping these wonderful Christ-followers is a matchless privilege!

We said goodbye to John after those three centers and went on to Kathmandu in Nepal. It was our first visit there, and its beginning was just a bit scary, even for old-timers like us. We landed late at night and our host wasn't there to meet us. We had no Nepalese money, couldn't say a word in that language, had no idea where to find a hotel, and there wasn't an English-speaking person around.

Somehow Willys inveigled two young fellows to drive us – complete strangers, you understand, and I wondered if they'd rob us and leave us stranded by the side of some road and no one would ever know what happened. I still don't understand how all that impossible situation worked out – I just know that somehow we ended up at the hotel where our host was waiting for us, he paid the taxi and we settled down peaceably to meet the delegates the next morning, twenty or so fine men.

And that's surprising, because Nepal has been a completely closed country until just fifty short years ago. Remember that chorus the Vineyard people taught us? – "All over the world the Spirit is working." That really is true, even in Nepal, the land we had prayed for almost forlornly way back in college days. We visited our School of Evangelism there, then met with leaders of DAN – the Decade of Advance in Nepal – for future plans for that country. What a privilege!

Then on we went to Myanmar, that's the new name for Burma, and what a surprise that country was! Our pastor there reminded us that Adoniram Judson had labored for six years without a single person becoming a Christian – I wonder if he can peek down from heaven and see what's going on now. He'd know that it was all worthwhile, the suffering and destitute life he had endured for the cause of Christ. ER has two Schools of Evangelism in that country, and the converts from Buddhism seemed to radiate the joy they have found in the Lord.

May found us back in the office trying to catch up on the business and correspondence that had piled up in our absence. At times it all seemed a bit burdensome, but it was wonderful being home again. How we loved it!

June was crammed with details getting ready for ER's annual board meeting and dinners, writing and helping to prepare the video presentation, sending out invitations, arranging all the details for *that highlight of the year. And then came July's Board meeting, with lots of heavy discussions, and you know, it seemed strange for Willys to be so insistent that someone must be appointed to the home office, someone he could mentor. That was agreed to, and we laid firm plans for Steve Liversedge and Dr. Bob Volk to accompany him to the conferences in India. I agreed wholeheartedly to that arrangement and to my staying home to work with Wes Eisemann and our fine part-time helpers to keep the office going, but I remember saying somewhat plaintively, "I don't know how I'll be able to manage without you, honey, for all that time."*

The dinners that followed, in Wilmore and Mansfield, were excellent – but there was that disturbing five minutes at the Kahls' breakfast table when Willys mentioned that his hand had gone limp and his speech was just a bit garbled. The weeks that followed had somewhat irksome lab tests, consultations about proper dosages and the like, but there was so much challenge in the work that there wasn't time to let it bother us too much. Instead, besides the regular office schedule we prepared material for the India conferences, got the October NEWS and the November Talking Turkey ready for the printer.

Summer was almost perfect. I do believe the weather was the finest since we moved to Kentucky, and how Willys loved his flowers and fruit trees! We had lovely visits with the Eisemanns, our cherished next-door neighbors, and celebrated together our 62nd wedding anniversary! Life was almost idyllic.

And then came the last day of September when my beloved Willys left me suddenly, not for India, but for that mysterious journey into the very presence of our Lord.

The family rallied around beautifully – I still wonder how Chris and Marcia got here so soon from Ivory Coast – just one day after the homegoing! They joined Paul and Nancy in helping with the funeral arrangements and entertaining, and the distant grandchildren came – Josh from California, Alicia from Wheaton College, Mike and Meredith from Somerset, Kentucky and Matt from Cedarville University in Ohio – to join Mindy, here in Wilmore. "How you'd love this reunion, dearest!" I found myself whispering. And then it occurred to me – maybe he was enjoying it.

Remember when we used to sing, "I'm so glad I'm a part of the family of God"? Never have I felt it more deeply. When I was feeling more alone than I had ever been in all my life, that family of God rallied around. Dr. Spann flew in from Mississippi, Roy and Katie Parsons from California, other Board members from Florida, Ohio, Indiana – from all around, and the pastor and friends of First Alliance Church here were kind beyond measure – there is no way to express my gratitude to all. John Musick worked day and night to prepare the video of Willys' life for the funeral that was really a celebration, not so much of Willys' life, but of all that God had meant to him.

Hundreds of kind friends from all around the world have sent their messages of condolence with tributes to Willys' life and ministry. I read them and then find myself saying, "Yes, but that's only a part. You can't know how wonderful he was!"

. . . .

The opening lines of the Rose Letter carried this quotation: "*Love deeply, but remember, it comes at a cost. It will mean to grieve deeply as well.*" I must confess that I have learned the truth of those words since that closing day of September in 2003. We had loved deeply, Willys and I, and the end had come so suddenly that the shock was intense.

But always I have known that I have been supremely blessed. The Lord whom we loved and served had given us sixty-two wonderful years together, years of adventure and joy, years of no regrets.

Possibly you noticed that over and over again Willys wrote in relating the ministries, "Thelma and I". That expression was not accurate; in most instances the "Thelma and" should have been deleted. Willys did the pioneering, dreamed the goals, worked laboriously to actualize the vision God gave him. I had the honor and delight of standing by his side, encouraging him in the dark hours and celebrating with him in the times of triumph. In most instances the "Thelma and" was a product of his humble spirit – and of his love.

It was a remarkable life that we shared, and through the blessing of the Lord the product goes on and on. Ellen Keller, who traveled with us on that first journey to the field and introduced us to Congo, wrote recently on her hundredth birthday, "The work Willys did will continue till Jesus comes." We are trusting God to make that true.

And it is my heartfelt desire that this book of his life will bring glory to the God who poured out His love and blessings so undeservedly upon us through the many years He allowed us to live and love, and that because of it some of today's young people may echo the title from the depths of their hearts, "Here am I, Lord. Send me."

- Thelma Braun